# Representations and Contradictions

To J. M.
with thanks

# Representations and Contradictions

*Ambivalence Towards Images, Theatre, Fiction, Relics and Sexuality*

Jack Goody

Copyright © Jack Goody 1997

The right of Jack Goody to be identified as author of this work has been asserted in accordance with the Copyright, Designs and Patents Act 1988.

First published 1997

2 4 6 8 10 9 7 5 3 1

Blackwell Publishers Ltd
108 Cowley Road
Oxford OX4 1JF
UK

Blackwell Publishers Inc.
350 Main Street
Malden, Massachusetts 02148
USA

All rights reserved. Except for the quotation of short passages for the purposes of criticism and review, no part of this publication may be reproduced, stored in a retrieval system, or transmitted, in any form or by any means, electronic, mechanical, photocopying, recording or otherwise, without the prior permission of the publisher.

Except in the United States of America, this book is sold subject to the condition that it shall not, by way of trade or otherwise, be lent, resold, hired out, or otherwise circulated without the publisher's prior consent in any form of binding or cover other than that in which it is published and without a similar condition including this condition being imposed on the subsequent purchaser.

*British Library Cataloguing in Publication Data*

A CIP catalogue record for this book is available from the British Library.

*Library of Congress Cataloging-in-Publication Data*

Goody, Jack.
    Representations and contradictions : ambivalence towards images, theatre, fiction, relics, and sexuality / Jack Goody.
      p. cm.
    Includes bibliographical references and index.
    ISBN 0–631–20525–X — ISBN 0–631–20526–8
    1. Culture—Philosophy.  2. Image (Philosophy)—Cross-cultural studies.  3. Representation (Philosophy)—Cross-cultural studies.
I. Title.
GN357.G665   1997
306'.01—DC21                               96–40927
                                                      CIP

Printed in Great Britain by T. J. International, Padstow, Cornwall

This book is printed on acid-free paper

# Contents

| | | |
|---|---|---|
| Acknowledgements | | vi |
| 1 | Representations and Cognitive Contradictions | 1 |
| 2 | Icons and Iconoclasm in Africa? Absence and Ambivalence | 35 |
| 3 | Relics and the Cognitive Contradiction of Mortal Remains and Immortal Longings | 75 |
| 4 | Theatre, Rites and Representations of the Other | 99 |
| 5 | Myth: Thoughts on its Uneven Distribution | 153 |
| 6 | Objections to the Novel | 182 |
| 7 | Representations of Sex and their Denial | 204 |
| 8 | Culture and Cognition | 238 |
| Bibliography | | 271 |
| Index | | 286 |

# Acknowledgements

The book explains itself. I have described the genesis of my interest in the subject in the first chapter. It takes up an aspect of one theme in *The Culture of Flowers*. I am especially indebted to the National Humanities Center, Research Triangle Park, North Carolina, 27709, for the facilities with which they provided me between September 1991 and January 1992, and to fellow members of the Performance Seminar – Victor Mair, Margaret Clunies Ross, J. Richard Green, Graeme Clark, Steven Lonsdale and Mary Hunter – for stimulating me to look further into this topic. I am also indebted to the Getty Center for the History of Arts and the Humanities, to the Smithsonian Institution and to St John's College, Cambridge, especially to Richard Beadle, John Kerrigan and Joe MacDermott, for the help they have given.

Since I am straying more than usual outside the bounds of my personal knowledge, I am more than ever grateful for help from colleagues and friends. With Cesare Poppi of the University of East Anglia I have co-operated before; his background in art history has been of help at various junctures, as was the invitation he arranged with Steven Hooper for me to spend a term as visiting scholar at the Sainsbury Research Centre, Norwich. Juliet Mitchell's background in literature, psychoanalysis and cultural history has been of great assistance to me throughout and she has read each chapter with care and attention. Stephen Hugh-Jones has done his best to turn my eyes from Africa to South America, above all in dealing with myth. Gilbert Lewis has contributed to my understanding of representations, Peter Brooks answered my queries on the antitheatrical and anti-novelistic prejudices, and Heather Glen too has supplied me with references on the latter. Esther Goody has commented on the cognitive side which has also benefited from my talks with Mike Cole, Phil Johnson-Laird, Steven Levinson, Dan Sperber, Pascal Boyer and Scott Atran. Knowledge of the theatre in Africa has profited from discussions with Karen Barber, Alain Ricard and Mary-Jo Arnoldi. Kum Gandah has read the material on Africa and Deborah Swallow that on India.

A version of chapter 2 has appeared in French in *Annales ESC* (1991) and I have given papers based on other chapters at the Smithsonian, Washington; the Sainsbury Centre, Norwich; the Departments of Anthropology at Manchester, University College and Belfast; the Humanities Center, Atlanta; the American Museum of Natural History, New York; the Ecole des Hautes Etudes, Paris; the Centre for African Studies, Northwestern University; and the Institute of Mediterranean Studies at the University of Malta where Paul Sant Cassia gave me the opportunity to spell out my ideas (as he has also done at Durham).

Asha and Suhrid Sarabhai helped me to see and understand something of India, Helen Hung-far Siu of China, and Shigehara Tanabe of Japan. Martha Mundy has always been willing to share her knowledge of the Muslim world.

I wish to thank Ruth Daniel, Stephen Hugh-Jones and Gilbert Lewis for helping with the proofs. My thanks also to Sue Kemsley for wordprocessing and other help.

Jack Goody
Lacapelle, September 1995

# 1

# Representations and Cognitive Contradictions

*'Man has doubts and does not have sufficient self-confidence.'*[1]

I am interested in the resistance to (or absence of) certain kinds of representations, images, theatre, relics, myth, novels and representations of sex. This may seem an arbitrary selection from the wide gamut of possibilities, and so in a sense it is. But it includes some central artistic and religious forms of representations (icons, theatre, novel), which are present in some societies and absent (or contested) in others, a fact that raises in my view questions about the very nature of representations. An element of selection nevertheless remains; I do not intend to cover the totality of representations where ambivalence or absence may arise but ones where this problem has impressed me with the need (and potentiality) for some kind of general explanation. For when reasons have been put forward in the past, they have tended to be historically specific and embedded in the European or Near Eastern experience. I am less concerned with the particular grounds for the rejection, suppression or absence of these activities in any one society as with the question of what this widespread feature implies for the nature of representations, which are so central a

[1] Wang Ch'ung 1911.

feature of human life. What are we talking about when we refer to representations? Re-presentations are basic to human communication, to human culture. Durkheim spoke of collective representations as the central concern of the sociologist or anthropologist. Art is representational; language, too, as in the word 'horse' for the animal horse. It may also be mimetic, as when 'pitter-patter' imitates the raindrops. I am largely concerned in this book with a category of artistic representation that falls somewhere in between, initially in figurative representations, images, in painting and sculptures, and also in the theatre, as well as extending the enquiry into the worship of relics (which stand for the person) and in fictional presentations of the world.[2]

My interest in these phenomena lies in two major aspects: firstly, in their uneven distribution in human societies, and at different times in the same society namely, their occasions of absence; secondly, in the objections that have been made to their presence, sometimes individually, sometimes in a more general fashion. I hope to indicate that these two aspects are interrelated. Let me deal first with absence.

## *Absence*

I want to begin to elucidate this theme by explaining how I first became interested in the absence of figurative representations. When the subject of discussion at a seminar or in private conversation turned to 'African art', the anthropologist Meyer Fortes would remark that the Tallensi of northern Ghana had none. One can dispute his use of the term 'art'. Obviously it is an outsider's, possibly a European or Eurasian, concept which we understand in the context of art schools and art museums. Equally obviously the Tallensi exercised judgements, including those we would call aesthetic, in relation to objects (let us set aside for the moment the verbal or musical arts), that is, they cherished some more than

[2] For a fuller comment on the notion of representations, see 'Endnote on Representation', p. 31.

others, and they decorated their houses as well as their persons with favoured designs. It is perfectly easy to see what Fortes meant, however. If we go to any ethnographic museum, the African displays are often dominated by startling Liberian masks, by delicate Dan sculpture, by massive Benin bronzes or by earlier terracottas from Nok. Nearly all this work is figurative, sometimes representing animals, more usually humans or anthropomorphic beings. Of these forms of representation the Tallensi had nothing, or virtually none. That was also true of some other types of artistic representation; they had no theatre in the restricted sense of the word; neither did the LoDagaa, who lived nearby. But the LoDagaa did have some figurative sculpture in wood. A similar difference obtained with the distribution of myth rather than mythology, using myth in the sense of long, rhythmic recitations involving supernatural or even elemental forces.[3] The LoDagaa had the 'myth of the Bagre';[4] the Tallensi had no equivalent.

In trying to explain this situation of presence and absence I looked back at my study of the uses made of flowers in different parts of the world. There I found some 'evolutionary' reasons for the absence of domestic flowers in Black Africa. By and large flowers are domesticated only in societies where there is an advanced, intensive agriculture of the kind found after the Bronze Age, that is, after what the prehistorian, Gordon Childe, calls the 'Urban Revolution' that produced plough agriculture, writing systems and advanced crafts of various kinds.

While this evolutionary process opened up possibilities, it did not necessarily mean that they were exploited. In classical times southern Europe had a vigorous culture of flowers but this declined dramatically in the early Christian period. Here we have evidence not simply of the differences between cultures in space but within one society at different times, raising quite other questions. In Europe, such decline is sometimes attributed to barbarian invasions (of the Celts and others) and to the associated falling off in the economy. Those factors were undoubtedly present. But the

---

[3] For an insistence on this distinction, see also Halbertal and Margalit 1992:264.
[4] Goody 1972; Goody and Gandah 1981; Gandah and Goody, forthcoming.

decline in the use of flowers and other items deemed to indicate luxury was not only passive, subject to the play of external forces, it was willed by the actors – or at least by some actors holding hegemonic positions. Many of the early Fathers of the Church condemned the use of flowers especially when arranged in the shape of crowns or garlands. This they did for a number of reasons. Firstly, these were used in pagan sacrifices; secondly, to God one offered prayer but no gifts; thirdly, they were part of a culture of luxury, an early consumer culture, emphasizing status, hierarchy and an unnecessary use of scarce human resources. One's duty was to give to the living rather than to the dead. The reasons were, in a word, puritanical.

Over the centuries these notions were gradually modified in Christian Europe. It took a long time for the culture of flowers to return in full bloom and even then it suffered a further period of decline in the sixteenth and seventeenth centuries with the coming of the Reformation and, more particularly, of the Puritans. In other words, the use of flowers was deliberately rejected by some societies at certain periods of their history.

Regarding spatial differences, it would have been easy to say, as Lévi-Strauss does with regard to mushrooms, that some cultures are floriphobe and some floriphile. That is true at any one point in time. But the inevitable implication of such a characterization is that this feature is buried deep in the mentality of a particular society, with the English, for example, being at once floriphile and fungiphobe. We have seen, however, that this situation can change over time. Consequently, to regard this feature (perhaps almost any feature) of human behaviour as part of a quasi-permanent, deep structure does not take into account the more temporary historical aspects of culture. While it is offered as a 'culturalist' explanation, the implications are quasi-genetic. But the use and display of flowers are not rooted in the cultural genes, even when the features appear persistent over time.

So it is not only a question of looking at changes over space but also at changes over time. Why should societies (or rituals) change from thick to thin cultural forms, rejecting what was once so central to their whole existence? The most striking example is what happened in Europe after the Greeks, to whom we often look back as laying the foundations for many of our cultural and intellectual traditions. It was the eighth century BCE (Before Common Era) that saw the beginning of Greek expansion, the rise of the city state, the development of writing and of that 'pre-eminence in the arts which forms a large part of what we understand by classical Greece'.[5] To which we would certainly add the virtual beginning of European literary contributions in a wide range of fields. For what is remarkable is not only the quality but the sheer quantity of works using the written word. In particular, Greece was noted for its drama, still performed in the West after 2500 years, sometimes in the original language, more often in translation. Greece is noted, too, for its architectural forms that have provided the West with models for banks and offices, for temples and palaces. And again, for its extensive sculpture, copies of which have become the furniture of our social space where the intention is to impose. Nor were these the superficialities of cultural expression.

## *Objections*

The question of absence in European societies, as distinct from those of Black Africa, raises the problem of intentionality, of deliberate objections, for example, to the use of flowers. It was the same with images and with the theatre, which formed part of Plato's critique of cultural representations. That critique was the point of reference for a long tradition of alternative views about such manifestations which the contemporary observer finds difficult to understand and the significance of which observers of other and earlier societies often fail to comprehend. Plato was concerned with mimesis to which, in effect, he objected that it was not the thing itself, not what it represented. Indeed, how could it be? What I want to point out here is that the human situation itself depends on re-presentation and this, whether linguistic, figurative or theoretical, can never be what is originally presented. Hence there is

[5] Dunbabin 1957:24.

always a potential problem for humanity in doubting or even denying what it has created.

Mimesis is a concept that has received a bad press from many recent and especially post-modern writers because it is taken to relate, mechanically, to the reproduction of culture, to 'imitation' in Tarde's sense, and especially to the repetition of language or of images. Mimesis therefore embodies a conservative ideology, denying creativity. Plato, on the other hand, saw mimesis as subversive of order; for example, when people imitate the behaviour of others, especially actors of rulers. The principle aspect of mimesis that concerns me here is the representation in art of the external world, of existence itself, the problem raised in iconophobia, in the anti-theatrical prejudice or by anti-novelistic attitudes. In these contexts, one is reproducing in a different medium; hence creativity is always involved, not endlessly repeating what is already a representation.[6] Like mimesis, the idea of representation receives short shrift from Barthes as 'an instrument of subjugation within the symbolic order',[7] a view that has little to commend it since it skirts around the notion of how that 'symbolic order' is constituted in the first place.

This critique is related to what Prendergast calls 'the uncertain status of representation as such . . . the permanently unsettled condition we inhabit related to the "mimetic" order'.[8] The uncertainty follows Barthes's 'wholesale attack on the idea of representation' which seems to me to call not for a prejudged dismissal ('an instrument of subjugation within the symbolic order') but for clarification.

There is a general problem about mimesis. Few people like to be imitated, except in very specific teaching situations. Yet imitation remains critical to learning; it seems to be, if not an exclusively human activity, at least one that is limited to anthropoids, not being found in monkeys.[9] But more relevantly, mimesis

---

[6] For a discussion of these problems in the context of French literature and thought, see Prendergast 1986.
[7] Cited by Prendergast 1986:14.
[8] Prendergast 1986:94.
[9] Whiten and Ham 1992. The authors consider different mimetic mechanisms

is a form of re-presentation; it is not the action itself, it is a re-enactment. From another point of view it may be seen as a falsehood.

In this discussion, mimesis tends to be equated with representation. Yet that tendency may overlook a useful distinction. At one point mimesis is related to 'mime' which, in Rome and Greece, referred to a 'simple farcical drama, . . . characterized by mimicry and the ludicrous representation of familiar types'.[10] That definition implies there is a non-ludicrous form of representation and mime is also seen to be '[The art of] gesture, movement, etc. (as distinct from words) used to express emotion and dramatic action or character; a dumb show'. But mimesis is applied more widely, to 'a figure of speech whereby the words or actions of another are imitated', and (in sociology) to 'a deliberate imitation of the behaviour of one group of people by another as a factor in social change'. Mimesis is usually seen as the imitation of people's behaviour; hence gesture and speech, but not writing, are called mimetic. Writing occupies a 'third place', whereas speech and gesture are dyadic, unmediated; even if one addressed a crowd, the crowd is one in a sense that the readership of the written word is not. But from another point of view any words, spoken or written, may be excluded from mimesis since only rarely do they imitate: except for onomatopoeia, they are arbitrary signs. Certainly written words imitate nature only in an indirect way, whereas gesture, sculpture, even mimicking someone's voice do so very directly. In themselves words represent rather than mimic.

Similar doubts about the status of representations appear in the philosophy of science. In discussing realism and anti-realism, Ian Hacking remarks:

> By attending only to knowledge as representation of nature, we wonder how we can ever escape from representations and hook up with the world. That way lies an idealism of which Berkeley is the spokesman. In our century John Dewey has spoken sardonically of

---

which resemble imitation such as stimulus enhancement. Metarepresentation, which goes along with 'mindreading' and deceit, is also associated with imitation.

[10] *The Oxford English Dictionary.*

a spectator theory of knowledge that has obsessed Western philosophy. If we are mere spectators at the theatre of life, how shall we ever know, on grounds internal to the passing show, what is mere representation by the actors, and what is the real thing?[11]

Here Hacking's attitude towards representation becomes clear. Theories 'merely represent'; they are not the real thing. At another level, what is re-presented (the theatre) exists in the real world. But it does re-present an original in that world and therefore must raise problems of truth, falsity or distortion of that original, problems that are not only involved in the correspondence theory of truth.

Clearly representation is central to human communication. Indeed, Hacking has proposed to characterize humans not as *homo faber* but as *homo depictor*: 'Human beings are representators;' 'People make representations.'[12] He continues: 'People make likenesses. They paint pictures, imitate the clucking of hens, mould clay, carve statues, and hammer brass.' Representations are not simply the internal ideas of French and English empiricists, as was Kant's *Vorstellung*, because they are public. Indeed, above all, Hacking refers to physical objects, and he imagines 'pictorial people making likenesses before they learn to talk'.[13] There is not much evidence for this statement, except that it is probable that dogs, for example, do represent in dreams, and presumably do so visually. Early humans used linguistics at the same time as pictorial representations. But language certainly greatly extends our powers of representing; for example, Hacking sees the theories of physics as constituting no final truth but only a 'barrage of more or less instructive representations'.[14] A plurality of representations necessarily invokes scepticism, doubt, and is related to the split between appearance and reality.

Scepticism, 'serious scepticism' according to Hacking, is inevitable with representations 'for if the atoms and the void

---

[11] Hacking 1983:130.
[12] Hacking 1983:132.
[13] Hacking 1983:134.
[14] Hacking 1983:145.

comprise the real, how can we ever know that?'[15] The kernel of doubt is always present, ever since Democritus formulated atomism, as Plato notes. Firstly, how can we check out any particular version of the Democritean dream? Secondly, there is the fear that it is only a dream: there are no atoms, no void, just stones. Thirdly, there is the doubt that if his story is untrue, how can we aim at any knowledge but only 'the contemplative ignorance of the tub'.

Hacking contrasts these statements with what he would call non-representative ones, such as 'my typewriter is on the table'. Of that we can say it is true or false, whereas representations involve doubt. But such statements also involve representations (the word 'typewriter' represents a machine); while scepticism and doubt of the same kind are certainly not involved, there can also be questions about linguistic representation and the 'reality' of words.[16] I would agree that these are of a different order and it is significant that I begin with a consideration of pictorial (indeed figurative) representations and that most of the book involves a visual dimension. But I also deal with one aspect of linguistic representation in discussing the myth and the novel.

Figurative or pictorial representations are basically what C. S. Pierce, distinguishing three kinds of representation, calls those based on similarity; the others are causal or metonymic (part for a whole) and conventional (for example, linguistic).[17] But the distinction must not blind us to the similarities and to the fact that actors themselves may shift from objecting to or encouraging one to treating another in the same way. While Judaism does not forbid figurative depictions of the deity, some later commentators claimed that 'the very art of interpreting anthropomorphic images literally is itself idolatry'.[18] It is not clear from the Bible whether or not God has an image, though Maimonides denies the possibility. What is clear is that any attempt to provide figurative

---

[15] Hacking 1983:141.
[16] See, for example, the experiments of Scribner and Cole among the Vai (1981).
[17] Pierce 1931–1938:8.
[18] Halbertal and Margalit 1992:35.

representation of a verbal image is forbidden.[19] That would entail a loss of uniqueness; the prohibition is not based upon a fear of substitution (taking the representation for the represented) but because it would be a mistaken or inappropriate representation.[20]

In this enquiry I am concerned chiefly with certain kinds of representation, namely, figurative icons, dramatic performances and relics (remains). At the end I extend the discussion to myths and, in a peripheral way, to narrative (in the sense of fiction, words used in particular ways). I use the term in a relatively simple way as a physical re-presentation either of an object (as in the case of an icon or image), or of acts (as in drama, mimesis). The representation of concepts or ideas, Platonic or otherwise, is marginal to my theme.

My first example of this dilemma comes from the classical world. Writing of the influence of art on religion in the classical world, Lane Fox calls attention to the way that ever since the age of epic heroes, 'statues and painting had become a fundamental influence on the way the divine world was "envisioned"'. Homer's gods, he argues, have at first no separate identities, appearing in disguises, since portrait statues were not widely available. 'As Greek scuplture developed, it fixed mortals' ideas of their gods as "individuals"'.[21] It must also have raised doubts, questions and controversy of the kind we find in Plato. If you create an image of an angel, it is almost inevitable that some will feel impelled to give a different type of consideration to this physical representation, perhaps critically, perhaps materially, leading them to reflect upon the physical space it occupies and how many 'real' angels could stand on the head of a pin. There is a concreteness, as Lane Fox notes, that clashes with the necessary vagueness, fluidity, of the imagined object, the verbal 'image' without icon.

There is a special problem for many groups or societies in representing the divine pictorially because of its otherwise immaterial status; that quality increases the possibility of perceiving discrep-

---

[19] Halbertal and Margalit 1992:47.
[20] Halbertal and Margalit 1992:48.
[21] Lane Fox 1987:153.

# Representations and Cognitive Contradictions 11

ancy between presence and absence, between image or word and referent. For many societies the problem is particularly acute for the High God who created all and cannot therefore have been created. But while in many cases the reluctance to represent centres upon the unique Creator, that in itself sheds some doubt upon the whole process of re-presentation, secular as well as religious; the two are not wholly detached.

What is also remarkable in the subsequent history of Europe is the way that those products of the arts, above all in sculpture and theatre, which constituted the greatest artistic achievements of those very societies to which the continent traces its roots (not to speak of democracy, widespread literacy and the accumulation of written knowledge) were rejected by those who followed. Why?

The decline in Europe after the fall of the Roman Empire has been attributed to the barbarian invasions of the fifth century and earlier. It has also been attributed to the collapse of the economy which Pirenne sees already setting in at the end of the third century. The disappearance of these artistic forms, however, was only partly due to the invasions. Although the decline in the economy, in the life of cities and in trade, all played a part, it did not prevent developments taking place in the sphere of architecture, for example, in the construction of great monastic and ecclesiastical buildings, in providing the House of God and dwellings for God's servants. Indeed, the decline was in part the result of a self-inflicted wound. There were many reasons why important elements in Christianity objected to theatrical performances, to dramatic representation, as well as insisting upon the dominance of the religious above the secular in these and other literary fields. These features had been characteristic of life in 'pagan' Greece and Rome, under which Christians had suffered from the theatricality of gladiatorial combats. 'Pagan' sculpture too was closely linked to 'pagan' worship.

These arts might have been turned to new ends had not the activities themselves also been considered luxurious – and hence as unnecessary diversions from the real business of living – not only of time but of money. On an ideological level all were representations of reality rather than reality itself. The physical side came under the ban on the graven image, as re presenting, re-enacting God's creation, that is starkly stated in the Ten Commandments and that had such a significant impact on artistic life in Israel, and indeed in Jewish history under the Diaspora. The concentration was upon the written word, the holy word, rather than on the banished representation in visual form.

Secular paintings too all but disappeared, leaving Europe with relatively few such works, even in the ecclesiastical sphere, until the advent of the *primi lumi* of the Renaissance. The naturalistic paintings of the classical world exemplified in the wall-paintings uncovered in Pompeii in the eighteenth century had no real successors, although the parallel Celtic tradition that dominated much of northern Europe had considerable achievements to its name in the sphere of zoomorphic art.

But what is most remarkable is the virtual disappearance of the art form by which classical civilizations are largely remembered, namely sculpture. That cannot be described as an entirely religious art; not all sculpture was concerned with worship. But worship was part of its undoing. Greek sculpture was taken over in its entirety by Rome, which borrowed, copied or built on their forms. It spread through the Bactrian Greeks. to give rise to the Graeco-Buddhist Gandāra school by fusion with local Indian motifs. It transformed physical and theological notions in Buddhism which had earlier been aniconic. It then travelled eastwards with Buddhism to China, Korea, and Japan where its forms continued to dominate important aspects of the sculptural traditions. But in the West that tradition disappeared for many centuries.

Once again the medieval world saw a disastrous falling off from the classical period, at least in terms of the secular theatre, secular painting, and to a lesser extent of secular literature. That absence in time is connected with absences in space, for both are linked, as I hope to suggest.

So it is not so much the presence as the absence of representations that holds my attention. 'Artistic' representations are unevenly distributed in human societies, and accorded uneven weight, for example, in the matter of fiction and non-fiction. Behind this unevenness I discern a fragment of doubt about their presence, a degree of ambivalence founded upon contradictions of a cognitive kind.

Surrounded as we are by the proliferation of representations that characterizes mass culture, the mediatic empire, today we may not even recognize this absence as raising an intellectual problem. In any case, what we find in storehouses such as museums, libraries or cemeteries are inevitably the instances of presence not of absence; the picture rejected, destroyed or not created, the books burnt, the missing offerings, these we do not see, any more than 'some mute inglorious Milton'. Yet that is not entirely the experience of other cultures today or of our own culture in the past. Even in our present the impulses that push towards absence exist but take other forms, such as abstraction or objections to realist theatre.

## *The Written and the Oral*

How do we link the spatial differences between cultures and the differences over time? Our knowledge of the latter is largely confined to cultures with writing since we need the records to establish change. It is in those cultures too that we find explicit discussions of absence that show intentionality, as in iconoclastic doctrines, and that give reasons for that phenomenon. For example, the changes and differences in the culture of flowers can be understood as related to the presence of a hegemonic literate world religion which forbids certain cultural manifestations because of its theological views or its attitudes to luxury. The absence of icons in Islamic Africa can also be seen in those terms; so too the aversion to theatre and perhaps partly to fiction.

But it is not only literate religions that make us iconoclasts or alternatively iconodules, the breakers and lovers of icons. It is we humans that also make religion in our image. The problem of antipathy to icons, for example, is wider than this Near Eastern tradition; it appears in early Buddhism and partly perhaps in Confucianism. It raises an explicit response in these literate civilizations where the arts are often associated with luxury in one form or another. And luxury was one of the targets both of philosophers and religion. Christ spoke out against the rich and championed the poor. The origin of Buddhism lay in the rejection of the luxury which the king of Kosala provided for his son, Siddhārtha, to make him unaware of the poverty, sickness and death that existed in the world. But the son renounced that life to live in poverty and meditation. For those who dwelt in luxury, it was necessary to be charitable to others, not only to the poor but to the arts, as in Mogul India.[22] Confucians, such as Mencius, took a similar line. Max Weber sees this renunciation as an aspect of the rationalization of religion, seen as the preliminary to the rationalization of society, and 'tied to a theme that is common to all world religions: the question of justifying the unequal distribution of life's goods. This *basic ethical problematic*, which bursts the bounds of myth, arises from a religious explanation of suffering that is perceived as unjust.' For that to happen suffering has to be revalued, 'for in tribal societies suffering counts as a symptom of secret guilt'.[23] 'What is new is the idea that individual misfortune can be undeserved and that the individual may cherish the religious hope of being delivered from all evil . . .'

In his discussion Weber follows his usual practice of putting forward a hypothetical evolutionary sequence to explain, at least in part, the phenomenon under consideration. I believe he is correct in stating that advanced agricultural societies raise, in an acute form, the problem of the unequal distribution of resources. But there is no evidence that this development is related to new notions of suffering and is totally absent earlier. Coveting one's neighbour's goods occurs in 'tribal' societies as in others. For instance, among the LoDagaa specific steps may be taken to prevent the less fortunate from wanting to damage one's abundant crops or cattle. The essential difference is that in post-Bronze Age societies such differences are structurally much more significant, that one gets whole social categories of poor who have no access to the means of production (and not simply the disabled, but the obviously fit).

[22] Habib 1963:57.
[23] Habermas 1984:201.

Initially I am trying to pursue an argument regarding cultural activities in the restricted sense of artistic and aesthetic ones, that I have put forward with regard to kinship and other forms of social action. Briefly, it is this. Across the multitude of dissimilarities between the cultures of particular groups,[24] there are certain broad similarities among the major societies of Asia and Europe (and I deliberately emphasize this particular order) that sets them apart from those of Black Africa. This is the case in many aspects of artistic representation which I want to discuss. That difference has something to do with the use of language, especially in its written form, which in turn is related to the economy.

While written language may be used to exhort, and is performative in that sense, more usually it is concerned with representation. Hence the written 'sciences' represent in a way that those in an oral culture do not. They are further removed from 'the action'. It is that very distance that makes the written word 'good to think' in a special way. And, as I have elsewhere discussed in relation to 'rationality' and 'logic', that is one factor bringing those major Eurasian societies closer to one another than they are to Africa.[25]

But that does not exhaust the argument. As Evans-Pritchard maintains, against the earlier Lévy Bruhl, even Azande witchcraft has its own logic, an informal logic that on one level of generalization we find in other oral cultures and which persists into written ones. The difference is that 'logic' in its Aristotelian sense, and in the Buddhist and Hindu equivalents found in India, China and Japan, constitutes a formalization of those procedures, a process which in some instances can be described as making the implicit explicit, and in others as a distancing, as giving them a broader context and a more abstract frame.

That is what I want to argue about the construction and destruction (or perhaps deconstruction) of representations. In discussing pictorial images, icons, I begin with Africa and suggest that some

---

[24] I use this phrase deliberately since I do not believe we can profitably speak of cultures except in relation to collectivities, or rather to people as members of collectivities in however loose a sense.

[25] Goody 1995.

of the notions that we find explicitly expressed not only in Europe but in Eurasia, and most persistently in West Asia, can perhaps be perceived in Africa in an implicit, embryonic, state. I shall try to adduce the evidence but it is sparse for it is not easy to get at beliefs that, while explicit in many written cultures, are implicit in oral ones. Parallel problems in the nature of representations seem to me suggested by the uneven distribution of imaged subjects and imaging cultures, that is, by their absence in some societies and their presence in others – in Africa, as in Eurasia. That distribution is not simply to be attributed to 'culture', the weakest of all possible narratives, but rather to an ambivalence in the human conceptualization of 'images' themselves.

## Change and Cognitive Dilemmas

I see this argument as bearing directly upon the discussion of 'modes of thought', certain aspects of which display developmental features, as with modes of communication and production. It is not enough to set societies one beside another in relativistic display (nor even to consider each instance as unique in itself, though in some particular respects that is necessarily the case); we have also to raise the question of how societies shift from one mode to the other, for otherwise one can understand neither the Eurasian past nor the African present.

Widespread cognitive aspects of the human situation give rise to ambiguities, ambivalences and hence to doubts, leading to variations in the way individuals and societies deal with that problem. One problem I have touched upon in earlier work and return to in the final chapter relates not only to the taking of human life, sometimes condemned, sometimes praised, but sometimes to the destruction of any 'life', soul, breath, which may be seen to threaten our own existence. It is necessary to live and eat; yet these activities may be deplored and even feared. The way such problems are dealt with at a particular time and place will depend upon a number of factors, 'solutions' passed down and adapted in the community, the explicitness with which alternatives are discussed in written texts, reaction to earlier solutions, and so on. These differences in the response may vary in various categories of society, for example, between written and oral, between hunting and industrial, between Eastern and Western. Nevertheless the core of the problem lies in the general human understanding of the alternative possibilities that are prompted by ambivalent cognitive situations. Those solutions that are different from our own we sometimes think of as hedged round with 'taboos' which are seen by moderns as irrational, as magico-religious prejudices, as primitive, for the word itself was borrowed from the Polynesians to provide precisely these implications. A more neutral designation would be 'prohibitions', or, in order to include positive as well as negative injunctions, 'customs' or even 'culture' which, as Gellner (1992) has argued, tends to get opposed to actions based on rational calculation. Unlike the notion of taboo, prohibitions and avoidances have an intellectual element; even those that are magico-religious have congnitive aspects, some of which have general roots in ambivalence and cognitive contradiction and it is those that interest me in trying to account for diversity.

It might be suggested that this programme proposes a return to what the Durkheimians dismissed as the 'English intellectualism' of the nineteenth-century anthropologists, Tylor and Frazer; I return to this point in the final chapter. It is correct to perceive an implication that the alternative approach of analysing the data to reveal underlying homologies among collective representations is insufficient for my purpose. The cognitive element is of primary significance, especially in accounting for change and difference, whereas the reference to deep-seated symbolic correspondences leads to the positing of a static structure. With oral societies, I do not claim to be analysing explicit statements displaying ambivalences about icons, for example, or about homicide. But absence of such statements should not result in limiting the examination of social action either to a purely functional or to a purely symbolic analysis, for it should include an enquiry into the cognitive potentials in the human situation, an indirect understanding of which can be gained from the explicit statements on these subjects found in written cultures. And there are also implicit aspects that can be deduced from the beliefs and practices of oral ones.

In the chapters that follow I try to show that while opposition to the presence of icons, the theatre and other cultural items highly valued in other contexts and in different circumstances, is more explicit in societies with writing, where it is given an ideological form, such contradictory views are not altogether absent from oral cultures, at least implicitly. They will inevitably be more difficult to detect. But I suggest they may account for the absence of such features from one oral culture to another, in other words for their uneven distribution. If this is so, ambivalence and cognitive contradictions about representations would be found across the range of human societies, though not necessarily in all, but the responses would be differentiated according to the nature of the mode of communication. That is the theme I intend to explore.

## *Puritanism*

The cognitive ambiguity or ambivalence behind the treatment of flowers touches upon a further problem which also arises with artistic genres. Apart from the religious question of paganism, of what others do, there is that of cultures of luxury, which were necessarily hierarchical. They contain features that radically differentiate the richer from the poorer, especially in the days before mass production and consumer cultures. Where the poor are seen as suffering, the use of flowers often encourages a puritanical countersentiment.[26] Should we not give up flowers in favour of growing crops that would fill the peasant's rice bowl? 'No more washing machines to Düsseldorf but tractors to the Third World', as Harold Wilson proclaimed in 1964.

I see a similar, but by no means identical, cognitive problem of

---

[26] I use the words 'puritan' and 'puritanical' in a generic way, as Gellner does, to indicate an approach to life characterized by 'moral rigour', by a rejection not only of luxury but of many aspects of what others consider the 'good life'. While there are dangers in using a specialized term for a general feature, I can find no alternative and plead that I follow common usage.

a puritanical kind behind re-presentation whether as icons, especially sculpture, or as drama. Are not these artistic forms luxuries that are dispensable in certain contexts (especially religious ones) and hence possibly in their entirety (since doubts are raised)? That was even true of music, which is a non-representative art in my restricted sense and hence less readily rejected. Some forms are at times inappropriate. The shutting of opera houses in continental Europe was normal for Easter; the secular and the dramatic were banned and, in eighteenth-century Germany, the oratorio took its place. Indeed, music was absent from worship in the early Middle Ages. In the later tenth century, Gerbert of Aurillac, later to become Pope Sylvester II, who travelled widely including to Barcelona, was said to have brought music and astronomy back to Italy whereas 'Gaul had known nothing of music for a long time'.[27] At the Reformation some sects again banned music, from the home as well as from the chapel, especially in Quaker and Puritan circles. Judaism also excluded dance from the synagogue, a ban that is perhaps more readily understandable than music, or rather instrumental music.

Although it has certainly been reduced, a recent ethnographic example shows that the rejection of representations is not entirely dead, although at the same time this raises problems for individuals that may lead to change. By the end of the nineteenth century Calvinism was beginning to lose its grip on Scotland and there were protests even within the different branches of the Presbyterian Church against the doctrine of predestination. Nevertheless the puritanical character of the religious life persisted. In his autobiography, the Orkney poet, Edwin Muir, writes that he had been aware of religion

> chiefly as the sacred word, and the church itself, severe and decent, with its touching bareness and austerity, seemed to cut off religion from the rest of life and from all the week-day world, as if it were a quite specific thing shut within itself, almost jealously by its

---

[27] Richer, quoted in Murray 1978:157. Northern Spain was also the place in Latin Christendom where mathematics was taught (159); did music and mathematics have some 'elective affinity'?

whitewashed walls, furnished with its bare brown varnished benches unlike any other in the whole world, and filled with the odour of ancient Bibles. It did not tell me by any outward sign that the Word had been made flesh.[28]

In his commentary on Muir's Orkney background, Marshall comments:

> The outward sign is necessary to the poet. Ultimately, it was for its rejection of the image, of the Incarnation in its fullest sense, that Muir found the Church of his youth wanting. He saw its faith as one of abstraction and rejection of life.

That feeling is expressed in his poem, 'The Incarnate One':

> The Word made flesh is here made word again,
> A word made word in flourish and arrogant crook.
> See there King Calvin with his iron pen,
> And God three angry letters in a book.

The word constitutes a minimal representation, dominating the visual, the outward sign, for it is an internalized one. As a visitor from the Faroes remarked, Scottish services are colder, excluding the senses, 'admitting neither altar, altar-pieces, lights or organ'. Originally musical instruments were forbidden and there was no singing except the Psalms (the very words of God), although hymn books were gradually introduced as were organs, beginning in 1863 (in Orkney in 1875). But the heart of the Presbyterian service remained neither music nor ceremony but 'the preaching of the Word'.[29] So Muir had to find that incarnation he was seeking in the formerly Catholic cathedrals of St Andrews or St Magnus in Kirkwall, but above all in Italy.

In the form that appears in Muir's autobiography, the rejection of such activities is much reduced compared with earlier times. People are now less worried by these countercurrents. This is due partly to the process of secularization in so far as religious rejec-

---

[28] Muir quoted in Marshall 1987:277.
[29] Marshall 1987:126–7.

tions are concerned, though it still makes itself felt in extreme forms of Protestantism, in certain aspects of Judaism, certainly in Islam, and in another way in some revolutionary movements. In these cases religion adds a further dimension. But there is a secular dimension related to the luxury status of many earlier artistic forms. That changed with the advent of the mass media. Now we are faced, as Walter Benjamin proclaimed, with the virtually unqualified dominance of iconographic and dramatic re-presentations in a way that has probably never before been paralleled in human history. Changes in the media have resulted in a mass culture of representations. The overwhelming dominance of icons and of drama runs in contrast to the explicit problems that some earlier societies faced in their regard and that made revolutionary movements, like that in France in 1789, condemn them both. That is not to say that doubt has now been eliminated; quite the contrary. 'The printers', wrote Jefferson, 'can never leave us in a state of perfect rest and union of opinion.'[30] And the printers have been followed by the electronic media. But the doubts have largely been diverted from the nature of representation itself. Nowadays, the alternative to inconographic re-presentation is abstract art. Realistic drama, drama itself, is criticized by dramatists, while some expressions of drama get so closely tied up with life that listeners and viewers send wreaths when a character in a soap opera dies.[31] Were they participating in a game or confusing fact and fiction? The two activities are not so distinct as they might appear. Both are of long-standing concern in this and other cultures, as we see in Nelson's account of Renaissance fiction (1973). The confusion of fact and fiction is one of the features of drama that Puritans and their ilk worried about, and the reason why no plays were performed on the Edinburgh stage for 200 years. Mimesis in the form of entertainment is mistaken for life.

Perhaps the earlier ambivalence now takes another different shape and I will later suggest, as indeed has Besançon, that abstract art is also a kind of iconoclasm. So too there are countercurrents

---

[30] Quoted in Innis 1950:24.
[31] For a reference to the reaction to the death of Grace Archer, see Ife 1985:50.

in the theatre that reject theatrical activity and in the novel that reject the narrative base; the rejection, however, is usually made in terms of the genre itself. In *Tristram Shandy* (1759–67), Sterne subordinates the narrative to his free associations and digressions; but the nearly plotless books still retain some temporal shape. Brecht objects to the illusion of the theatre as 'bourgeois drug dealing', a carousel ride on a wooden pony'. 'Alienation' should be the effect of dramatic representation but, as Adorno points out, the playwright can only succeed in shifting the ground of illusion.[32]

Why should such opposing attitudes be so widespread? I suggest because they arise from problems inherent in the process of representation which take the form of cognitive contradictions on the societal level and ambivalences on the personal one. Let me turn to the question of ambivalence.

## *Ambivalence*

The concern with ambivalence in people's thinking and feeling derives partly from Freud (*The Psychopathology of Everyday Life*), partly from T. S. Eliot's literary criticism and his discussion of the role of irony, partly from more general sources. It is a notion that is very explicit in the poetry of John Keats and is associated with the fleeting nature of beauty and joy:

> She dwells with Beauty – Beauty that must die;
> And Joy, whose hand is ever at his lips
> Bidding adieu; and aching Pleasure nigh,
> Turning to Poison while the bee-mouth sips:
> Ay, in the very temple of delight
> Veil'd Melancholy as her sovran shrine . . .
>
> 'Ode on Melancholy'

Being in two minds, looking both ways, is an approach that has been overlooked in a good deal of structural, and even poststructural, analysis much of which harks back to a linguistic model

---
[32] Burwick 1991:5–6.

of binary opposites, of allocating concepts to one box rather than another, especially where polarities appear in the rows and analogies in the columns of decontextualized tables, giving a permanent quality, for example, to the equation Female = black = night = sinister = witchcraft, excluding any use of the equation 'black is beautiful' which obviously obtains in Africa. That failure to be flexible is not remedied by those post-modernist approaches, like that of Derrida, that tend to reject the binary categories, say, of orality and literacy altogether. There has to be a third way that treats such concepts contextually.

In this enquiry I try to relate ambivalence to the fact that in many societies we find an absence of cultural activities, such as figurative sculpture or the theatre, which are quite at home in others. In a recent work (1993) I argued that the relative absence of any aesthetic use of flowers in Africa was largely (but not entirely) due to the level of agriculture. However, when we look at the more complex societies of Europe and Asia, at some times and in some places we find not only that flowers are absent, contextually or in their entirety, but that there are tendencies towards their deliberate rejection – for both secular and religious reasons, including their status as luxuries.

The latter was the case during the Cultural Revolution in China when people had more important crops to cultivate and when aesthetic activity as a whole became treated as an unnecessary luxury. I have also made the same suggestion regarding the rejection of elaborate cuisines by revolutionary regimes or by puritanical sects, though that rejection was perhaps less widely practised than in the case of flowers. I argued that the contradictions involved in the use of luxury items in the midst of poverty created a potential cognitive problem for some; there was an underlying contradiction which under certain conditions would be recognized by some participants, giving rise to an alternative valuation of these activities, that is, to ambivalence. This contradiction was noted not only by some of the poor (who suffered) but by critical commentators of the type of Thersites, by the King's fool and similar licensed speakers, as well as by philosophers involved in ethical and moral enquiry.

Here I was referring to forms of internal criticism and contradiction that arose from the stratified nature of the cultural regime, of 'luxury cultures' where one stratum was radically distinguished from another in terms of its style of life. Both luxury and poverty are relative concepts, indicating conditions that are particularly characteristic of the major Eurasian societies after the Bronze Age. In Africa such differentiation was comparatively muted and it is difficult to speak of cultures of luxury in the same way. But in Eurasia luxuria was conceived of as a sin, when some consumed over-elaborated food while others went short or lived on more spartan diets. Flowers were rejected partly for similar reasons, as products of 'aesthetic' rather than utilitarian horticulture. In addition the offerings of flowers to deities or to ancestors could be seen as gifts to the wrong gods, or as the wrong gifts to any god if he is better worshipped with words rather than with material objects.

I want to extend this approach to treat of the ambivalences involved in representations, which may also have an element of luxury about them. Representation is often considered unproblematic, especially for Africa, by many historians of art and students of performance. Art and performance are seen as universal. That may be the case if we merge together figurative and non-figurative graphic activity, or treat ritual and drama as interchangeable. As a result it overlooks the absence of certain types of representation (for example, pictorial ones), treating this question as unproblematic, or at best as a matter of accidental (or 'cultural') distribution. My broad argument is that such a view neglects an important aspect of the actor dimension, which includes an intentional, intellectual element. The explanation takes me outside any particular group (although the touchstone is still my own experience in northern Ghana) and outside Africa, since I want to establish that if Black Africa is different, it is different in an understandable way, not simply 'cultural', 'primitive'.

But it is not only a question of ambivalence arising in luxury cultures. Ambivalence is involved in the very process of representation in language-using animals. I use that circuitous phrase rather than 'representations in language' in order to convey the idea that even visual representations are altered by the presence or advent of language. Representations are always of something; hence they are re-presentations, not the thing itself, *der Ding an sich*. Yet they appear to present themselves as that thing (here understood as any entity whatever, including imaginary ones). So there is always the possibility that the signifier, words, actions, images, may get confused or overly identified with the signified, bringing about a situation in which that relationship needs to be made more distinct. For instance we may realize, perhaps as the result of a wish not granted, that the icon of Christ is not Christ himself, nor does it necessarily partake of the powers claimed for him; that relics, as parts, do not necessarily stand for the whole; or that the suspension of disbelief which the theatre calls for is never complete; or that reading novels or romances may lead us to tilt against imaginary windmills. In other words we may realize that there is some difference between image and 'reality' (though in other terms the image constitutes another level of reality), between the metaphorical and the literal (to take up a theme of Lloyd 1991), between truth and fiction; these antinomies are not to be dissolved by some wave of the post-modernist wand. For the problems, that I refer to on a societal level as cognitive contradictions, are built into the use of language itself, in other words into the definition of the human.

Hence the objections to representations follow from the use of language itself. It is language that enables us to develop tenses other than the present, to conquer time and space by representing imaginings.[33] The very fact that we can do so may harbour questions about the reality of the process, and raises 'a kernel of doubt', especially about creative activities such as painting, sculpture, drama and even literature. All those activities depend upon the fact that language enables us to handle, in an explicit way, the future (and the absent) as well as the present (which we later relocate in our memory store), that is, it enables us to deal with hypothetical situations (which do not exist and perhaps never have done or never could do) as well as with those we are experiencing or have experienced.

[33] Good 1995:140.

Language explicitly re-presents an image of the future as well as the past and present, and in each of these tenses it can in fact also misrepresent. Recall that passage from Samuel Johnson's *Rasselas* (1759):

> 'Dear Princess,' said Rasselas [to Nekayah], 'you fall into the common errors of exaggeratory declamation, by producing in a familiar disquisition examples of national calamities and scenes of extensive misery which are found in books rather than in the world, and which, as they are horrid, are ordained to be rare. Let us not imagine evils which we do not feel, nor injure life by mis-representations.'[34]

That statement pertains to books rather than the word more generally and it is a theme that crops up again in Jane Austen's *Northanger Abbey*, in Gustave Flaubert's *Madame Bovary*, and much earlier in Miguel de Cervantes' *Don Quixote* (1605). In all representation, however, including the use of language itself, there is a further element of misrepresentation in that even if the representation is 'correct' in Rasselas' terms, it is still not the thing itself. In presenting itself as such, in fiction dressed up as realism in the manner of Defoe, or perhaps even in a 'Once upon a time' sense, it runs the risk of being treated as a lie or, if intentionality should not be presumed, a falsehood. This realization can give rise to criticism of representation itself, even of language.

It is plainly not always easy to tell whether an image, an object or an act is a presentation or a re-presentation. The dogma of the transubstantiation of the host into the body and blood of Christ, which was proclaimed in 1215, meant that the bread and the wine were no mere symbols, but rather the real presence.[35] So too it was the real presence of the relics of the saints that often justified the 'idol', the statue or the reliquary that surrounded them. *Presentia* was a word long associated with the relics of saints, just as the term 'images' often evoked a fiction or '*une relit faible et appauvrie*'.[36] But

---

[34] Johnson 1759:xxviii.
[35] Luther's consubstantiation was in effect the symbolic version.
[36] Ginzburg 1991.

while that presence might be proclaimed in the official doctrine of the church, it was not always sufficient to dismiss all the doubts of the congregation. On the one hand the host was also used by the populace for 'magical' purposes because of the power attracted to it; meanwhile 'heretics' were led to distinguish between the 'actual' (real) body and blood of Christ and their 'imagined' (imaged) appearance in the host. It was the latter trend that was incorporated in the 'rationalized' or 'sanitized' doctrines of the Reformation; the re-presence could never be the same as the presence. That is to say, quite apart from the problems offered by any analytic definition of representation (which is obviously based upon European experience), there is the question of the actor's often changing perception of what is presented and what is represented. Take, first of all, performances that from some external points of view may resemble one another, that is, theatre and funerals; William Ridgeway even argued that Greek drama had emerged from funeral rites. But funerals do not re-present in the same kind of way as drama; they are among a category of repeated acts (rites, rituals), but ones that repeat each other. They do not re-present in the way that, say, *Hamlet* re-presents on a stage a series of imagined actions from life itself. Rather they act, in and of themselves.

Some rites are both re-enactments and efficient at the same time. The Mass can be said to re-present the death and resurrection of Christ. But while that aspect might make it powerful to some, to critical spirits ('heretics') within the same general cultural tradition it rendered the ceremony suspect. For many Puritans, no representations at all were acceptable, especially religious ones, because of their intrinsic falsity; re-presentation was not the real thing, it was illusion. As with the priest, it interposed itself between people and God.

Discussions of the simpler societies often assume that images are taken as the real presence, as in the concept of the fetish or in the figure of the enemy into which pins are stuck. While some assumptions of this order are undoubtedly made by the actors, and more frequently than in Europe, they do not always go unchallenged. At times there is a measure of scepticism expressed by those who are led to question the identity of object and image. In that very questioning we may also find a genesis for the elaboration of such techniques in one society and their virtual absence in the next. The 'Third World' is not so ideologically or conceptually monolithic as it is often presented, if one takes presence and absence as indicating an implicit acceptance or rejection of the image about which there is potentially a kernel of doubt.

I see the ambivalence that lies behind these doubts and their cultural products as arising from cognitive contradictions that are inherent in the human situation regarding representations, that is, the situation of language-using beings. My use of the word cognitive and my reference to language suggest the need to relate this argument to an important approach to cultural phenomena that has recently been developed by a number of anthropologists in France whose work harks back in some respects to that of Lévi-Strauss, of Chomsky and more particularly of cognitive scientists and linguistic philosophers. This approach, which I discuss in greater detail in the final chapter, is associated with the work of Dan Sperber and his colleagues, Scott Atran and Pascal Boyer. It looks at certain widespread features of human societies, in religious beliefs for example, recognizes them as not tied to specific cultures and argues, as Chomsky did with language, that their origin was built in to the human mind. My own argument differs in that I see problems to do with representation not as actually wired in but as arising from the cognitive contradictions in human life and as becoming explicit only when a written language makes this kind of discussion inevitable because it objectifies thought in a special way. Which is why I see a significant difference (based on common understanding) between societies with and without writing. Of course, speaking is important in both, but writing adds a distinct dimension. Hence, I am quite opposed to Derrida's claim that reading the stars is the same as reading a text, or the (post-modern) attempt to blur the notion of text with that of utterance.[37] Derrida's statement was

---

[37] See D. Olson, *The World on Paper*, 1994.

presumably in Lacan's mind when he declared that to read coffee grounds is not to read hieroglyphics. Natural symbolism is not the same as the symbolic.[38] I want to maintain a delicate balance, as I have tried to do elsewhere, between universal or widespread, transversal, tendencies and the way these are brought out, made explicit, and hence changed, with the increased reflexivity which writing brings.

This ambivalence about representations seems to me to lie behind a number of phenomena central to cultural history which Western historians and others have looked at in a much too specific way as being characteristic of their own tradition, in particular of the Christian one, and its controversies. I refer here to iconoclasm (a term I extend, as do many art historians, to the rejection of visual images more generally) and to anti-theatricality, as well as to some similar rejections. The latter topic was the subject of Jonah Barish's book *The Anti-theatrical Prejudice* (1981), the former of Alain Besançon in *L'Image interdite; une histoire intellectuelle de l'iconoclasme* (1994), both of them valuable books to which I am much indebted. The first deals with the actual banning of theatres, the latter concentrates, as its subtitle indicates, on the intellectual history, largely of representations of the divine, which raise special problems (can one create the Creator?) Both begin with Plato and assume that they are dealing with phenomena that need to be examined only within the Western tradition. That is a notion I wish to challenge and extend.

In discussing the intellectual history of iconoclasm Besançon argues that:

One begins, in Greece, with a situation of innocence. Greece, like Egypt and Mesopotamia before, gives its gods a figure. Then, at the

---

[38] 'What was the meaning of my lecture last night on the training of analysts . . . it is essential to carefully distinguish between symbolism properly so-called, that is, symbolism as structured in language, that in which we understand one another here, and natural symbolism. I have summed this up on the epigram, to read coffee grounds is not to read hieroglyphics.' Lacan, Seminar 13, Bk 3, *The Psychoses* 1955–56. London 1993 [1984 Fr. ed.].

very time when Greek religious art established itself, developed and approached its perfection, an equally religious element of hellenism, philosophy, began to reflect upon this representation, weighing its agreement and disagreement with the civil notion of the divine and the received forms of its representation. And so there opened up, beginning with philosophy, a cycle which would in future be characterised as 'iconoclast'.[39]

That is very true, except for the impression given by the opening sentence. Was the world really innocent of such thoughts before the Greeks? Did philosophy (Greek philosophy) change the situation? I would argue that this is a Western humanist view that disregards the manifestations of iconoclasm in other parallel societies as well as its proto-manifestations in simpler ones (of Africa, for example). Philosophy, as a literate discipline, did a lot to formalize and to develop the notions present in pre-literate societies, but it did not create the ambivalence towards representation that Besançon describes; it made explicit that which was already implicit, but did not initiate the impulse. Nor is that impulse confined to the divine, though this was undoubtedly of special significance.

The question of iconoclasm is not simply a matter of the uniqueness of the Western tradition, nor yet one of intellectual history as commonly understood (that is, in a highly literate way), but of the nature of representation itself, indeed of the origin of cultural forms. It is possible with images, the theatre, and imaginative literature to trace out an interrupted tradition of rejection from Plato onwards. Empirically that procedure is not altogether satisfactory since we find these objections outside the Western tradition, and indeed, implicitly, even in societies without writing. Writing creates philosophy as we know it, creates a constant reference back to the literary works of others – at least for the elite. But there is another possible view that sees philosophy not as the creator but as the created, as the written expression of doubts, ambivalences, questions, that inhere in the human situation, in

---

[39] Besançon 1994:9, my translation.

the interaction of animals talking with one another and, internally, with themselves. Writing makes those thoughts more explicit, and in so doing changes them. But the basis of the tradition lies not so much in a handing down as in a persistence of the original doubts about representation, that it is never altogether what it seems.

## *Endnote on Representation*

The word 'representation' has a plurality of meanings. The first thing to say is that I am not concerned with political representation of one human by another, the kind of sense used by Pitkin in her book on the subject where her interest is 'primarily in political representation'.[40] I use the word in the Latin sense of re-presenting, the literal 'bringing into presence of something previously absent', nor yet simply 'the embodiment of an abstraction in an object',[41] but as presenting something in a different way, as in a painting of a dog. It nearly always has a visual aspect, since that is the way of the world, but it includes the representation of abstraction such as courage referred to above; indeed the very concept of courage is a re-presentation of something else. That is to extend the idea; I do not really see music as re-presentational, except in some obvious ways (for example, in Britten's War Requiem), but it may present experience of a different kind. In order to be representative a picture has to have 'an arrangement of elements analogous to the arrangement of salient visual elements in the object';[42] intentionality is critical. Representation means a presenting again, a presenting of something not present, which may take a linguistic as well as a visual form.

In the social sciences, the concept of representation forms a central part of the Durkheimian legacy to social science, as in Hertz's important essay on *'la représentation collective de la mort'*

---

[40] Pitkin 1967:6.
[41] Pitkin 1967:3.
[42] Pitkin 1967:67, 71.

(1907), although the concept is present in the work of Freud and earlier writers. In Durkheim's 'collective representations', according to Parsons, the phenomena of the external world are 'reflected in the mind of the scientist in systems of data and concepts'.[43] It is a name for the scientist's subjective experience of the phenomena of the external world, the term 'collective' referring to the social environment, whereas the individual representations refer to heredity and the environment. While the first notion is in common usage, the latter is an interpretation singular to Parsons. In fact, these writers were referring primarily to customary notions, as well as acts, relating to death, and on the other hand to individual conceptions. More recently the word 'representation' has become widely popular in the jargon of the social sciences and the humanities.[44] There is the inclusive view, especially prevalent in France, which refers to linguistic usage and to processes of thought, in a wider, and at the same time, looser way.[45] Sperber writes of 'widely distributed, long-standing representations' as being the primary referent of 'culture'.[46] A representation, he explains, involves a relationship between three terms; an object is a representation of something for some information-processing device. For this purpose he distinguishes two types, mental and public representations, the first has to do with the intra-subjective (psychological) processes of thought and memory, the latter with the inter-subjective ones whereby the representation of one subject affects those of other subjects through modifications of their common physical environment.[47] There is a fundamental difference between 'internal' and 'external' representations; by internal representations is meant what is often referred to as 'the expres-

---

[43] Parsons 1937:359. I find his discussion of the difference with 'conscience collective' obscure, partly because Durkheim's usage seems to change over time (389).
[44] See Ginzburg 1991.
[45] For example, Augé (1982) in an anthropological context, Fodor (1984) in a philosophical one, Sperber (1985) in an epidemiological one.
[46] Sperber 1985:74.
[47] The former are internal objects in psychoanalytic terms.

sion of thought', usually by words, either orally or in writing. What is distinctive is that there is no clear division between the signified and signifier; what is represented may be part of the representation itself. But there is a second relationship since the linguistic expression may refer to experiences of various kinds with the world outside.

In the psychologist, David Olson's, account of the impact of writing, representations are modes of description, which always involve intention and interpretation. But he also proposes a much narrower category in which he would include seventeenth-century Dutch paintings but not medieval icons.

I use the word in the more specific sense but not in as limited a as Olson. All kinds of figurative painting of humans or the world are re-presentations. They do not have to be realistic or even mimetic, as often understood, but in the figurative representations with which I am largely dealing in this essay, the presentation of reality involving a measure of correspondence, is always one element. What distinguishes representational art is not accuracy; representation, as Gombrich has declared, is never a replica. Only abstract art would escape, although even here there is an argument to be made. There are clearly degrees of realism in painting or sculpture as there are in drama or in other literary forms. But figurative representation entails a degree of mimesis, although it is frequently more than that word often implies; it refers back to the original but does not copy it.

The process of representation is basic to human social life. Indeed the complexity of representational systems may already be a major vector in animal evolution. With humans, representations are mapped on to an externalized language. But even apes have developed a 'Machiavellian intelligence' without the use of language which may involve some kind of representation. In the work on the evolution of intelligence, special attention has been given to the role of deception in anthropoids, which has the particular quality of challenging the other to outwit the deceived. The human skill of pretending, however, may have depended critically on the linguistic representations of intentions because it requires the concurrent maintenance of two levels of belief.

Language enables one to represent (not figuratively, of course, but arbitrarily) what is not there. Indeed, from this point of view language itself is a deception; the word 'horse' is not a horse but can represent the animal in its absence.[48]

---

[48] Freud saw the child expressing in language its appearance and disappearance in the mirror by the words 'gone' and 'here' as a way of conceptualizing the absence of the mother – Lacan's 'mirror phase'. On relevant literature from other fields in the social sciences, see also Barnes 1994 on lying, to which I return in the chapter on the novel.

# 2

# Icons and Iconoclasm in Africa? Absence and Ambivalence

*What are the roots that clutch, what branches grow*
*Out of the stony rubbish? Son of man,*
*You cannot say, or guess, for you know only*
*A heap of broken images, where the sun beats,*
*And the dead tree gives no shelter, the cricket no relief,*
*And the dry stone no sound of water.*

T. S. Eliot, *The Waste Land*

Africa is often seen as the continent of figurative icons, of masks, of sculpture, bronze-casting and of 'fetishes'. In museums the remains of blood offerings are splattered over their surfaces, showing they were actively involved in cult, not made for aesthetic display alone. The figurative sculptures of Africa dominate many collections of non-European art and have had a profound influence on European artists earlier this century. The well-known case of the Fang mask acquired by Derain and admired by Picasso was certainly not unique.[1]

Despite the frequent appearance of figurative, three-dimensional forms, there are large gaps in their distribution. This is particularly true of representations in metal and to some extent

[1] Willet 1971. Masks are, of course, not necessarily figurative. Nafana wooden masks are 'abstract', so in a sense are raffia disguises. But they move and are associated with human beings.

of sculpture in wood which is more common in the forest. But there are regions and peoples where little or no figurative art at all appears, or does so only in restricted contexts, suggesting that more is at stake than access to raw materials. Among the Frafra (including the Tallensi) of northern Ghana one finds virtually no figurative art, nor is there very much among some other peoples of the region, including the LoDagaa and the Gonja with whom I worked.[2] On the other hand their near neighbours to the west, the Senufo of the Ivory Coast and the Lobi of Burkina Faso, are noted for the richness of their sculptural traditions.[3] But it is not only a matter of the general weight given to representation in a culture, but of its absence in certain specific contexts.

A number of neighbouring groups in northern Ghana display a similar lack of interest in sculptural traditions. For the Sisala, Nunley (1976) attributes this situation to past political and social upheaval when slave-raiding and immigration inhibited the establishment of an artistic tradition. Such upheavals may have played a part in the case of the Sisala as there is some evidence of an earlier masking tradition[4] which might have been suppressed by the Muslim raiders. But it seems very doubtful if this thesis has a wider application, for many of those with sculptural traditions were acephalous peoples who were similarly raided for human booty.

One factor in this general unevenness has been the influence of

[2] On the Tallensi, see Fortes 1945, 1949; on the Gonja, see E. Goody 1982, 1973.
[3] On the Senufo, see Holas 1960; on the Lobi, see Labouret 1932, Père 1988 and Meyer 1981. In numerical terms this difference was brought out when I examined a record of the 445 items in the Smithsonian collection in Washington D.C., that came from Ghana, Togo, Burkina Faso, Benin and the Ivory Coast. The distribution of anthropomorphic or zoomorphic representations was very uneven. There were many artistic objects from Ghana but with the exception of those from north-west Ashanti, none was masks or figures. To the east there were three from the Republic of Benin; apart from two from the Mossi of Burkina Faso (possibly from a subordinate group) and four from the Bobo in the north, the rest were all from the Ivory Coast to the west, twenty-eight in all. At the level of indigenous societies such differences were of course more marked than between the new nations as units.
[4] Rattray 1932.

ideas about representation that derive from Near Eastern religions. The attitude of Judaism is enshrined in the commandment of the Old Testament, 'Thou shalt not make unto thee any graven image, or any likeness of anything that is in heaven above, or that is in the earth beneath, or that is in the water under the earth.' This injunction applies not only to religious icons, but to any pictorial representation of humans, animals, plants or natural object. Of course, there were illustrations in Jewish manuscripts but painting was not a major part of that tradition in Europe until recently.

Most historians do not regard the prohibition on images of living things as absolute but Josephus forbade them entirely. During the Roman period there were no human figures on Jewish coins and 'not a single statue of a Jewish worthy has either been recorded in literature or revealed by excavation', even in medieval times. But some non-human figures did appear later on Jewish coins and the prohibition applied to whole not to mutilated statues. Moreover, throughout Jewish history a distinction was made between *intaglio* and *rilievo*, between graven and other images. Consequently embroideries, woven with figures, and wall paintings were allowed for use in synagogues.[5] In other words, casuistical arguments got around the absolute prohibition, but it remained very significant.

In their fascinating philosophical enquiry on *Idolatry* (1992), Halbertal and Margalit see the notion of idolatry associated with iconoclasm and with monotheistic religions; it is the worship of other gods, of strange gods, as well as a ban on certain ways of representing the right God, a ban on visual images (but not on linguistic ones). 'Strange' is seen as other gods and other ways of worship. The rejection of 'idolatry' is a question of 'sensibility', deriving from the relation between concepts and feelings. It is not simply the worship of 'other gods' but a 'pagan' threat to monotheism, the exclusive worship of a single God. Idolatry is pagan which they interpret as more than the worship of the other or others' worship; it pertains to non-monotheistic practice. The problem with linking idolatry, both the worship of strange gods and their embodiment in figurative representation, so closely with

[5] Elmslie 1911:74–5.

monotheism (and hence 'non-paganism') is that objections to and the rejection of images occur in other situations, so that the explanation offered is philosophically and analytically inadequate.

While God was not imaged pictorially, physical descriptions of him are offered in words. In speaking 'the language of the people', the Torah speaks about God in the concrete ways that the masses can understand, metaphorically. The question raised by Maimonides is whether language does not also misrepresent God. Maimonides criticized idolatry because it was too anthropomorphic, a projection of human qualities on to God, due to the lack of power of abstraction and the inherent limitations of human language.[6] Language, he concludes, is in fact bound to misrepresent in the same way as pictorial representations, which leads him to the Wittgensteinian conclusion that 'Silence and limiting oneself to the apprehension of the intellect are more appropriate'.[7] Such a statement leads directly to meditation and to mysticism.

It is interesting, and logical, that questions of representation should emerge most clearly and most often with regard to the Creator. But is it right to consider these doubts about whether it is possible to approach God through language as doubts about linguistic representation *per se*? If we take pictorial art, that would in many instances be the case. The aniconic approach to deity is generalized to the creations of the deity. But language we humans cannot do without; we have to use it but we may worry at times about its arbitrary nature, as when we fail to tie down the concepts of right and left, or when a hysteric refuses to settle for the arbitrary (symbolic) nature of language, or when a philosopher declares 'A white horse is not a horse'.[8]

In Russia, the situation for Jews changed at the beginning of the twentieth century with the revolutionary explosion of 1905. Shortly afterwards, in 1907–1908, we find Marc Chagall starting to paint. A young Jew could now devote himself entirely to

---

[6] Halbertal and Margalit 1992:238.
[7] Halbertal and Margalit 1992:61–2.
[8] For right and left, see the work on dyslexia (Goody 1977); for the references to hysteria I am indebted to J. Mitchell; for the Chinese discussion of the white horse, see J. Goody 1996a:1.

painting. 'This decision', writes Lucien Goldmann, 'implied a complete break, if not, as has sometimes been said with a formal prohibition, at least with a very strong tradition (born in part perhaps out of the prohibition on representing God) which meant that painting was not a Jewish metier.'[9] In deciding to become a painter the young Chagall had already marked himself off, distanced himself from his own social group. So while he continued to seek his subject matter in the Russian village, in 1910 he left his homeland for the West for four years, and in 1922 decided definitively to settle in France. Exile left him freer to explore pictorially his own background.

In Judaism the rejection of icons was directly linked to the uniqueness of God's creation. In the earlier period the aniconic doctrine was vigorously taken up in Islam, although possibly only by later authors of the Hadith for whom attempts to represent God's creation pictorially were sacrilegious.[10]

This was partly related to the problem of 'the creation' which is a widespread, if not universal, feature of human cultures before the predominantly secular societies of our times. One dominant way of accounting for the existence of things is by attributing their origin to the unique act of the Creator God which the creation of images by humans may be seen to threaten. The logic of the ban

---

[9] Goldmann 1960:669.

[10] Cole (1989:12) defines an 'icon', in an African context, as a visual representation which achieves 'compelling prominence through frequent repetition in sacred or secular arts'. The sense the word has acquired in the context of the development of 'iconography' is even wider though always relating to sculptural or pictorial form.

Its earlier use in the Orthodox church was for 'religious icons', or 'figurative icons' when the reference is to likenesses of the object of God's creation including man. An alternative is 'image', which, especially in the form of 'imagery', is much used to refer to the 'mental images' or perhaps visualized representations conjured up by poetry, by words generally and by reflection. There is overlap in the usage of all these terms. For this reason some would see any differentiation as unnecessary; all are 'symbols', 'representations'. But my problem, which I also argue is often a problem for the actor, has to do with why these forms of 'symbols' differ in different societies, why you get figurative images in one context and not in another.

on images in the Ten Commandments is that attempted repetition might be taken as a challenge to the Creator.[11] Indeed, in a well-known Islamic tale, the creation of a perfect garden is deemed to be an imitation of Paradise and so has to be destroyed.[12] While there were times in the history of Muslim societies when this prohibition was overlooked or overcome, by and large Islam continues to reject figurative representations, especially in mosques. With few exceptions they were particularly excluded from the sacred space, which confined itself to abstract designs, including the dancing rhythms of arabesques and of calligraphy.[13] The word was dominant over the image, the abstract over figurative representational forms. Aniconism was directed not only to the representations of the gods but to humans and animals too, anything with a soul.

In the Arab Hall which the Victorian painter Frederic Leighton (1830–1896) built in Holland Park to display the tiles he had brought back from the East, one ceramic from Isnik shows two birds whose throats have been 'cut' in the glaze.[14] The tiles no longer represented living creatures but dead ones, so did not rival God's creation.[15] At the Hindu temple of the Maharana of Mewar at Eklingi near Udaipur, the Moguls (whose advance had been resisted for so long) broke off the trunks of sculpted elephants on the temple friezes as well as damaging the noses of gods; they were literally defaced (or rather denosed), and were therefore no longer what they purported to be.[16] If the major *lingam* shrine (the phallus dedicated to Siva) was damaged in this way, it could no longer be

[11] Marçais 1957.
[12] Schimmel 1976.
[13] Clément gives four cases of mosques with images (1995:21).
[14] See the catalogue of the Leighton House Museum, n.d., Royal Borough of Kensington and Chelsea. I am grateful to Dr Cesare Poppi for drawing my attention to this and many other relevant matters.
[15] On ways of avoiding the accusation of imitation, see Clément 1995:24ff. These included miniaturization (25).
[16] For the damaging of statues in Mesopotamia, the effacement of names and the insertion of curses, see Bahrani 1995. In Judaism, an idol could be desecrated (and rendered harmless) by cutting off the tip of the ear, the nose or finger, or by battering it (Elmslie 1911:4–5).

worshipped by Hindus since it would no longer be perfect. For when the icon is consecrated, it becomes the god for the worshippers in a real sense, even though the deity is recognized to be both there and not there. So that such an act is sacrilegious and destructive of more than a representation.

When Islam entered East Africa by sea and the West across the Sahara, there came a religion not only of the written word but one that was largely aniconic in this wider sense of being against the representation of living things. It was not the case that no representative art, even of anthropomorphic figures, was found in the Muslim-dominated areas of Africa.[17] In the first place, Muslims were rarely completely dominant in the cultural, or even in the political sense; they often lived in multi-ethnic communities with a plurality of religious practices. Moreover, marriage and hence kinship were not confined, as was the tendency in Eurasia, to particular social groups. In the formerly independent kingdom of Gonja, for example, since there is neither endogamy, hypergamy nor yet hypogamy as a social rule or norm, cultural practice flows through the community, leading not only to the automatic conversion of a non-Muslim woman (even of a royal daughter who marries a Muslim man), but to frequent apostasy, as when a Muslim woman cannot escape from participating in the ways of her non-Islamic husband.[18] The situation makes for fluidity of practice, including a modification of Muslim dogma about representation. For example, among a number of peoples in West Africa, including the Muslims of the Gonja town of Bole, the masked rites of the Do society were performed at night.[19] Because of a commitment to the Qur'an and its commentaries, such practices laid themselves open to attacks from the righteous. In Bole the advent of a 'Mahdī', a self-proclaimed messianic deliverer, in 1917 led to a stricter application of the laws of God, as a result of which such dancing was officially prohibited.[20] Even the local

---

[17] Bravmann 1974, 1981.
[18] J. Goody 1970a.
[19] We hear of 'masques' in North Africa (Clément 1995:31).
[20] J. Goody 1970b.

autochthones were affected; they use masks in the villages but not in the town. The very nature of the written Islamic canon meant that there always existed the possibility that some individual or group might come to power, locally or nationally, by claiming to go back to God's word and his ways which had been neglected by other commentators or by later followers. The new purists would insist upon a return to basics, to the aniconic fundamentals.

Such aniconic dogmas did not go altogether uncontested even in the more central regions of Islam.[21] The Mongol conquests brought the Near East into closer contact, both for trade and for art, with influences from China from whose borders the new rulers had come. Under the Safavids, Persia saw a vigorous development of representational painting beginning in the fifteenth century but picking up the threads from the earlier iconic traditions of the area and spreading practices to the Mogul regime of North India.[22] Nevertheless, the aniconic tradition persisted in the religious sphere. Paintings were largely secular and no images of any kind were allowed into the mosque except under the rarest of circumstances.

A similar tendency was found in early Christianity which, like Judaism, has been described by Grabar as 'aniconic.'[23] Even in the third century CE, when figurative representations are found in the Christian community, one section of the faithful continued the fundamentalist rejection, placing their faith in the literal interpretation of Biblical sources.[24] A number of the early Fathers of the Church – including Justin Martyr (d. *c.*165 CE), Athenagoras (*c.*177 CE), Minucius Felix (*c*,200 CE), Tertullian (*c.*200 CE), Clement of Alexandria (*c.*200 CE), and Origen (248 CE) – objected to the use of images in worship as being characteristic of the ways of the pagan. The first three authors rejected the possibility of

---

[21] See Clément 1995:24ff, who seems to argue that 'la révolution des images' that has occurred recently (with photography, cinema and television) was in a sense prepared for because the ban had never been absolute.
[22] Gray 1930.
[23] Grabar 1968.
[24] Pelikan 1990.

worshipping God through images, the immaterial through the material; the last three objected to any image-making as an activity, although queries about notions of divinity were also involved.[25] In Tertullian's eyes, the devil had introduced artificers of statues and images into this world; every 'form' was an idol.[26] The whole status of religious images was raised in acute form by the eastern Iconoclasts of the eighth century, a movement that began after the rise of Islam in an area it had come to dominate.[27] Some recent interpretations of early iconoclasm in Europe and the Near East have stressed the particular historical context. That is certainly one aspect of those events, of *'histoire événementielle'*. But the problem of religious images runs much deeper for we have to place those happenings in the more general context of repeated events over the past centuries and in different parts of the world.

The iconoclasts objected to images in places of worship and many were destroyed. But of three-dimensional ones, there were already virtually none to destroy for their production had almost ceased with Christianity. They were not only deemed too realistic, feigning appearances, but resembled pagan idols and challenged God. One of the most remarkable features of the history of European culture is the virtual disappearance of sculpture in the early centuries of Christianity, although that art form had dominated the heritage from the classical civilizations of Greece and Rome. It did not return in force until the Gothic period, perhaps even the Renaissance.[28]

---

[25] Justin Martyr, *First Apology*, ch. IX; Athenagoras, *A Plea for the Christians*, ch. XV; Minucius Felix, *Octavius*, ch. XXXII; Tertullian, *On Idolatry*, ch. III ('every art which in any way produces an idol [=form] instantly became a fount of idolatry'); Clement of Alexandria, *Stromata*, bk. V, ch. V (the Mosaic prohibition); bk. VI, ch. XV, *Pedagogus*, bk. III, ch. XI (no faces for idols); Origen, *Against Celsus*, bk. IV, ch. XXXI; bk. VI, ch. LXVI ('not to form representations of things contrary to reality', 'feigning the appearance', but 'to have regard to the truth of each individual thing'; 'the evil handiwork of painters and moulders and sculptors').

[26] Elmslie 1911.

[27] Sahas 1986; Schmidt 1987.

[28] For some earlier examples of European statuary see J. Goody 1993a.

Even then the aniconic tendency continued as a sub-motif. The victory of the Iconodules in the east provided no permanent solution to the question of images. In the first place, the decisions of Nicaea, which established that victory were not accepted by the Western Church. In the second, the text of the Commandments of the Old Testament remained a continuing point of reference. In the third place, the ambivalence about representations lived on because it depended neither on theology nor on text but on a problem inherent in conceptualizing the immaterial. The aniconic trend continued in Western Christianity and was taken up by various heretical sects, especially in relation to religious images in places of worship.

Then, in the sixteenth and seventeenth centuries, Calvinists in Western Europe set about clearing the churches of visual representations, although often proliferating the secular variety at home. Part of the Puritanical wing carried the objections to representation still further, in refusing to accept the division between the religious and the secular, at the same time as radically simplifying the architecture of tombs, banishing theatres, forbidding traditional rituals and creating what, from the standpoint of performance and art, was a cultural desert by rejecting many of the rich manifestations that society had developed.[29] They were set against any notion of representing the divine. Such representations and performances were held to hide, rather than reveal, the true nature of the world;[30] there was unease on this wing not only about religious images but about all images, as untruths, deceptions.

The practical result of these doctrines is illustrated in the fate of the great Norman cathedral in Durham. Little change occurred at the time of the Reformation. The monastery was dissolved in 1539, but the prior became the dean of the cathedral. In 1553 a new reforming dean was appointed. He began the work of destruction by smashing up a good deal of the stained glass and removing

---

[29] Freedberg 1985; 1989.
[30] Marcus 1986.

the effigy of St Cuthbert. In Elizabeth's reign a new dean, Whittingham, who had spent part of his exile in Geneva,

> had all the carvings defaced, and got rid of all brasses, especially those with any imagery on them. The holy water stoups and memorial stones were put to use in his kitchen and stables. To him they were monuments of idolatry, which had not only to be removed but also downgraded, lest any superstitious reverence should still cling to them. His wife burned the famous Banner of St Cuthbert on 'her fire, in notable contempt and disgrace of all ancient and goodly reliques'. Priceless works of art were destroyed at the Whittinghams' hands.[31]

Tombstones were used for building: it was rumoured that the peal of four bells was to be sold. The new approach to religion was established despite the populace of whom one preacher wrote in the reign of Edward VI:

> They come to church to feast their eyes, and not their souls; they are not taught that no visible thing is to be worshipped. And so, because they see not in the church the shining pomp and pleasant variety (as they thought it) of painted clothes, candlesticks, images, altars, lamps, tapers, they say 'as good as go into a barn'.[32]

Conflict between the Puritan wing and the Laudians, between Calvinists and Lutherans, continued for many years. Ritual, images and music made a partial comeback under the latter, only to be suppressed again under the Commonwealth. The Scots had occupied Durham in 1640 for five years, displaying reforming zeal: 'they smashed the font, and began to wreck the organs . . .'[33] The bishopric was abolished, the dean and chapter suppressed. Scots prisoners were housed in the Cathedral and did further damage so that by the time of the Restoration, things were in a bad shape physically and financially.

---

[31] Stranks 1973:40, 43.
[32] Stranks 1973:44.
[33] Stranks 1973:52.

The continuing manifestations of iconoclasm arose because, despite these objections, there was a tendency for the visual to creep back in. The early Christians had started to use abstract signs as symbols for divinity, then moved to image signs and then to figurative representations of the Apostles, of Christ and later even God the Father (but not in three dimensions). That movement was partly the result of a recognition that the illiterate masses needed such visual symbols, especially as they could not read and hence could not directly appreciate the word of God, which was primarily available as a written text. Partly too because in the West there had existed an earlier Roman tradition of representing patrons. Partly again it was because of a widespread tendency to embroider and elaborate forms of social action such as ritual and gift-giving, so that the mere word was never quite enough, even for the literate.

Like Islam, some Protestant branches of Christianity were set against any notion of representing the divine, except possibly for 'educational' purposes, and so objected to all icons of that kind, partly for theological reasons (as 'idols'), partly because they were unnecessary luxuries. The destruction of images was taken up by local breakaway churches, such as that of William Harris who came to the Ivory Coast from Liberia in 1914. Other branches of Christianity were less severe and permitted images of their own, for painting and later sculpture had, of course, been developed within the Christian church. Icons, in the restricted sense, even of the Eastern Church made their way north of the Alps as the result of gifts but did not become established there before the thirteenth century.[34] The influence of Byzantine art was especially strong in Ottonian painting in Germany. The introduction, however, of the reliquary-statue, a development of the Carolingian West, did help to solve the problem since it meant that adoration was given to the relic (the person itself) and not to the image.[35]

The eastern tradition of icons was directly linked to earlier Graeco-Roman practices, such as the mummy portraits of Egypt, with dead saints replacing the secular dead. As we have seen, it was

---

[34] Wirth 1988:15.
[35] Wirth 1988:15.

established in the face of the objections of a section of early Christianity to figurative representations in general and to images of the deity in particular, the rejection of which was associated with its Judaic roots. The theological justification of the new attitude was that, in Christ, God had made himself flesh, become visible through the Incarnation and had thus overridden the proscriptions of the Old Testament.[36] Indeed, in the Eastern church it was sacrilegious to claim that one could not represent divinity.

Like others Besançon has contrasted a '*divin païen, immanente au monde*', with the '*Dieu biblique, transcendent, invisible, inimaginable par essence*'. The first gives rise to an infinitude of plastic forms; the latter to ambivalence.[37] As a result of Christ's Incarnation of God in human form, Besançon sees Christianity as creating a situation in which the image is unstable and 'history presents an alternation of glory and extinction'.[38] The problem of iconoclasm is located firmly in the Judaeo-Christian tradition. Rejection also has a hierarchical facet, for he sees the populace as being drawn to idolatry, with iconoclasm being the doctrine of the elite.[39] In that there is some truth, though it is not only true for Christianity.

Besançon sees the return of the icon, like its disappearance, as due to special circumstances in Latin Europe. The consideration of 'things' as neither divine nor yet bereft of divinity, ensured a fruitful exchange between divine and profane images, a relationship that modern science has tended to destroy, so reviving earlier iconoclasm. Without denying the special features of Christian Europe, it is helpful to see the aniconic tendency in a wider perspective. We have already seen that Islam had an even more pronounced tendency in that direction, but that can be understood as related to the Judaeo-Christian tradition. In other literate civilizations of Eurasia, however, we find examples of the same kind, including overt expressions of the dangers of representation other than by the word.

---

[36] Pelikan 1990.
[37] Besançon 1994:505.
[38] Besançon 1994:506.
[39] Besançon 1994:506.

Implicitly at least, and often explicitly, early Buddhists recognized the problem involved in making material images of the immaterial divine. Even when they began to represent his life in visual terms, the figure of Buddha himself was absent. Only centuries later was he introduced.[40] When this happened, the process once again gave rise to conceptual problems: no longer how to represent the unimaginable, but how to imagine he who has not hitherto had an image. It was not only that a switch occurred at a specific moment in time; the ambivalence remained in one form or other, with one sect more reluctant to create 'idols' than another. It was Hīnayāna Buddhism that remained longest without icons. Was the defacement of Roman coins around the Krishna valley in South India the result of Hīnayāna Buddhist iconoclasm, as has been suggested?[41] In fact, the dating of the entry of Mahāyāna Buddhism into Gujarat in the third or fourth century CE is based upon the appearance of various figures of Buddha in the archaeological record. Previously, the caves contained nothing of that kind, although a rock inscription has been found at Junagadh. For a later period, is an ambivalence towards sculptural images of deity perceptible behind the fact that the figure of the Buddhist 'goddess of mercy', Kannon, at the Sensōji Temple in Tokyo has remained hidden since the seventh century as the result of a revelation from the goddess herself?

A similar sectarian divide appeared among the Jains. One division of the Digambara (or 'sky-clad') Jains, founded in the sixteenth century, is known as Táraṇapantha, or Samaiyāpanthī, because it rejected 'the worship of idols' and revered only the sacred books (*samaya*), that is, the holy word. They were against caste distinctions (though these have subsequently re-emerged) and dispensed with outward worship and study. The other major division of Jains, the Svetāmbaras (or 'white-robed'), also gave birth to an iconoclastic sect, the Sthānakavāsīs. They arose out of the older Lonkā sect founded in 1474 CE by a rich and well-read

---

[40] Hyers 1989; Pal 1989; J. Huntingdon 1985; S. Huntingdon 1985; Snellgrove 1978.
[41] Thapar 1992:18.

merchant of Ahmadabad who rejected even the use of temples. These later iconoclastic sects (together with Terāpantī founded in 1817) seem to have been influenced by the advent of Islam. 'No oriental', writes A. M. Stevenson (Mrs Sinclair Stevenson), 'could hear a fellow oriental's passionate out-cry against idolatry without doubts as to the righteousness of the practice entering his mind.'[42]

A less-pronounced form of ambivalence marks that other major Indic religion, Hinduism. There exists a proliferation of images: 'Brahminism established status through the ritual of sacrifice. In Purāṇic Hinduism . . . the temple housing an image came to symbolize the sacred place and worship . . .'[43] But these are sometimes seen as necessary only for the unenlightened. One local commentator notes:

> To the Hindu, the omnipresent God, who is the father of the universe, appears to reside in everything, as much in the loving heart of the devotee as in sticks and stones. His God may or may not be conceived as anthropomorphic; the form of the conception depends upon the stage of advancement of the worshipper in the culture of divine knowledge and spiritual wisdom. To a *yōgin*, who has realised the Supreme Brahman within himself, there is no need of any temple or any divine image for worship; but to those who have not attained this height of realisation, various physical and mental modes of worship are prescribed, and rules of various kinds are laid down in relation to conduct. The Hindu *śāstras* prescribe image worship to weak unevolved persons in particular.[44]

These doubts are quite explicit in the canonical literature. The *Jābāla-upanishad* asserts that 'images are meant for ignorant men'. Their worship is said to bring on rebirths from which the *yōgin* desires to free himself. So the images of the Hindu gods and goddesses are 'representations of the various conceptions of divine attributes' but they inhibit true understanding.

---

[42] Stevenson 1915; Jaini 1979:310; Dundas 1992:210.
[43] Thapar 1992:32.
[44] Rao 1914:i, 26.

The proliferation of images of divinities raised another philosophical question for the Greeks, as we have seen in the previous chapter. The provision of bodily images of gods usually means that they are individually differentiated, each one given its own rank and duties, its own name and form. Individuality is clearly established. That notion was contested by 'marginal sects and by philosophers' who saw the evil of this world as due to this very individuation.

> For them perfection belonged only to the one, to the unified being, to the High God who was the sole (important) god. Anaximander was the first Greek to propose a system which brought the world under a single principle, that of *arché*, which was not that of a particular element, like water, but was capable of giving birth to everything.[45]

Xenophanes himself criticized the multiple gods of Homer, fashioned after the image of man, an idea that he rejected.

This ambivalence about images is manifest in the belief that they are meaningful for the masses rather than for the enlightened few. But in India there were times when they were rejected by some or by all sects. For example, according to Max Müller, 'The religion of the Vēda knows no idols', which he regarded as 'a later degeneration'.[46] This notion of degeneration apparently represents the view of an iconophobe and is not shared by all commentators; nevertheless, the earliest representations (for example, the Linga at Guḍimallam in South India, which carries the image of Śiva) date from the second century BCE, while the cults and icons of Śiva and Vishṇu appear only later in a developed form.[47] Even then, the third element of the Hindu trinity, Brahmā (to be distinguished from Brahma or Brahman, 'the omnipresent God', the absolute), who is the Creator God, is sometimes said not to have his own cult, temple or *pūjā*. In fact, there are some exceptions, and many temples contain a bearded image of Brahmā to which a daily

---

[45] Besançon 1994:31.
[46] Müller 1868–75:i, 35.
[47] Rao 1914:i, 6–8.

offering is made.[48] In the Near Eastern religions the aniconic trend was made explicit in the written word and that was to some extent true of the East. But the existence of these general problems in Buddhism and Hinduism means that outbursts of iconoclasm have to be seen not only as part of reversions to the text – taking a close (or literal) rather than a distant (or allegorical) reading – but also as attempts to solve the insoluble. That is the crux of the matter.

## *General Doubts About Icons*

One constant problem with figurative images is the tendency to identify them too closely with reality on the one hand and with the deity on the other. That is especially clear where not simply the deity but the image itself is held to have acquired life, to have moved from the inanimate to the animate, as the result, for example, of having its eyes painted in, as is the case with all Hindu sculpture. The larger-than-life wooden sculptures of the *bhuta* cult of coastal Karnataka are images of the spirits of deified heroes, of fierce and evil beings, of Hindu deities, of the mother goddess, of animals and the serpent spirit. The carving is naturalistic without being realistic, and represents the various *bhutas* in their corporeal existence. They are coloured and then lacquered except for the eyes which are left untouched until the final ritual of *pranapratishtha*, or 'breathing-in of life', when the deity is said to descend to the sculpture and occupy it. But, in invoking the spirit rather than the image itself, a human impersonator or *patri* is entered by the *bhuta* who possesses him. The continuity displayed in crossing the boundaries between image, deity and human being is undoubtedly of comfort to some but capable, at the same time, of raising a cognitive problem about the status and relationships of the entities involved.

This problem touches upon that of domain specificity, discussed by cognitive psychologists and anthropologists, because the very attempt to translate immaterial to material involves just this

---

[48] Rao 1914:ii, 502. One consort of his is Sarasvatī, the goddess of learning.

crossing of a boundary. The boundary is potentially breached by any representation of deity but the act of installation itself raises the contradiction in precise form which is more likely to induce an ambivalence in the minds of the actors.

Reference to Hinduism and Buddhism shows that the iconoclastic ideology found in Christianity was itself a manifestation not simply of a local theological dispute but of a wider intellectual problem concerning the nature of the deity and of communication with the gods which is intrinsic to humanity's notions of the supernatural. Beyond the question of divinity lies a further ambivalence about representations themselves. That is to say, if we see the problem in a limited historical, theological, contextual framework, we fail to understand an important part of what is going on. Comparison is not something to be added to an enquiry into local knowledge; it is part of any wider understanding of the situation. The rejection of the bodily image of gods, and especially of God, the Creator God, was part of the contradiction involved in conceiving gods anthropomorphically and then having them create humanity or order its life in ways that were possible only to non-material beings. That contradiction is particularly acute in the case of the Creator God but it exists for all other supernatural agencies because of the opposition of the material to the immaterial, the sacred to the profane, of humanity to deity and of the natural to the spiritual. It expresses some more general doubt about representations.

These wider intellectual problems associated with the iconic are four in number. Firstly, the very creation of images, of likeness, may appear to duplicate the unique act of creation itself. Secondly, the creation of religious images raises the specific issue of how to put the immaterial, the spiritual element, into 'human' form, and at times into any form at all. If we want to communicate with the divine, we have to establish a point of contact, an altar, and that may involve the creation of an image of an anthropomorphic kind. There is a potential tension between the fact that a shrine, any shrine, is likely to be a human artefact and the fact that it represents an immaterial essence. The more specific rejection of religious images may allow for secular representations while eschewing the sacred. Thirdly, there is the special situation of the High God, of representing not the Creation but the very Creator, which combines the hesitations embodied in both the first two objections. Finally, there is the broader trend that distrusts images because they are deceitful re-presentations of 'reality'.

That is to say, iconophobia was not only a matter of rejecting the images of false gods; it also had a philosophical dimension that involved rejecting all images of divinity, all religious images, and at times images of all that divinity has created or even, in the extreme mode, images that humanity has forged. These tendencies appear to be widespread but often sub-dominant in human cultures. In the case of divinity the reason is clear. Making the invisible visible – creating a material image of something immaterial, divine, supernatural, associated with the spirit, with the breath, with *anima*, with the soul – presents obvious problems.

One solution to the problem of representing the divinity is to avoid the image altogether and to rely solely upon the word. Hence the stress on the word of God in Israel, in early Christianity, in Islam, under Protestantism and in Zen Buddhism; there the word is diametrically opposed to the image. On the altar, in the temple, there is no figurative representation, and the only offerings are words, prayers and hymns, possibly without any accompanying 'music'. In Africa, Muslims and Christians are known as those who pray in contrast to those who make offerings of other kinds, especially blood sacrifices. Such material offerings themselves involve a series of further contradictions; the paradox of divine sacrifice at the material level is that the gifts cannot be consumed by immaterial agencies in the usual human way, and so have to be distributed among the givers, the congregation, or abandoned altogether.[49] That paradox may be 'resolved' by shifting gifts to the verbal level, or alternatively, by offering the immaterial 'soul' of the gift or letting a vital element, such as the blood or the libation, soak into the earth. The paradox of sacrifice is linked to the way that divinity is conceived, as non-human but with human attributes.

[49] J. Goody 1981.

These intellectual problems about the nature of divinity bear upon the question of conversion. Divinities always turn out to be somewhat less than satisfactory; they never give us entirely what we want. While the privileged may be able to rationalize the situation of the God who failed, that may not always be the same for the masses. The potentiality for conversion or for the adoption of new cults, new panaceas, is always present; if Saint Antony of Padua offers no relief, we turn elsewhere for help.[50] But conversion, which is a shift of allegiance of a more radical kind, does not only result from promises of a better future or even the association with a higher culture. The post-Roman missionaries had little of either to offer northern Europe in the fifth and following centuries of our era, yet they achieved the effective conversion of much of the population of Western Europe. Looking back, from an essentially Christian, literate or Western European point of view, the abandonment of the 'old religion' in favour of something higher, purer, truer, may seem unproblematic, though the countercultural persistence of its supposed rites through the ages, even down to modern London and California, has also been remarkable. But the rapid adoption of the new and the virtual abandonment of the old was and is problematic not only in Europe but in contemporary Africa and the Pacific. Why should people set aside basic religious beliefs with such apparent ease? Part of the answer has to do with the presence of dilemmas inherent in conceptions of divinity. Do we give words or things? Do we represent in visual or in verbal terms? If so, how is this to be done? These questions in themselves raise the problem of the relationship between the human and the spiritual and the way the latter is conceived anthropomorphically. How is the spirit to be made flesh? The weakness and contradictions of one solution may lead to the adoption of the alternative, even though the answer may not in the long run be more satisfactory. That long run may not be just a matter of alternation, but of a certain (or uncertain) vectorial movement. The less than satisfactory results of material offerings, the greater awareness of outcomes encouraged by education

[50] J. Goody 1975, 1986.

and the advance of scientific knowledge, may encourage the trend towards a more 'abstract' faith.

These problems have undoubtedly affected the conversion of Africans to Islam and Christianity, resulting, in some cases, in aniconic trends, often of a selective kind, that we discussed in opening this chapter. Aniconic doctrines imported from the north affected Black Africa in a variety of ways. While some authors have pointed to the continued manifestations of the visual and other arts under Islam, practitioners of that religion also destroyed many 'idols' because they stood for pagan gods.[51] These figures could also be considered as representations of 'reality', a divine reality, which was not allowed to be recreated by mortals. In addition, dancing and masquerades were subject to attacks by reformers even when these performances had been largely islamicized, with the result that here too representations were discouraged, especially those involving disguise.

Nor did the danger come only from Islam. Christians and their converts destroyed much African art largely because they thought of it as representing false gods, fetishes, devils. Pagan idols, as the Jewish Mishna explains, might be dead or they might have a devil lurking behind.[52] Christian iconoclasm of a kind penetrated the African continent from the north and west. Nor was it only a matter of annihilating the gods of 'others'; for some missionaries all representation of divinity was suspect. But, irrespective of these outside influences from the written, world religions, did these underlying cognitive problems of understanding divinity, and perhaps of representation as such, feature in native African societies? Are they to be found only in literate societies where they are certainly more explicit, or is there any evidence of them in oral cultures? And can they conceivably account for the uneven distribution we noted at the outset? In other parts of the world we learn about these problems largely from written sources, not simply because they provide a record but because they also provide a performative text which is often more explicit in these matters than is

[51] Bravmann 1974.
[52] Elmslie 1911:42–3.

usually possible with utterances in oral cultures. In Africa we have to look at ways of examining implicit rather than explicit understandings.

The situation in that continent is complex. No one would ordinarily consider aniconic tendencies to be a feature of cultures which, from the European standpoint, are characterized by idolatry, animism (even the trees are worshipped) and, above all, fetishism – in its original Portuguese sense (the worship of an inanimate artefact), in that meaning with which Marxists have endowed the word (of over-evaluation), and in the way it is used by psychoanalysts (an object associated with potent sexual significance). Masks and sculpted images proliferate. All of these supposed features, not to mention the worship of the ancestors, of the Earth, of other agencies, are concerned with objects and have therefore been taken by some to indicate lower levels of spirituality, a too-concrete relation with the divine which is often imaged in anthropomorphic or zoomorphic form. In fact, as we have seen, figurative images are found only intermittently. Altars may take a non-figurative, abstract shape as readily as a figurative one. In the extreme and crucial case, which we will now consider, there is no form at all.

In Africa the indigenous Supreme Deity, who is usually referred to in English as the High God, and who is often identified with Allah and Jehovah by the actors themselves, as well as by the Muslims and Christians, rarely, if ever, takes a figurative form. He is not represented, imaged, iconed, and, with occasional exceptions, not even given an altar, a material focus, not even a twig or pebble. The observant Dutch factor, Bosman, declared in the early eighteenth century: 'By reason God is invisible, they say it would be absurd to make any Corporeal Representation of Him'. They make them only of lesser deities which are intermediaries between God and man. Those other deities may be seen as what Evans-Pritchard called 'refractions' of the spirit or the High God, although the phrase perhaps underemphasizes their own individual status since for most of the people most of the time, these others are the important agencies in their spiritual lives, as much, if not more so, than the patron saints of popular Mediterranean

Catholicism.[53] To these refractions, sacrifices are constantly offered. In this the actors contrast themselves with followers of religions of the Book who, in the area of West Africa in which I worked, as in many others, are distinguished as people who '*puoro Nãã-aŋmin*', which is translated locally as those who 'pray to God'; it is perhaps more accurately rendered as, 'to greet God', greet him in the same way you would an elder, though by speaking (in prayer) rather than by making material gifts.[54] In contrast both to the sacrifices made to lesser deities and to the prayers of the world religions, one does not generally make any direct approach to the Supreme Deity. In local practice there was rarely any way of communicating with God at all, either by words or by gifts, since there is no shrine, no altar. Certainly people do not offer sacrifices in the way that they do to lesser immortals. We get some glimpse of this special position of God as the Creator in a LoDagaa tale in which the Hare outwits God, only to be outwitted in turn by the Partridge. The story ends with the sentence 'How can a creature be wiser than the Creator?'[55]

What I am suggesting here is that the African attitude to the High God displays some of the complexities, the necessary contradictions, that arise in the process of conceiving the immaterial. Why should African religions display this reluctance to image the Creator God or often to approach him even with verbal requests? Part of the answer lies in what philosophers and theologians refer to as the problem of evil. The act of creation, which led to humans inhabiting the universe, was not an undiluted good. Evil made its way into the world and its presence had to be explained. Why should a perfect God create an imperfect world and then refuse to set things right? The Genesis story presents one version, attempting to locate the fault as that of Adam, or rather Eve. A Chinese folk-tale tells how the Creator, P'an-ku, fashioned men and women out of clay, but a storm came and damaged his work. 'This is the reason why now there are lame, blind, deaf and other

---

[53] Evans-Pritchard 1956.
[54] J. Goody 1962.
[55] Bemile 1983:87.

ill people on earth.'[56] In Africa, a very frequent answer is that, unlike his 'refractions', God has largely withdrawn from human affairs.[57] But there is another aspect to the question.

In discussing supernatural beings, psychoanalysts and anthropologists have both spoken of the mechanism of projection. Humans are seen to create their gods after their own image, a reversal of the theistic approach. In so doing humanity becomes involved in giving a shape to the shapeless, a form to the formless. This Africans may do for lesser agencies but the inherent contradictions in the process may be resolved or mitigated by avoiding any type of material altar or image for the High God, the Creator God, as is the case in Islam.

This aniconic trend is but one facet of the process of conceptualizing the supernatural. At the same time, as we have seen with Christianity and Buddhism, there is also the continuing pressure to represent, to find a way not only of conceptualizing and communicating but of imaging. For verbal images are frequently present either on a personal or a 'poetic' level, so that in making an icon one may be giving shape to an already existent imagining. That is the case in the Bible and it is the same with the Bagre myth of the LoDagaa. A recognition, however, implicit or explicit, of the difference in the materiality of icons (as distinct from words) and in the deliberate process by which they are created is particularly relevant in the special case of the Creator God in Africa. It is true that it is occasionally reported that he has an altar, for example, the *nyame dua*, the tree of God, of some Asante. But that is certainly not an image, a likeness, nor is it in essence an object of man's creation, though perhaps one of his arrangement; it is not an arte-

---

[56] W. Eberhard 1965, *Folktales of China*, Chicago (original edn 1937, New York).
[57] He may have been distanced by the world, as in the Asante folk-tale where he is driven away by the pestles of women, thrown high as they are pounding yams in their mortars, a theme that resembles the story of Adam and Eve in that crucial human activities have distanced humans from God, thus dealing with the problem of evil. One of the consequences of the notion of distancing is that since he was once in contact with humanity, there may be circumstances in which God can be brought back again. For the implications for temporary cults and more permanent 'conversion', see J. Goody 1975.

fact, but natural rather than artificial. Similar focuses exist in a few other parts of West Africa and libations may be poured at these points. But even in these instances there is often a problem in knowing whether the tree is an altar to God or to one of his refractions.[58] In any case the order of spirituality could be considered higher rather than lower than in Christianity, since there is no figurative image, and only rarely an altar.

Before considering how this argument applies to other categories of spiritual being in Africa, I want to clarify a point about the nature of altars, for their presence or absence says something of human relations with those agencies. The altar may take an abstract form, as with the cross, or a figurative one, as with the crucifix, and the difference is often of supreme ideological significance to the actors. So too is the question of whether the altar is being treated as a point of communication or as an agent itself. Cases of 'fetishism' of this latter type are explicit in the history of the Christian church. At those times queries are raised as to whether one is offering reverence or worship to the image or the altar, as distinct from what it represents, a problem that tends to be heightened when the question of likeness is introduced. Is the likeness deity itself or only a material representation?

But the identification of agency and object may take quite a different form from 'fetishism' and indicate another conception of spirituality. If God is everywhere, and the world is but his 'refraction', then it makes little sense to image him, although it might be proper to address oneself directly to one of his creations, for

[58] This is not the place to discuss the complex nomenclature of divinity in West Africa, but among the LoDagaa *ŋmin* have shrines, for example, *saŋmin*, rain-shrine, *bagŋmin*, Bagre deity, *sāāŋmin*, deity of the ancestors; only *nāāŋmin* ('the head divinity') does not; the concepts are complicated by the fact that the word *ŋmin*, or its alternative *wen*, is related to the word *ŋmintɔŋ* (or *muna*, or *wen*) which means the sun. *Ŋmin* shrines can be stones found on a path. In Gonja too the name *ebori* (High God) is found in the form of *bori* which refers to a supernatural agency of lesser status (and with shrines) as well as to the rain. In both cases the identity with sun and rain is denied. Such complex networks of meaning are frequent in West Africa and make the reference of any particular statement not easy to discover. Indeed the ambiguity may be present to the actor.

example, to a tree. That is pantheism, the belief that God is not a personality but is everything everywhere; likewise everything everywhere is God. From a pantheistic standpoint it is more logical not to re-present God but to present him, to address his presence directly in the shape of one of his own creations rather than one of ours, that is, in manifestations or refractions of God rather than in images of representations of him. We address ourselves directly to the rocks, stones and trees which believers in a more 'personal' God, that is, a more personified deity, imagined after a human image, regard as the objects of nature-worship, as idolatry without the manufactured idol. That was the case in Judaism and to some extent in Christianity.

There is obviously a point of overlap between the manufactured image, the icon, and the natural object with which humans have not interfered at all, for some icons are constructed from natural objects which have been rearranged by people. In the Judaeo-Christian-Islamic tradition, all are idols, sticks and stones. Nevertheless, pantheism is held to be a more respectable version of 'animism' or the worship of trees, rocks and other natural objects, because one is worshipping the God beyond and only offering reverence to those objects in themselves. It is a notion embedded in European thought like that of other 'great traditions' and one of the classic expressions was given to it by William Wordsworth in autobiographical passages in *The Prelude* as well as in his Lucy Poems: 'Rolled round in earth's diurnal course,/ With rocks, and stones, and trees'. The notion that God can be discerned in the natural beauties of this world, in the objects of his creation, is familiar in Christian thought, certainly in Western thought, but it becomes extended to the use of man-made 'images', pictorial icons, and indeed to the architecture of churches themselves; Abbot Suger argued that the beauty of the stained glass in St Denis turned man's thoughts to God.[59]

A type of pantheism can also be seen in Ch'an (or Zen) Buddhism in China, the origins of which go back to the sixth century. The sect claimed that Buddha-nature is immanent in all

---

[59] Panofsky 1946.

beings and that its discovery, through meditation and introspection, brings release from illusion.[60] Distrusting even words, especially book-learning, its followers felt that life lived in close communication with nature was conducive to enlightenment, a notion influenced by Daoism. Zen doctrine, however, was only one aspect of the new religion that came to China from India; in place of the nature spirits and divinities of earlier times, Buddhism offered 'gods of great color and warmth, magnificent ceremonies replete with music and symbolism, and spiritual rewards undreamed of in the old religion'.[61] In other words, this religion of the books, of the illustrated books, of the temple and the monastery, tended to demand representation of various kinds. But this approach may be seen by some as less directly related to the divine than was the natural world the divine has created. Zen attempted to express this alternative line of thinking and to stress the link with nature. Nor was it altogether alone. In China there is a more inclusive tension in the uses of painting between the Indic Buddhist trend and the local Confucian one, the latter being more ascetic, rejecting colour and concentrating on secular representation.

Confucians were often opposed to the use or creation of figurative images, especially sculptures. For example, there was a reaction against existing ones when Confucian images were replaced by spirit tablets in 1530 following a memorial by grand secretary Chang Fu-ching which incorporated large segments of the arguments of Chi'u Chün (1421–95) who objected to their vulgarity. He saw them (probably incorrectly) as having been introduced by Buddhism and as profaning the invisible realm. 'The physical form of a concrete figure impedes an effective apprehension of the spirit . . . it would attempt to represent.'[62] In his writings Chi'u Chün referred to earlier works that objected, for example, to the tendency in popular religion to anthropomorphize mountains and rivers, conceived as ducal lords. Some allowed that,

[60] A. F. Wright 1959:78.
[61] A. F. Wright 1959:82.
[62] Sommer 1994:6.

as in early Christianity or the Reformation, images might have didactic value, but Chi'u Chün adopted a more extreme stance that has been compared by Sommer with Byzantine iconoclasm. Confucian temples then became quite different from Buddhist and Taoist ones. That move was in line with the worship of the ancestors where images were rejected in favour of written tablets; for the Confucians writing was the dominant form of representation. Other changes in ritual were taking place at the time, largely in opposition to Buddhism. It was a time when in South-west China Buddhist lands were being confiscated and handed over to the gentry, on the understanding the proceeds would be used for schools or similar purposes.[63]

These general considerations have been brought out in order to place the religions of Africa in the same overall logical (though not always theological) frame as the Eurasian ones, so that we can approach the question of figuration of other orders of supernatural being in Africa,[64] Are there any traces of the same factors at work in the conceptualization of the two other major levels of supernatural being, namely, ancestors and (lesser) divinities? I concentrate here specifically on Ghana since my argument has to do with differences in conception among neighbouring peoples and I need to deal with the region I know best. In terms of form, ancestral shrines show an interesting span of diversity ranging from the quasi-anthropomorphic figures of the LoDagaa, to the personal stools of the Asante, to the 'abstract' pots of the Tallensi.[65] The first represent the dead man in a general way, the second are seen as imbued with his particular body fluids, the last have no personal connection with him at all. In addition, the Akan (a term that includes the Asante) of southern Ghana go even further towards portraiture and make terracotta heads as funerary sculptures to be used in ancestral cults. They have the generic name of *mma*, meaning children or little people. These sculptures have

[63] Shyrock 1932:138–9.
[64] Some general differences I have tried to explain in *The Logic of Writing and the Organisation of Society* (Cambridge, 1986).
[65] In the death-mask of the Asante king and the bronzes of Benin royalty, we find yet greater emphasis placed on likeness.

been made for centuries, at first to honour deceased chiefs and queen-mothers but later for any notable man or woman. The heads 'were regarded as an actual portrait of the defunct personage' and hence resembled the death-masks made of Asante kings and their reconstructed bodies.[66]

The same source shows a chair (stool) of Nuna (Burkina Faso) origin, resembling similar Lobi ones. Like other personal property such as headrests, pipes and spoons this becomes 'intimately associated with the spirit of the owner and after his death may be placed on the family's ancestral shrine' as a vehicle for communication from one generation to the next. 'Neither the Nuna nor the Lobi carve ancestral figures, but such heirlooms stand in the place of such figurative portraits.'[67] The neighbouring LoDagaa do have ancestral figures, of a very simple kind, with stylized head, body and legs, which are in no sense portraits but represent the human form in a generalized way. And, indeed, I have in my possession one that is carved like a stool.

One can see these forms as functionally equivalent; they all 'symbolize' the dead. But the choice between portrait, generalized figurative representation and non-figurative associated object is not, I suggest, purely accidental, but at one time embodied intentionality and had specific meanings for the actors. We get some idea of this difference in discussions of the neighbouring Senufo of the Ivory Coast, who produce an extraordinary range of sculptural forms. Nevertheless, these do not include portrayals of humans. 'The idea of sculptural portrayals of a living person fills the Senufo with horror. It was regarded as a dangerous and threatening act, inviting a curse on the head of the person depicted or, in the case of a woman, rendering her sterile. The sculptors say that if such a statue was made, it would be to harm a person', for instance, a girl who had refused you in marriage.[68] The same prohibition applies to dead ancestors. There can be no clearer expression of the fear of iconic representation.

[66] See T. Phillips 1995:449. Also E. L. R. Meyerowitz, *The Akan of Ghana: Their Ancient Beliefs*, London, 1958.
[67] T. Phillips 1995:522.
[68] T. Phillips 1995:458.

A similar range of objective correlatives exists for divinities. Despite popular western belief major divinities are not often portrayed in African sculpture, although all have non-figurative altars where communication takes place. Most masks and figures have to do either with so-called bush-spirits, what I call 'beings of the wild', or with the dead.[69] Even with the ancestors, with those who have lived as human beings, there can be a problem about representing the supernatural in too precise a form, not about giving the immaterial a material correlation, since clay, wood, stones or shells provide a focus for worship, but in approximating its form to that of living things.

We posit cognitive operations, dilemmas and contradictions within cultural situations that have become customary. If I ask a Muslim why there are no figurative icons in the mosque, he may reply, 'that is our custom, our way, our culture'. He may not refer to, may not even know of, discussions in the Hadith about representations. But these discussions did occur, as the result of which Islam adopted (in general) one position rather than another.

Did the same situation exist for an African people like the LoDagaa? If you ask them why a certain supernatural agency is not figured, they may likewise reply, 'That is not what we do'. Is one therefore entitled to assume a problem about representation? There is a general reason to suggest that a contradiction emerges between deity and shrine ('fetish'?), between immaterial and material. Can one go further and assume not only an implicit questioning of the relationship, but that at some point in time, as in written cultures, the LoDagaa have actually 'talked themselves into' this situation, or alternatively talked themselves out of icons (at least in some contexts). On general grounds I believe one can assume that certain cognitive problems are not confined to the heirs of Near Eastern cultures, to users of the text, but occur in less explicit form in oral ones as well. The suggestion regarding icons (which does not necessarily *require* the positing of a 'talking into' phase) is strengthened by looking at the context in which the fig-

---

[69] The 'beings of the wild' are often known as 'fairies' or 'dwarfs' in West African English or by Muslims as '*jinn*'.

urative representations are forbidden, namely for the High God and for many 'serious' deities. For them the LoDagaa 'prefer' non-figurative forms, about which there are fewer problems.

The existence of such problems, whether explicit or implicit, may lead one group to choose one course of action, another a different one, each subject to change over time. These alternative possibilities for action, embedded in the logic or rather the cognitive contradictions of the situation, might then account both for the distribution in neighbouring regions of abstract forms and figurative images as shrines to the ancestors or divinities, as well as for the differential stress placed by these societies on all representational images. As a result of such implicit notions, Islamic and Christian injunctions to destroy the images of their former gods may have struck a chord in the existing thinking of the inhabitants and been more acceptable to them than might appear at first sight. In other words their resistance may have been undermined by the pre-existing ambivalence about representing the immaterial.

Of course, they were being asked to destroy not only anthropomorphic or figurative images but all representations of, or altars to, a divinity. For the LoDagaa these agencies were usually considered to be living things, even if they were not given images as such. I found a persistent preoccupation in serious discussions with whether 'gods' (*ŋmin*) had 'life' (*nyovur*, literally, breath). Plants clearly did not have life in this sense but there were arguments on this topic about supernatural beings that are reflected in the long recitation of the Bagre. At one point in my first transcription, published in *The Myth of the Bagre* (1972), the Earth shrine is made to break into speech and to protest at human beings striking his surface ('skin') with stones at the time of sacrifice. As we were working on checking the translation, my collaborator, S. W. D. K. Gandah, burst into laughter at this incident which displays that agency in a quite atypical way, as having not only 'breath' but speech and sensations. The 'beings of the wild' (*kontome*) do have these attributes and it seems natural to have them speaking to humans in the course of the recitation. They are, after all, intermediaries with somewhat the forms of men and women, living in the hills and rivers, herding wild animals as their flocks, teaching humans the basic features of their culture, and communicating to them when they divine what has been revealed to them. Virtually alone among the LoDagaa, they are given human images in sculpted form. Figurative representation, 'breath' and resemblance to mankind are closely intertwined.

The result of the ambivalence towards figuration, especially of the divine, emerges at a more inclusive level than the individual or the society. I have deliberately used the term 'regions' since the broad differences are not so much between societies as between groups of societies. They do not lie at the level of a single 'culture' but of a 'culture area', the boundaries of which change over time. To explain this distribution in terms of diffusion is not very helpful, although clearly the practices of neighbouring groups often affect each other through their interaction. But even internally those practices are not simply transmitted between the generations in an unquestioned way, for the ambivalence towards any aspect means that it is subject to reselection and change as the result of the interplay between internal and external factors.

Is there any evidence of the possible dynamic for such changes? One case in the recent past emerges in Schildkrout's account of the history of Mangbetu sculpture where she points out how little anthropomorphic art they created before the colonial period. The reason she sees as lying in their attitudes towards materials which have meaning and power without further elaboration. When sculpture did develop among the Mangbetu in the early colonial period, it seems to have had 'an entirely materialistic significance; it simply had no place in their world view'. Ancestors were venerated by way of trees, not by way of sculpture. Creating things of beauty was 'an entirely secular business'. However, occasional sculptures have been found in the context of funerary practices which suggests that they were used as an embellishment. 'Secular' sculpture itself developed only as the result of the market that Europeans encouraged. Today a further change has taken place. Little anthropomorphic art is now made because the market has collapsed. In other words, there has been a shift from 'abstract' to anthropomorphic and back again, the iconic element being largely a response to early colonial demands. Carvings, 'fetishes', were what the Europeans wanted; carvings, 'fetishes', were what they got.

Nor was this the only area where figurative art expanded in this period. Writing about brass masks in eastern Nigeria and western Cameroons, Kandert remarks that 'As a type, masks are in the overwhelming majority of cases connected with the arrival of the Europeans into the area'. For the last seventy or eighty years they have been cast for the market, especially the European one. However, they may possibly have had predecessors in metal-covered wooden masks, although a shift in the practice of representation is equally possible.[70] What we find among the Mangbetu is an ability to switch between figurative and non-figurative modes within the framework of a general reluctance to represent divine agencies in sculptural form. Pantheistic notions, the veneration of an ancestor through a tree, even the worship of sticks and stones, can be seen as an alternative to figurative representation of an anthropomorphic kind, as also in the case of the early symbols of Christianity and Buddhism.

With the outright rejection or limited use of all figurative images we enter into a state of thin as against thick, art, ritual, or 'culture' (though these are not necessarily homologous). Situations of this kind recur constantly in the history of human religions – and in some non-religious fields as well. One thinks of the Cathars, of Bernard of Clairvaux and the Cistercians, of the Calvinists of the early Reformation, above all of the Puritans of Old and New England, as well as the Presbyterians of Scotland, who entirely rejected major aspects of their cultures of performance.[71]

Above all it was the Zwinglians who placed so great an emphasis on the text that 'they feared the visual image which they considered so powerful that the ignorant might take it as a substitute for the

---

[70] Kandert 1990. There are many other examples of the way that the largely European demand of the art market has stimulated the production of figurative forms, for example, Olmec stone masks, East African sculpture and Senufo figures, some of which represent innovations, others increased production.

[71] On Puritanism, see Kibbey 1986; Ludwig 1966; Stannard 1977; and J. Phillips 1973.

real thing'.[72] The image was confused with reality. 'Such an error would lead to the worship of a graven image or the idolatry condemned in the commandments. To depict God, the Holy Family and the Saints was not only dangerous but a travesty, for no artist could know the truth.' This point of view did not, however, deny the efficacy of instructional prints but artists must find other means such as classical figures to convey God's message and not depict holy people. Or, they must single out texts dealing with a generic woman whose virtues could be captured in visual imagery without running the risk of idolatry. This aversion to the icon was essentially religious, against the depiction of the divine. It could be avoided by painting other non-biblical or generic figures that did not try to represent the holy as real.

Such reactions for or against the icon are time-specific, not embedded in the cultural genes, in the deep culture, but stimulated by particular situations and based on contradictions implicit in the human conception of divinity. Actions tend to become ritualized (that is the nature of repeated behaviour) which may lead in turn to them being queried, hence encouraging some generative diversity of response. Images tend to creep back when they have been excluded; drama emerges in the interstices of ecclesiastical performance; flowers are rejected and then reappear; the material icon raises questions about the nature of 'spiritual' beings, which in turn reacts upon the icon. The movement has a dialectical tempo about it, even if the swings of the pendulum are of very different duration.

With the overwhelming dominance of the image in modern culture, aniconic tendencies have been largely engulfed by the processes of mechanical reproduction.[73] Can we discern the partial continuation of the problems posed by representations of the divine in the work of modern abstract painters? Besançon speaks of the 'iconoclasm' of one of the first of these, Kandinsky, as having a distant relationship with ancient and medieval examples. But it is very distant for above all that painter reproached nineteenth-century

[72] Hufton 1995:30.
[73] Benjamin 1968.

painting for its 'futility. To paint this world was not worth an hour's trouble. Nothing was worth representing but the absolute.'[74] In a sense this attitude embodies the very opposite of iconoclasm since it refuses to represent lesser objects, only God, the absolute, Himself. For Malevitch who followed but arrived at non-representation by a different route, the desire to reproduce existing forms rather than to create new ones was a sign of savagery.[75]

Besançon sees the French school as taking another road, indicated by Kant and Hegel as well as by Fromentin, to an abstract art different from that of Kandinsky and Malevitch because it is profane and agnostic rather than mystical. The advent of abstract art was associated with the notion of purity which was related to an essentialist metaphysic.[76] Essentialism involves the search for immutable essence or truth and the concomitant division between reality and mere appearance. Plato inaugurated this discourse in Europe – look for the truth rather than appearance. Truth is immaterial, the material is untruthful, but memory can give access to truth. This theme was taken up by Gauguin in 1888 when he wrote about a portrait he was painting and could not get the result he wanted: 'Maybe I shall do him from memory, but in any case it will be an abstraction.' This approach marked a shift from Impressionism which, in its turn, represented a rejection of naturalism although it concentrated on the effects of light and colour. Gauguin moved to Synthetism which led to yet more abstract forms. That further step distinguishes the School of Paris around 1950 with its attachment to the '*délicieux concert des gris, des azurs et des argents*', enjoyed for itself. In this way, Besançon argues, the aesthetic of doing and seeing results is a new attitude towards the image which one hesitates to attribute to iconoclasm and is rather a form of iconophilia or of iconolatria, leading through the disappearance of the represented to 'a hyperbolic exaltation of forms and colours'.[77]

The shift from figurative to abstract art is also a feature of other

[74] Besançon 1994:476.
[75] Besançon 1994:485.
[76] Cheetham 1991:xi.
[77] Besançon 1994:331.

traditions. Tantric art of India is largely geometrical, though not exclusively so. 'Geometrical forms dominate the whole range of Indian symbolism, particularly in Tantric diagrams and formulae. In these the motifs aspire to absolute "geometrical purity".'[78] Figurative art was considered to be superficial, not reaching the underlying reality; this represented the abandonment of external reality for inner searching, for the One without a second. The essence of every thought and every idea originates in sound (*nada*) and is connected with an abstract design and a verbal formula or mantra. The notions are not dissimilar to that of the Russian abstract painters of the twentieth century. Indeed, in his discussion, Mookerjee quotes Kandinsky as saying: 'Sound, then, is the soul of form'; the abstraction of music relates to the aim of non-figurative art.[79] Indeed, the shapes of geometrical Tantric art resemble those of the abstract painter Rothko.

So far I have talked of icons and iconoclasm largely in the religious context, for that was the focus of African image-making. In those cultures there is little separation between the religious and the secular. Especially in the West, on the other hand, increasingly secular times are marked by a prevalence of icons, of logos, paintings, photographs, representations of all sorts. But while religious attitudes play a smaller part, the contemporary world continues to have its own iconoclasms, usually of the temporary political kind, directed to the overturning of specific heroes rather than the idea of imaging as a whole. This is the phenomenon of the 'false god'. I was present in Italy in 1943 at the time of the fall of Mussolini when the *fasces* were stripped from the façades of public buildings; in Germany, too, when Hitler fell and the swastikas disappeared. I was working in Ghana in 1966 when the fall of Nkrumah was followed by the toppling of his statue outside the Parliament building. Walking around the town that day I met an electrician in a bar drinking beer out of the frame of the neon sign that had been used to light up the words, Kwame Nkrumah Circle. Many other political changes have seen the dis-

[78] Mookerjee 1966:13.
[79] Mookerjee 1966:16.

mantling of public statuary of the previous order, the undoing of Queen Victoria in Bombay, the dismissal of Stalin in the Soviet Union, not to speak of the disappearance of reminders of the earlier Tsarist regime and now of Marxist-Leninism more generally. All this is a question not simply of removing the memory, the model, but of the semi-magical destruction of one's own experience and the questioning of the process of image-making, the cult of personality. It is also a matter of cleansing the world, creating a *tabula rasa* and starting afresh. In the pursuit of this end, pictures and statues are put up and taken down with the rise and fall of dynasties.

Antipathy to representations may also take the much wider form of an attack not only against the previous order but against images as deceitful, or as manifestations of luxury, when artistic and decorative objects are prime targets. Those objects have a special character: literature is normally rejected by being banned or censored, although some has been destroyed in the burning of books; in the era of print this was effectively a token destruction owing to the nature of literary reproduction. But creative art is largely unique and can therefore be physically destroyed or at least damaged. Much has disappeared as the result of the destructive power of war, which may not be intentionally directed against such objects but which consumes them or more usually seizes them as booty. In addition there has been the iconoclastic annihilation carried out by regimes such as that of Pol Pot in Kampuchea and by the Cultural Revolution in China. While these phases were points in the history of particular movements, they represent a common feature of many revolutionary acts, the desire to start all over again, to create a new future and to rid oneself of the past, especially the past of privileged groups which graphic art largely represents – again in partial distinction from the word which tends to command a wider audience.

In a stratified culture icons are mainly luxury items. But in any case the character of the image's materiality and in many cases its uniqueness makes it especially vulnerable (as well as valuable) in terms both of the loss to the owner and as a reward to the attacker. In other words, such iconoclasm is part of a cleansing of the social order of which we may detect other manifestations in contemporary Western societies. Iconoclasm has been present in many revolutionary movements. Andalusian anarchists regarded the Church as having buttressed the position of the ruling class. 'Iconoclasm led crowds to destroy pictures of popes and images of saints as well as convents, monasteries, and homes of priests, whenever the opportunities arose.'[80] But while the anarchists hated the institutional Church, women in particular did not abandon the Church *per se*.

In those revolutionary situations that were backed by an atheistic ideology, religious objects were especially vulnerable to attack. Only recently are the paraphernalia of Buddhist, Daoist and local cults returning to inhabit the domestic landscape of China. While temples were sometimes destroyed, secularization also changed the functions of those that remained, leading to their adaptation as factories, theatres, schools or as store-rooms, as well as to their demolition for new developments – a similar kind of well-meaning destruction, for a lot of iconoclasm is well-meaning in this sense, that swept the towns of Britain in the 1950s and 1960s. Their buildings were often no longer protected either by their sacredness or by a respect for the past; they were destroyed to make way for a 'better world'.

So atheists are not only destructive agents; indeed, in Eastern Europe they were sometimes the most dedicated conservers of old buildings, provided their use was changed, and even when that was preserved as in the case of the Communist governments of Bologna or of Prague. On the other hand some of the most radical attacks on religious objects, as in the iconoclasm of the Byzantine world, has come either from within the Church or from the newly dominant practitioners of other religions. While the practice has become less common of late, many Christian missionaries in Africa encouraged their converts to destroy their idols as a sign of their attachment to the new faith and of their rejection of the old. Sometimes religious destruction of this kind was self-inflicted. The history of cargo cults in the Pacific and of chiliastic movements in

---

[80] Kaplan 1977:85.

Europe provides examples of the wider destruction of property in order to gain new spiritual strength, which could also be seen as an avenue to greater wealth, to more cargo.[81]

Such deliberate destruction of property, such explicit rejection of images, are not common in indigenous Black Africa, except in situations of conversion and under the guidance of religions of the book that take a less eclectic view of the universe than do local systems of practice and belief. Nevertheless, the widespread reluctance to create representations of some divinities, and the uneven distribution of cultures that produce any form of three-dimensional image, suggest that we may be in the presence of implicit aniconic, or even iconoclastic, attitudes similar to the more overt types that have occurred in the history of Europe and other societies with writing. Of attitudes, that is to say, that hesitate to provide an image of deity, especially any objective correlate of the High God, and sometimes any representation of His unique act of creation. Or attitudes that encourage the destruction of the images of others, whether of other religions, other dynasties or other classes, especially the enjoyers of luxury, since the destruction of objects then feeds the ideas of levelling that so often accompany the existence of cultures heavily differentiated by styles of life. The presence of any such attitudes could provide a dynamic for the differences that we find in neighbouring groups and regions as well as offering another example where written cultures make explicit the contradictions and problems that are implicit in oral ones. I make this last remark neither to resort to the kind of vague cultural distinctions involved in many binary classifications of 'primitive art' or society, nor yet to take refuge in a minute contextualization, but to try to avoid 'the demeaning of Africa' by pointing to a possible explanation not only of the similarities in the intellectual problems but of the differences as well. What I have tried to show with icons in Africa is that, on the implicit level, we find a similar kind of ambivalence about figurative images, especially of gods, and more particularly of the Creator God, that occurs explicitly in iconoclastic movements and aniconic tendencies in Europe, and

[81] Worsley 1957.

in Asia too, through the existence of writing. At the implicit level, these basic manifestations are widespread, transversal characteristics of human understanding. In Africa we see this ambivalence in the reluctance to image the High God and, I suggest, in the uneven distribution of figurative images of other gods, or even of humankind and nature themselves.

# 3

# Relics and the Cognitive Contradiction of Mortal Remains and Immortal Longings

After pictorial images, I consider another form of metonymic representation, namely, relics in which not only does the part stand for the whole but in the case of bodily relics, the inanimate for the animate, the dead for the living. If the relics are other material objects, there is the problem of 'idolatry'. We have already seen that in early-Christian Europe, figurative statuary was permitted when it acted as a container for a human relic of the saint, which justified the attention given to the image itself. The evident emotional and cognitive opposition between the two may raise the question of the validity of this 'standing for' in people's minds, leading to opposed reactions and different customs.

Living, as I do, for part of the year near Conques, the site of the ninth-century reliquary-statue of Sainte-Foy, I am accustomed to hearing expressions of the negative as well as the positive attitudes to relics. The positive attitude cherishes and respects the remains of the dead; the negative attitude treats them with fear and loathing. While, psychologically, respect and fear may have elements in common, even be seen as two sides of the same coin, the practices associated with these sentiments are very different. For early Christians the bones and other relics of their earlier dead, especially the saintly dead, were preserved and endowed with supernatural powers. In theological terms, these were remains of those who, by virtue of their sanctity, could act as intercessors with God. Such relics were kept in special containers or reliquaries which, in later times, sometimes took the shape of sculptural forms, figurative 'representations' of the dead as in the statue of Sainte-Foy or in the many crucifixes that adorned the great cathedrals. Here it was the relics, the actual remains of the dead, that justified the representation, since graven images themselves were forbidden in the Old Testament and discouraged by the writings of many early Fathers of the Church. The reliquary-statue, a development of the Carolingian West, meant that adoration was given to the relic, the person himself, and not to the image, the representation, although the relic was also a metonymic representation.[1]

The use of relics expanded throughout Christendom, though more vigorously at some times than at others. Moreover, there was always a negative undercurrent that drew its strength, firstly, from the excesses of the cult of relics, in the shape of the promises of salvation by 'pardoners', and the proliferation of items that were manifestly more false than others; secondly, from the biblical injunctions against the worship of anything or anyone other than God himself; thirdly, from the more general phenomenon of 'the God who failed', the inability of relics to live up to the promises made on their behalf. That negative attitude was embodied in the beliefs of heretics and reformers of various kinds.

## Pilgrimage

The earliest Christians had rejected the notion of *loca sancta*, even of a temple. It was for that reason they attacked the Jews[2] and were in their turn attacked.[3] It ran against the notion of the omni-

---

[1] Wirth 1988:15.
[2] Acts 7:46–49.
[3] Minucius Felix, *Octavius* 10, 2–3.

presence of God, who was of the sky and the earth and did not inhabit temples built by the hands of men.[4] There was no sacred place and so, according to Hunt, pilgrimages to the Holy Land were not made before Constantine, although that chronology is disputed by other writers.[5] In any case, they began 'timidly', reserved for scholars seeking to complete and make more concrete their understanding of the Holy Scriptures.[6] In 325 Helen, mother of Constantine, made her voyage to the Orient and stimulated others to visit the Holy Land, to see the places recorded in the Scriptures and to recite the events that took place there. Especially at Easter time in Jerusalem, the services re-enacted those earlier events for the benefit of the pilgrims.

Many wanted a souvenir, a witness of their suffering, and at some places they were offered 'eulogies'. They visited the tombs of the dead and in the case of Saint Andrew and Saint Timothy, even the places where the bones of the saints had rested when they had been transferred to Constantinople. Such relics were covered by a cupola of the kind erected over the imperial throne, baptisteries and martyrs' tombs; all were pregnant with divine power.

These pilgrims were seeking for evidence of Paradise, or at least of its image. The very journey brought their faith to a pitch of religious fervour, which encouraged yet others to follow in their footsteps. That resulted in a transfer of huge funds from west to east for investment in basilicas, monasteries and hospices, while on the return journey they brought back eastern influences to the west.[7]

The use and value of relics in Christianity are closely connected with the memory of the saints, with pilgrimage, with miracles, with their transfer by discovery, by gift and by theft, with images, jewels and reliquaries, with the expenditure and acquisition of money, and with sectarian disputes. If saints are addressed through their relics, and if it is specifically these material objects that are seen to have 'power' on a part-for-whole principle (synecdoche),

[4] Acts 17:24, 27–28.
[5] Hunt 1982; Kötting 1950; Maraval 1985.
[6] Heim 1985b.
[7] Heim 1985b:208.

then there is a premium on approaching them physically, even on touching them. Such an approach is associated with the pilgrimage and its virtues. To visit the relics of Sainte-Foy at Conques in south-west France is more effective than prayer offered at a distance, partly because it involves a greater 'sacrifice' in making the effort to travel there and partly because of the efficacy of approaching, or even touching, the relics.[8] As a result their possession gave political power and wealth to the establishment that owned them as well as to the inhabitants of the surrounding settlement, since it attracted visitors from far and wide, exploiting its own marked site as the tourist industry does today. The attractions included the acquisition of merit (or grace), the bestowing of blessings and even the performance of miracles, as well as various secular benefits. All of these ends were, in principle, attainable through prayer, but they were even more readily available through physical contact with relics.

Pilgrimages were not always seen as unmitigated blessings. From the earliest times some eminent Church Fathers scoffed at the mania for travelling to the Holy Land because, to a true believer, 'God is everywhere'. Pantheism demanded no site. In the fifteenth and sixteenth centuries the Catholic Church forbade pilgrims to go to the Holy Land without official permission, on pain of excommunication, while Erasmus was scathing about pilgrimages on the grounds that the participants often lost sight of their objectives. As a result of these objections and those of the Protestants, there were fewer voyages and the costs mounted. From the Renaissance onwards, mass travel disappeared; voyagers went as individuals until the latter part of the nineteenth century.

Victor Turner saw the demise of the pilgrimage system as taking place because 'it no longer represented communitas, social anti-structure'; it became encrusted with customs 'denying its original

---

[8] Writing of the Carolingian statue of Sainte-Foy at Conques, Taralon notes its connection with the medieval cult of relics, which was the reason for pilgrimages. In this case pilgrimage took on a double aspect: the cult of the saint itself and its location at a staging point on the road to Compostella, where the relics attributed to Saint James were preserved (1978:9).

spirit'. A spate of relics arrived from the Holy Land through the activities of Crusaders, devolving the 'generalised "ludic" media'.[9] Yet while there was clearly a falling away, it is important to note that there was no perfect original; tensions and contradictions were there from the start of the cult of relics. As with the notion of pilgrimage, there were more general dilemmas. Turner treats iconoclasm in a similar particularistic way. The destruction of the Marian shrine at Le Puy at the time of the French Revolution is attributed to the troops who swept into the Cathedral and turned it into a temple of Reason. Many other famous medieval Marian shrines in France, Belgium and Luxembourg were damaged or destroyed in the same period, including at Rocamadour in the Lot. Elsewhere the agents of destruction were Henry VIII's commissioners, Cromwell's Roundheads, the Scottish Covenanters, the Hussites and the Huguenots. The iconoclastic phenomenon was not simply a feature of a single historical epoch; it derived from a tension in the minds of men, not from a failure of a mystical communitas.

## *Miracles*

The cult of relics has been described as 'the reason and goal of pilgrimages' in medieval Catholicism.[10] It was relics and the related tales of miracles that attracted pilgrims.[11] The idea of miracles lies, according to the medievalist Murray, 'at the very core of religion', since it embodies the question of whether power lies with nature and humanity or with supernatural agencies. 'If God is in charge, he needs propitiating.'[12] The notion of the miracle was linked to

---

[9] Turner 1979:197. On the ambivalent attitudes to the pilgrimage see Constable 1976. On the pilgrimage generally, see Sumption 1975 and other references in McKeon 1987:428, as well as to relics.

[10] Taralon 1978:9.

[11] It was only when the monks of Conques decided to acquire relics by a 'translation furtive' between 863 and 883 that the monastery's fame began to grow.

[12] Murray 1978:12.

that of the relic because miracles were bound up with accounts of the acts of saints as well as with those of Christ at the time they resided on earth. Now that those agencies are in heaven they are to be approached, literally, through the relics of their earthly lives. The miracles associated with them validate their power and their glory.

One problem with miracles is that few have seen them happen. Accounts of these events were embodied in stories that were read out aloud (*legenda*) but these reports were inevitably about the past, not the present. Why do miracles not occur at the present time? This potential contradiction between past and present was open to exploitation by sceptics but also raised questions to thoughtful believers about the difference between the everyday (usually present) and the unusual (normally past) happenings on earth. In the case of Aquinas, for example, it led to a consideration of the relative place of regular natural ('rational') laws that lay behind the everyday and those irregular divine ones associated with the miraculous. But that was not the only contradiction raised; there was also the question of where power, where the presence lay. Was it in the immortal figure who had departed from this earth, or in the mortal remains left behind? Were these remains marked by the 'real' presence or were they falsehoods, lies, relics empty of meaning?

A related problem was posed by the ceremony of the Mass in relation to the 'real presence', that is to the status of the bread and the wine as the body and blood of Christ. Any drama which represents a happening is a re-enactment. But in this re-enactment how much credence is to be placed upon the notion of transubstantiation, whereby the appearance remains the same but the essence changes? It was a problem that worried the Protestants (who adopted the ambivalent Lutheran doctrine of consubstantiation by which the communion wine was both blood and wine at the same time) as well as some recent Catholic theologians who developed the doctrine of transignification, putting the change on the level of meaning. For Luther, whose doctrine differed from Zwingli, the body and blood of Christ was in the bread and wine as fire is in a heated piece of iron. The problem revolved around the ambiguities residing in the use of the verb, to be: What did it mean to say, 'This *is* the body and blood of Christ'? Some earlier non-Christian authors had accused the early Church of advocating the consumption of human flesh. The physicalism of the Mass also attached to the cult of relics, which involved not only memorialization but the search for power. Moreover, that cult was also the subject of both sceptical comment and the objections of reformers. This reaction existed from the early days. In the fourteenth century, those comments received their classic expression in Chaucer's *The Pardoner's Tale*. One of the first measures taken at the Reformation, and enshrined in the articles of the Church of England, was a total rejection of them by the break-away churches. Relics could neither represent the saint nor had they any power to confer blessings and to perform miracles. The bones of the dead were not the dead, who were represented by the spirit or the soul, not by material remains. On the other hand, Catholicism and other major religions specifically urged their use. These contrary attitudes, it is suggested, rest on a paradox entailed in the employment of such relics which emerge as ambivalences, dilemmas or contradictions to humans actors, in the longer term. That paradox helps to account for the downright opposition accorded to relics in some societies, especially to bodily parts, as well as for their enthusiastic acceptance in others. Let us examine it in a wider comparative context.

## *Relics, Christianity and Continuity*

In anthropological and similar enquiries the acceptance of relics has been seen to pose few problems to earlier societies. In the article on relics (*reliquiae*) in *The Encyclopaedia of Religion and Ethics*, edited by James Hastings, Canon MacCulloch begins by referring to a previous entry on Cannibalism. He compares the gaining of power through eating part of the body with the benefits to be derived from touching objects associated with the deceased, and that in turn with the reverence universally offered to the dead. The attention given is valued in proportion to the qualities of the living individual with whom the relic was associated. That practice was adopted by Christianity. The early Christian cult of relics had already emerged at the time of Ignatius who died about 110 CE in Rome and whose bones were transported to Antioch. This act has been seen as an extension of the hero-cult of the Greeks, traced to the affection 'which makes the survivors cling to the mortal remains of a relative . . .'.[13] According to another commentator, 'nothing is more natural than that the pious solicitude felt by all men for the bodies of their loved ones should in the Primitive Christian Churches have been turned most strongly towards the bodies of those who had met their death in confessing their faith'.[14] But whereas the remains of the pagan heroes generally rested unseen in a grave, those of martyrs were exhibited in reliquaries and even subdivided to achieve a wider distribution of their benefits. Such proposed continuities were in fact more complicated than might appear, for the whole situation contained within itself the seeds of criticism (and therefore of rejection) because of the paradox of addressing the immortal dead through their mortal remains, to which one is both attracted (because of their power) and at the same time repulsed (because of death itself, our death, which embodies a lack of power).

The notion of continuity with earlier beliefs, and particularly with the hero-cults of antiquity, is contested by Peter Brown in the *Cult of the Saints*. He sees the Christian cult as breaking new ground in the Mediterranean world of antiquity; heaven and earth were now brought together at the graves of dead humans, joining worlds that had previously been kept scrupulously apart, the soul in heaven, the body on earth. The tombs of the saints were the privileged places where the contrasting poles of heaven and earth met. From the sixth century new centres of ecclesiastical life grew up around the Christian churches situated at these burial places outside the old towns. For the saint was present in a tomb and, having known intimacy with God, the resting place and relics of the saint were sufficiently powerful to be able to aid humankind.

---

[13] Relation of the martyrdom of St Ignatius, 12; MacCulloch 1918:653.
[14] A. H., 1911, art. 'Relics', *The Encyclopaedia Britannica*, 11th edn, vol. 23, p.59.

But these were visualized, Brown claims, in a quite different way from the cult of heroes which constituted their predecessor in time and which, for other writers, had been their progenitor as well.

While there were obviously differences between the Christian worship and earlier practices in the region, there were also important similarities with cults of the dead more generally. I refer not so much to the surface correspondences correctly pointed out in the encyclopaedic articles following the ideas of Frazer in Hastings and elsewhere to which I have drawn attention, but rather to the underlying paradox, the structural ambivalence, that marks such customary acts. For the concept of relics is characterized not only by attraction but also by repulsion, by an attachment to the dead as well as by a distancing from death, which readily becomes associated with our death. So too with the concepts of Heaven and Earth. This world and the other world are seen as distinct domains, but they are nevertheless joined together in religions other than Christianity for they constitute the dwelling places of the same individuals, the one in life, the other in death. God is our home as well as High Street, Harlow. Not only does an element of the personae of those individuals, namely the 'soul', travel to 'Heaven' at death, but that same element is often seen as coming from 'Heaven' at birth in the first place, and sometimes as having left behind a spiritual double who acts as a spirit guardian.[15] That intimate relationship between Heaven and Earth, both worlds being included in the locations of an individual's overall developmental cycle, may involve confusion as well as conjunction. Le Goff writes of the *'confusion entre le terrestre et le surnaturel'* surrounding miracles, the cult of relics and the use of phylacteries, a confusion that represents 'a common mental structure' found both in ecclesiastical and in popular (*'folklorique'*) culture.[16] This formulation raises the question of 'mentalities' to which many historians are

---

[15] The notion appears in Western writers, such as Wordsworth, but is more developed among some West African peoples. The classic account is that of Fortes (1983) for the Tallensi but similar notions appear among the LoDagaa and Gonja of the same region of Ghana.

[16] Le Goff 1967:785.

committed and which is based on the notion of a unique constellation of ideas and attitudes persisting in a particular cultural group over an unspecified period of time. Such a notion tends to overlook internal contradictions and their potentiality for initiating change. I would put this confusion at the level of a more all-embracing cognitive structure of belief in supernatural agencies which involves just such a paradox. But if there is a common element deriving from the paradox, the outcomes or solutions differ.

While all forms of reverence for the dead have some elements in common, Christianity developed a cult of physical relics which went far beyond the veneration (*veneratio*) allowed by many Fathers and partook of the worship (*adoratio*) to be offered only to the Trinity. As a result relics could act as talismans. Aquinus himself permitted the wearing of relics round the neck for protection, provided ostentation and superstition were avoided.[17] Christianity also concentrated attention of the physical remains of the dead in a manner that was promoted by the doctrine of bodily resurrection. While it is not incorrect to point to the common features of these phenomena, perhaps including cannibalism, these articles, written in the nineteenth-century tradition of comparative studies, tend to give the impression of an overly homogeneous state of affairs, in which all these items are linked at a universal level. Only in later civilizations, it is suggested, do we find objections to these practices embodied in the writings of some early Fathers such as Saint Augustine, which some commentators see as a prelude to their abandonment by civilized, especially Protestant, peoples. Indeed, MacCulloch concludes with the comment that the use of relics smacks of the 'barbaric' and is 'a forcing of . . . instinct beyond its legitimate place'.[18]

In fact, in both earlier and later societies, the use of bodily relics (and it is on these I want to concentrate) differs considerably.[19] Some societies employ bones of the dead for protection or for

[17] *Summa*, II, ii, qu. 96, art. 4.
[18] *de Opere Monachorum*, 28, *de Civ. Dei*, xxii, 18.
[19] The term *reliquiae* included objects associated with the saints during their lives or at their martyrdom.

curing, others for reverence. Yet others attempt to distance themselves from the dead, refusing to disturb or use their bones out of another kind of reverence, out of fear or out of notions of impurity.[20] I suggest that this distribution, whether of synchronic diversity or of diachronic change, can be explained only by taking into account the structural ambivalence, which makes both thesis and antithesis appear as possible outcomes. The normal notions of 'culture' and '*mentalité*' are too single-stranded, too rigid, to allow for an understanding of these changes and differences in certain widespread practices and attitudes over time and over space. They are potentially present because of the implicit or explicit contradictions that exist at the cognitive level, with the implicit becoming generally more explicit with the advent of writing and all that it entails. The continuity lies at the level of the contradiction, rather than of cultural practice or of '*mentalité*' which are notions that tend to freeze social action at the deep structural level, to embed it in concrete foundations and so inhibit the analysis of temporal changes and of spatial differences. For the notion of transformation is of merely formal interest without an understanding of the mechanism at work.

Let us return to the relics of early Christianity to give flesh to our understanding of these dry bones, especially those of the saints. We can trace the rise of the Holy Dead in Europe and their relationship with the power of the Church because the cult was officially approved, unlike in Islam where 'saints' are very much on the periphery of orthodoxy. Following the transport of the bones of Ignatius to Antioch a few years earlier, attention to the bones of a Christian martyr again appears in records of the *Martyrdom of Polycarp* which seem to be an account of an event taking place in 115 or 177 CE.[21] The relics of bishop Polycarp of Smyrna, a friend of Ignatius, were gathered together so that they could continue to be venerated on the anniversary of his death. After the body had been burnt, 'we, at last, took up his bones, more precious than

---

[20] I am indebted to the work of T. S. Strong who points out both the uneven distribution of the cults of relics and the paradoxes their use entails.
[21] Figueras 1983:11.

precious stones, and finer than gold and put them where it was meet'.[22] The Eucharist was subsequently celebrated at this spot and other members of the congregation then desired to be buried nearby to 'rest with the saints'. The practice of a second burial and the consecration of the remains has a long history in the Near East and the Mediterranean, especially among pre-Zoroastrian Iranians, who exposed the body and gathered up the bones in boxes. Elsewhere, as among the Etruscans, the same was done for the ashes. The practice of 'bone gathering' existed in Palestinian Judaism where many hundreds of ossuaries have been discovered in tombs and the practice was almost certainly carried on by Jewish Christians. These ossuaries date from the period of the Second Temple, stretching from about 530 BCE to 70 CE but continuing until the third century. The usage was later abandoned by the Jews and even condemned in some liturgical texts, perhaps in opposition to developing Christian practice.[23]

The cult of Christian relics seems to have gained ground as a private rather than a public practice. At the beginning of the fourth century, Optatus tells how Lucilla, a Donatist, was said to have 'kissed a bone of some martyr or other – if he was a martyr' before she received the Eucharist. The parenthetical remark referred to the prohibition on Catholics in Africa to honour any dead as martyrs if they had not been 'vindicated or canonised, for some had brought death upon themselves'.[24] The worry about whether relics were real was one thing, but there were other qualms because the trade led to the dispersal of a person's mortal remains. In particular, condemnation was directed at the custom of leaving the bodies of martyrs unburied.[25] In the course of that century the traffic in relics grew considerably and in the later half the custom of dividing up the martyr's remains became widespread in the East, representing important political transactions between churches

---

[22] *Martyrdom of Polycarp*, XVIII. 2, *The Apostolic Fathers*, ed. K. Lake, Cambridge, Mass., 1976.
[23] Figueras 1983:12.
[24] Optatus, *de Schism. Donat.* 1.16 (see Vassall-Phillips 1917:31).
[25] Athanasius of Alexandria, *Vita Ant.* 90.

and rulers.²⁶ That is what attracted particular disapproval. In a letter to the Empress Constantine in 593 CE, Gregory protests against the eastern custom of breaking up the bodies of saints. For the new basilica of Saint Paul at Constantinople the Empress had requested the head of the apostle or another part of his body. He answered that it was not the custom of the Romans to touch the body in any way when they needed relics but only to give a cloth which had been placed over the saint. The difference between an actual bodily relic and a non-human object sanctified by contact was stressed in an imperial edict of 26 February 386 which forbade the removal or dismemberment of the bodies of martyrs. Gregory tells the story of the fate of two Greek monks who wanted to take away the bodies of the saints by night;²⁷ that was considered reprehensible. On the other hand, and here the ambivalence becomes explicit, he sends to the king of the Visigoths some hairs of John the Baptist enclosed in a cross which itself contained a fragment of the true cross. His correspondence is full of references to the dispatch of non-human relics, or rather copies, especially miniature versions of the keys of Saint Peter.²⁸

According to Bernard of Angers it was the custom in the Auvergne and around Toulouse for a church to commission a statue of the patron saint to hold the relics; hence that of Sainte-Foy at Conques. In the north of France, on the other hand, it appeared wrong to erect statues to any but the supreme God, indeed only to represent our Lord on the cross. For saints, one had to rely on the written word or on paintings which reproduce their two-dimensional image on walls painted in colour.²⁹ In the Rouergue, in the south-west of France, things were different and the statue of precious metals was a way not of displaying a luxury item but of glorifying God, and, in Suger's phrase, of rendering the material immaterial. So relic and reliquary become identified. Taralon dates the wooden sculpture of the body of Sainte-Foy to

---

[26] Brown 1981:89.
[27] Cod. Theod. IX.17,7; Greg.1 *Ep.* IV 30. See Minard 1991:51.
[28] Minard 1991:52.
[29] Taralon 1978:10.

the end of the ninth century, making it 'the oldest statue of the West to come down to us'.[30] Did the *Majestés* of the south-west represent a precursor of the romanesque Renaissance? Taralon points out that after centuries of absence this practice constitutes 'a return to a kind of visual necessity to represent the human body not only by *imagines* in two dimensions but by statues in three'.[31] In fact, in some places, from the ninth century there existed reliquaries in the form of a limb, a bust or a head; moreover, statues of the Virgin, like figures of Christ on the cross, were permitted by the Council of Ephesus of 431, though that was in the East. What surprised Bernard was to find complete figures of saints in the West.[32]

Opinions about the use and efficacy of relics could be associated with the growing notion that material instruments could be the vehicles of divine grace. As a result, the cult of relics spread from East to West when the Crusades later gave direct access to the lands in which Christianity had originated. More churches were founded in memory of martyrs (as they had already been and still are) and in them relics of the relevant saint were placed, often in precious containers or reliquaries, which could be carried in procession on the consecrated day. So widespread did this practice become that by the Second Council of Nicaea it was obligatory to place relics under the altar (often in a cavity known as the *sepulchrum*) when a church was consecrated. All relics provided blessings, and some were also believed to work miracles. Where these miracles concerned healing, it became common from the fifth century to hang up models of the limbs that had been cured, giving rise to the custom found today in many churches in Spain, Greece and Mexico.

These latter, of course, represent the limbs of living mortals, not

---

[30] Taralon 1978:19.

[31] Whether statues had ever totally disappeared, or whether their return resulted from an evolution of forms accompanied by the transformation of techniques, whether they grew out of religious inspirations or whether they were of local origin in the southwest has been discussed by various scholars (Taralon 1978:19).

[32] Taralon 1978:22.

the relics of dead saints. But the cult of relics was later followed by the display of the corporal remains of ordinary men and women in medieval charnel houses and later in those Baroque chapels in Bavaria and Czechoslovakia that are decorated with elaborate arrangements of human bones.[33] Not only the bones of 'all saints' were preserved, displayed and venerated but those of 'all souls'. While the day of All Saints dates from the fourth century, that of All Souls only followed in 1048, even before the location of purgatory was established. Once they had been properly separated from the flesh, the bones were venerated. The process of separation was a source of weakness and tension as well as of power. The intellectual tension arose because there was a vital distinction between the recent dead and the 'dried bones', the clean bones. These latter one handled, but not the former, at least not without taking adequate precautions. That tension could give rise to criticism, since bones could be dirty as well as clean. So too could a reference back to the earlier biblical objections to the worship of the dead, which might be raised in opposition to later Christian practice.

At first sight, the sadness, the distaste, even the horror with which a corpse is viewed, the impurity of the dead body itself, are notions difficult to reconcile with the cult of relics and even with less marked forms of veneration for the dead. But in the case of medieval Christianity, that impurity was seen as purified by the process of burial itself, by the decay of the flesh and by the subsequent reinstatement of the 'clean bones', a concept explicitly used in consecrating charnel houses which were depositories for bones from which the flesh had disappeared. When cleaned up, the skull could be cherished, painted, enclosed in a reliquary, even placed on the chimney breast. The pollution had been removed. Nevertheless, as Strong points out in a useful discussion, a paradox remained. Relics 'are often objects that are normally considered to be impure – dead flesh, bones, and body parts – and yet they are venerated as holy'.[34] To this is added a further paradox: while

---

[33] See Goody and Poppi 1994. The striking example of Kutna Hora in Czechoslovakia I owe to Eve Danziger and Joseph Kandert. On Bavaria, see Legner 1989.
[34] Strong 1987:281.

bones are 'symbols of death and impermanence', they also represent a 'continuing presence'. There is a special case with beings that have once been human but are now spiritualized and regarded as saints, as supernatural agencies.[35] For material objects are clearly opposed to a spiritual (immaterial) existence in the afterlife. This opposition was particularly pronounced when the material object was translated from one place to another, that is, was disinterred from the place of burial and not only moved elsewhere, but sometimes moved through theft by those wishing to get their hands on a source of power and wealth.[36]

Apart from these cognitive problems, we have seen that the proliferation of relics and the question of their authenticity were already the subjects of critical comment at an early stage. Cyril of Jerusalem remarked that the whole world was filled with portions of the wood of the cross,[37] while other Fathers raised objections to the use of spurious relics.[38] Saint Martin of Tours miraculously exposed a 'martyr's' tomb as being that of a thief who had been executed for his crimes and was 'wrongly venerated by the populace'.[39] It is possible that the thief or burglar in question may have been a Celtic hero, celebrated by the locality, whom Martin was attempting to discredit.[40] In any case, there were both religious and political aspects in this unmasking of false martyrs. The bishop achieved a wider legitimation through this exposure (though creating some local enmities) as well as possibly offering a critical comment on his more credulous predecessors. This was not simply a local issue, however, but part of a much more extensive problem. The council of Carthage of 400 CE raised the general question of the control of private altars declared to be those of martyrs. Such

---

[35] That is largely the case with relics, although in Europe the Devil's footprints are sometimes pointed out.
[36] See Geary 1978.
[37] *Cat.* iv.10. *De Cruce*: ac crucis ligno universus jam orbis per partes repletus est. And XIII.4 . . . crucis lignum, quod per particulas ex hoc loco per universum iam orbem distributum est.
[38] Sulp. Sev. *Vita Mart.* 8; Aug. *De op. mon.* 28; Greg. 1. *Ep.* IV. 30, etc.
[39] Sulp. Sev. *Vita Mart.* II. See Fontaine 1967:277.
[40] Fontaine 1968:690–712.

rejection and authentication brought up the question of 'truth' and 'falsehood', and how this was to be established. For, if there were forgeries, there had also to be a body of relics that were authentic, and vice versa.

Behind these problems lay the more fundamental paradoxes and contradictions that were certainly apparent to some among the ecclesiastical commentators from earlier times. The Aquitanian presbyter Vigilantius (c. 400) rejected the belief that the souls of the martyrs clung to their ashes and heard the prayers of those who approached them. He called for a more radical separation between the material and the immaterial, describing the cult as embodying idolatry and insanity.[41] In doing so, he protested that 'we see something like a pagan rite introduced under pretext of religion; they worship with kisses I know not what heap of dust in a mean vase surrounded with precious linen'. Jerome, to whom we owe these words, objects in turn, saying we do not adore them with *latria*, like the Gentiles, but honour Christ through them. At the same time, he inveighs, in extreme terms, against those 'sacrilegious' beliefs which he relates to the Jewish notion of the impurity of the corpse. Vigilantius has opened his 'stinking mouth, casting a load of filthy rubbish before the relics of saints'.[42]

While his voice was discounted within the Church, non-Christians also inveighed against those practices. So too did the emperor, Constantine Copronymus, during the iconoclastic controversy, though not all at that time made the same objections. In the West, Claude, bishop of Turin (c.817), wanted to purify religion of the use of relics, of the intercession of saints and of pilgrimages to their shrines, causing such relics to be destroyed. Some medieval mystics objected to their use, as did major groups of reformers like the Waldenses and Lollards who preceded the decisive rejectionists of the Reformation. The late eleventh century produced a devastating satire on the cult of relics, entitled *The Translation of the Relics of the Martyrs Rufinus and Albinus*. This claimed 'Those who possess their relics are forgiven their sins

---

[41] Jerome, Esq. cix, ad Riparium, *c. Vigilant.* viii.4.7.
[42] Labourt, J. 1955 *Saint Jérôme, Lettres*, vol. 4, Paris, p.201.

forthwith.' Translations of relics from one place to another were common and in this case the move purported to be to Rome. The satire lay in the fact that these saints were known never to have existed; not only the relics but the saints too were false.[43] A similar ambivalence to that emerging in this work can be seen even in Aquinas who defended a modified cult of relics and the use of talismans. Following Augustine, he argues that the love of children for a father's ring or coat is legitimately extended to his body, 'for they belong to man's very nature'.[44] So we should venerate any relics of saints, 'principally their bodies, which were temples, and organs of the Holy Ghost'. At the same time, in dialectical fashion, he discusses the possible objections to such activities. These are, firstly, that 'to worship the relics of the dead seems to savour of the error of the Gentiles, who gave honour to dead men'; secondly, 'it seems absurd to venerate what is insensible'; thirdly, a dead body 'is not of the same species' as a living body. He answers himself, following Jerome, that we honour Christ through relics and worship the insensible body for the sake of the soul, with which it will later be reunited.[45] While the Council of Trent restated Catholic faith in validated objects, the progress of general secularizing and 'rationalizing' tendencies led away from their worship and even from their reverence; although they persist as attractions for (some) tourists and marginally as objects of pilgrimage and prayer, they have tended to play a decreasing role in recent years. In fact opposition to the veneration of relics and of saints has occurred throughout the history of Christianity, though more strongly at some times than at others. The most widespread heretical movements from the twelfth century were the Waldensians, the Joachites and the Wyclifites, all of whom objected to such practices, placing more emphasis on preaching the word of God. From then on opposition gradually spread to some rationalizing elements within the Catholic church itself, evidence of an underyling ambivalence about the use of relics.

[43] Murray 1978:72.
[44] *City of God*, I.13.
[45] *Summa*, III, qu.25, art. 6.

## Relics in Other World Religions

Christianity was not the only major world religion to embrace the use of relics and to experience concurrent contradictions. When the Buddha himself finally passed into nirvana, he is said to have instructed his disciples not to concern themselves with his physical remains at all but only with his teachings, with the word rather than the body. His cremated remains, however, were taken over by the laity and their possession became a subject of considerable dispute among the rulers of North India. In the Sanskrit legend of King Aśoka (Aśokavadāna), composed during the second century CE, the king is converted to Buddhism by the mystical deeds of a monk, Samudra, who told of a prediction of Buddha himself, that he 'would distribute his bodily relics far and wide', and build 84,000 stupas to house them. So Aśoka set out with an army to collect up the relics of the Buddha that at his death had been split up between the eight kings of northern India. In this he was not entirely successful but he shared out what he had into 84,000 boxes made of precious metals and stones, one of which was to be sent to every town on earth with more than 100,000 inhabitants. At each of these towns he ordered a stupa to be built, which were all to be finished and dedicated at the same moment in time, the moment when the stupa, like an image of the Buddha, 'comes alive' and 'when the Buddha is thought to be present in it.'[46] In this way his fame would spread throughout the world.

The establishment of these domed funeral mounds thus appeared to run against the wishes of the Buddha himself who had in any case overcome his physical existence in the course of achieving enlightenment, just as earlier in his life he had set aside the luxuries of the court in favour of the poverty of the *sanyasi*. That did not prevent the subsequent growth in the use of material objects such as icons, especially of the Buddha, nor yet the attachment of Buddhism to relics as in the Temple of the Tooth in Kandy, where it was treated much as a Hindu deity. Similar

---

[46] Strong 1983:115.

temples existed in Burma, Thailand and at Ch'angan, the ancient Tang capital of China. The famous Sensōji Temple in Tokyo has a hanging casket in the top room of the tower that contains relics of the Buddha brought back from Sri Lanka. Indeed, the origins of religious architecture under Buddhism are grounded in the construction of the stupa, which later developed into the pagoda. The building of such monuments was made possible by the generous gifts of princes and by the many contributions of pilgrims visiting the sites of holy relics, as was the case with some cathedrals such as Gloucester in the west of England, St Albans in the east and Durham in the north. In Tibet it was not only relics of Buddha himself that were valued but of incarnations of Bodhisattvas such as the Dalai Lama. In the Red Palace at Lhasa at the beginning of the twentieth century a 'Treasurer of Offerings' sold 'relics of His Divinity's dress and person as amulets'.[47] Outside India, Sri Lanka and Burma (Miranmar), however, the Buddhist world gave less attention to relics and (after an early aniconic period) more to the image and indeed to the word. The construction of religious buildings continued to be a way of acquiring merit but copies of sacred texts could also be used to give sanctity to the stupa.[48]

Like Christianity, Buddhism was not without its sceptics. In 819 CE, the writer and statesman, Han Wang-Kung, offended the reigning Chinese emperor by commenting upon the reverence given to a finger bone of the Buddha. His criticism led to his official degradation and he only narrowly escaped execution. The comment was not made in the spirit of frivolity and some of the general philosophical issues or cognitive paradoxes we have already discussed, were undoubtedly present. For example, many Buddhist teachers taught that the human body in any form is 'foul and disgusting'. This belief was related to the view of Hīnayāna ascetics as well as to the other-worldliness of the adherents of Zen, for whom 'celibacy and ritual acts of bodily mortification rendered a higher service to their parents than preservation of the body and

---

[47] Waddell 1905:397, who confirms Colin de Plancy's claim (in 1825) that these include a powder from his dried excrement enclosed in bejewelled boxes as well as his urine sold as *'un elixir divine propre à guérir toute espèce de maladie'*.
[48] Smith 1918:661.

perpetuation' of the family.[49] It was better, in other words, to get rid of the body rather than to retain it for reverence; for the latter one needed a constructed shrine (a written tablet for ancestors) rather than a 'natural' relic.

Looked at comparatively, Buddhism and Christianity are unusual among the major religions in their attachment to the physical remains of their holy individuals. In Hinduism, cremation does away with virtually all remains. Both Islam and Judaism, which were attached to inhumation rather than to destruction, firmly rejected not only images of such persons but any transactions with their bodies, much less bits of those bodies. For while the use of bodies as relics is clearly associated with the widespread if not general reverence that humans pay to their dead, especially to the heroic dead and to their personal ascendants, societies vary greatly in the use they make of their actual fragments. In Islam, the saints are honoured under ground; the bones are never disinterred and spread around. While in parts of the Islamic world, the tombs of saints receive much attention, in theory it is only God that is worshipped. As in that other monotheistic religion, Christianity, God receives *adoratio*, the holy dead only *veneratio*. It is more 'a cult of bodies than of bones; and those bones remain placed firmly under the earth.[50] Some Qur'anic scholars denounce even this veneration as *shirk* (polytheism), equivalent to idolatry. The opposition here is between the One God and other agencies, epitomized in the legends of mausoleums destroyed by the very saints they entombed because they objected to the cult devoted to them. As in the case of the Buddha, the celebration of the holy dead ran counter to their express wishes.

Similar notions of idolatry were found in ancient Israel where too great a veneration for the dead, including offerings of food, was considered to border on paganism. Such an attitude was reinforced by the fact that contact with the corpse was defiling, running up against the idea of the uncleanliness of the dead body (*Numbers* 19:11) and the importance given to burial under ground.

---

[49] Nakamura 1967:i, 24, 64.
[50] Strong 1987.

Nevertheless, as we have seen, bones were at times 'gathered up', even if they were not worshipped.

While Hinduism is neither monotheistic nor iconoclastic; it did not follow Buddhism in its attachment to relics. Pilgrimages are made to the sites associated with divinities and great teachers but veneration of their bodily remains plays virtually no part in cult activities. Death and the dead are considered highly polluting, the funeral stressing the total destruction of the body through fire. Even the ashes are taken to a river, if possible the Ganges, to be washed away in its waters, just as the indianized Balinese take them from the pyre to the sea. While notions of the illusory nature of reality and the doctrine of reincarnation are no less prominent in Buddhism, in Hinduism they are strictly applied so as to distance the dead from the living – except in thought alone.[51]

## *Relics in Oral Cultures*

The final part of my discussion relates to the distribution of the cult of relics among non-literate peoples. In his article on relics contributed to Hastings' *Encyclopaedia*, MacCulloch collects evidence from each and every continent to show the widespread belief in their supernatural value. In the Pacific, for example, some widows are said to carry around the bones of a dead man after they have been exhumed. As I have suggested, this very monolithic view of custom arises from the nature of the comparative procedure he adopted, the collection of examples of a particular practice from all around the world, without considering the implications of its absence, a fundamental methodological error. Although some uses are made of skulls for ritual purposes, no member of the societies I have studied in West Africa would behave in this way. While the skeletons of Asante monarchs received special treatment, those of other inhabitants did not.[52] In the north of Ghana with few excep-

---

[51] Jains have some stupas but nowadays no cult of relics.
[52] On the disintegration of the flesh of dead kings and the preparation of the skeletons, as objects of sacrifice, see Rattray 1927:114ff.

tions men and women were buried once and for all, both in states and in acephalous tribes. One case in which this did not happen was when a body of a man who had been sold into slavery was disinterred at night and reburied in the bank of a river so that the impurity would be washed out of the parish.[53] Another case, in some ways similar because running counter to normal usage, occurred in the rites addressed to the spirit-guardians of certain clans. I have never witnessed those performances, nor do I know of anyone who has, for they have fallen into disuse. But they are said to have involved drinking beer out of the skull of an individual, presumably a slave, who had been killed in order to consecrate the shrine. A related use of skulls may have occurred formerly in the New Yam performances in some Gonja divisions (and particularly in the Akan-speaking village of Kadelso near Salaga). These Asante-type rites were carried out by the executioners and the notion but not the practice of human sacrifice (although not of cannibalism) is very much to the fore, even today.[54] Otherwise the LoDagaa and the Gonja, like other peoples of the area, followed the (puritan) principle of leaving bodies where they have been buried and not tampering with the bones.

Apart from special cases of this kind, there is little that could be called a cult of relics. The worship of ancestors is a widespread feature of African societies, and in the case of the Asante, the shrine consists of a stool resembling the one on which a person sat during his lifetime. But it is in fact carved anew for the funeral. In other cases in West Africa the shrine consists either of some 'abstract' object such as a pot or stove, or occasionally, as among the LoDagaa, of a carved anthropomorphic figure that bears no specific resemblance to the deceased, nor is intended to. In some cases, objects associated with an individual may be buried alongside; more usually they are formally destroyed or, in the case of inheritable goods, ritually separated from the dead. The notion of a

---

[53] J. Goody 1962.
[54] For the rites surrounding the death of an Asante and for the Yam Festival, see Rattray 1927; the skull of the British general, Macarthy, became part of an Asante war shrine.

relic is not one that is encouraged, although in the area of Gabon and Cameroons there is evidence of the use of skulls and of reliquaries to contain them.[55]

In writing of the distribution of icons, I have remarked how adjacent 'societies', or more usually adjacent 'areas', take up different views towards figurative representation. Regarding bodily relics, these areas of similarity are much more extensive. Their relative absence in Africa contrasts strongly with the head-hunting, the display of skulls and the use of bones in many Oceanic societies. There are but few variations within the African continent. The influence of Islam is only part of the reason, as it was for icons. Nevertheless, the rejection of relics of the ancestors and the widespread use of dissociated objects in their place seem related to similar kinds of consideration that we have seen most explicitly in Christianity. There the paradox of attributing an active role to the material remains of the dead and, at the same time, dismissing the spiritual essence to another realm, the problems involved in breaching the separation between the living and the dead, between the material and the immaterial, the paradox of the burial of a human and the disinterment of the bones, appear to lie behind the general acceptance of the use of corporal relics by some and their rejection by others. Once again we find that what is explicitly formulated in written cultures is implicitly stated in oral ones; in different ways both point to the cognitive contradictions between the evident mortality of the body and notions about the immortality of the soul. It is the paradox of mortal remains and immortal longings.

---

[55] For example, Kota, Gabon; royal shrine, Bangwa, Cameroons; Fang, Bumba, Mashongo, Mahongwa. I am grateful to C. Poppi for these and many other references. See also T. Phillips 1995 and Anon 1986.

# 4

# Theatre, Rites and Representations of the Other

*Was Cressid here? This is, and is not, Cressid!*
Troilus and Cressida, V, 2, ii.

It is not only icons and relics whose use incurs rejection as well as acceptance, over time and over space, but the 'performance' arts as well, not ritual (though elaborate rites may be condemned) but, rather, the theatre. In cultural studies much contemporary usage looks at ritual, whether sacred or profane, whether secular or magico-religious, as belonging to the same analytic genre with theatre under the general category of 'performance'.[1] Clearly there are some similarities between masked dances (for example, among the Vagalla of northern Ghana or the Ibo of Nigeria), masquerades in the Italian Dolomites today and the masques among the English upper classes of the seventeenth century. At one level all are performances, all are in one sense dramatic. But bringing them together under one head seems to underplay the differences in detail that are often significant to the participants. In Western Europe we recognize points of similarity between rites and theatre

[1] For 'performance theory', see the works of Schechner in the bibliography. In this chapter, I have used the word 'theatre' in the narrower sense of what we think about as the stage. Drama I employ in a wider, looser way, more precise however than performance which may or may not be dramatic.

but separate them conceptually and practically because one is work (or at least serious) while the other is (literally) play. This distinction relates to special problems which the latter may engender. In a number of societies questions have been raised about theatrical representations (and less frequently about rites, on somewhat different grounds) which have to do with their presence and absence, with their appearance and disappearance, at various times and in various cultures. Could the presence of less explicit forms of cognitive ambivalence about theatre than we find in written texts have something to do with its uneven distribution and relative scarcity elsewhere? As with my earlier topics, it would be impossible to cover the world exhaustively, rather I want to indicate the range of societies in which these questions occur.

In non-literate societies, theatre in the more restricted sense is rare but not altogether absent and often forms part of a much wider category of play. That is not how it is seen by all. According to Turner, 'Tribal rites know nothing of modern distinctions between "work" and "play" or "work" and "leisure"; episodes of joking, trickery, fantasy and festivity mark the rituals of tribal society.'[2] The ludic (play) is seen as part of the ritual, 'vividly represented in liminality', which he contrasts with the division of work and leisure in modern (industrial) societies. It is obviously important to recognize the growth of institutionalized leisure in industrial societies, as well as the links between rite and drama in earlier ones. But the wider claim concerning work and play, such as the global use of performance, seems to fly in the face of many categorizations of cultural activity by the participants themselves. I hope to show that such distinctions do in fact exist in oral cultures and are related to the frequent absence of theatre.

But let me first concentrate on Europe and call attention to the claim, which was consistent with the view of magic giving way to religion and then to science, which the Scottish anthropologist James Frazer proposes as an evolutionary sequence, that theatre in the more restricted sense may have emerged out of rite, that there was a long-term temporal differentiation of performance, of 'play'

[2] Turner 1979:35.

from 'work'. Taking an 'anthropological' line, William Ridgeway argued that Greek drama arose from funeral performances, although later authors have suggested that its origin lay in the dramatic recitation of the Homeric epics which in historical times were part of the festival of the Great Dionysia in Athens.[3] The claim that there exists a genetic link between rite and theatre appears to be somewhat strengthened by the knowledge that, in later Europe, the virtual disappearance of the theatre, following the decline of Rome, was brought to an end by the revival of dramatic performances of biblical inspiration developed out of the musical tropes introduced into medieval church services from the tenth century onwards. These additions to the service led to the elaboration of the performances known as mystery plays throughout Europe.[4]

Under Christianity, the classical theatre of Greece and Rome vanished, but ritual obviously did not. Some may see the Mass as a replacement, the functional equivalent of earlier theatre. But that analytic view was not held by the participants themselves. Should we call liturgy drama, Tydeman asks, 'given that their originators probably saw them as no such thing'?[5] Although its boundaries varied over time as well as between different groups of people, firm distinctions were made between the liturgy and these dramatic interludes, not to speak of theatre, folk plays and similar performances. Specific objections were made by the Church to the latter, which continued to have a 'popular' audience. For these biblical tropes were only one of several elements leading to the renewal of secular theatre in the Renaissance, as indeed funeral or other rites

---

[3] Goldhill 1986. Ridgeway's work was part of a much wider tradition of enquiry at the time that saw Greek dramas as emerging from ritual (the *ludus sacra*), for example, F. Cornford, *The Origin of Attic Comedy* (London, 1914), G. Murray, 'Excursus on the ritual forms preserved in Greek tragedy', in J. E. Harrison, *Themis* (Cambridge, 1921) and J. E. Harrison, *Ancient Art and Ritual* (New York, 1913). The same notions have been applied to Nō theatre by B. Ortalan in 'Shamanism and the origins of the Nō theatre', *Asian Theatre Journal* 1:166–90 and more generally by V. Turner in *From Ritual to Theatre: The Human Seriousness of Play* (New York).

[4] See for example Meredith and Tailby 1983; Massip 1984.

[5] Tydeman in Beadle 1994:4.

must have been to the emergence of earlier Greek drama because the existence of these forms of 'play' are widespread.

The distinction between them and rites is clear because, despite the fact that much medieval drama took as its subject biblical themes, the sacredness of the story did not prevent constant attacks being made upon them. One of the most forthright of these attacks was the fourteenth-century sermon, probably of Lollard origin, entitled 'A tretise of miraclis pleyinge'.[6] Much of this work centres on the use of the word 'play'. Despite their religious content, such performances could be seen as 'playing' both with reality and with religious ritual. In Barish's words, the author of this treatise is 'mesmerized by the very word play, which in his eye affixes a stigma onto the whole operation that nothing can remove, and which makes the representation into a calculated affront to the thing it is attempting to represent'.[7] In other words 'play' is deliberately set aside from work, indeed, at one level, from 'reality' itself, which includes rites. 'Playing at' is contrasted with 'doing'. As in the title of Raymond Firth's account of the Pacific island of Tikopia, *The Work of the Gods*, rites are work, not play. Play is re-presentation, mimicry and at one extreme associated with carnival skits whose method and even whose truth is questionable, at least for the Lollards. Religious rites were not queried in the same way, though these do undergo some criticism for extravagance, for lack of efficacy, and in extreme cases even for their presence. The anti-theatrical notions of the Lollards went back to the early Fathers. But such ideas were not confined to the Christianity of that period and it would be a mistake to see them as only religious in inspiration, although that critique was particularly important.

I want to pursue the nature of the anti-theatrical activity in Europe that turned around this distinction, then ask if those objections are found in other literate cultures, and eventually see if there are any similar distinctions, manifestations and objections, at least

---

[6] Printed in T. Wright and J. O. Halliwell (eds), *Reliquiae Antiquae: Scraps from Ancient Monuments* (London, 1843).
[7] Barish 1981:68.

in embryonic form, in oral cultures such as those in Africa. Such an enquiry may tell us, among other things, whether we are dealing with an activity and attitude specific to Christianity and Europe, whether these are facets of literate cultures or whether we are in the presence of a more general feature of human interaction. My aim is to break down the concept of performance to show the cognitive tensions (sometimes contradictions) that lie behind theatrical re-presentations (and more rarely rites) that may lead over time to a swing between their acceptance and their rejection. Although discussion of this topic, as with the parallel one surrounding icons or relics, is often embedded in the Christian or the European context, I want to demonstrate that it also characterizes other major societies with literate traditions and hence requires a different kind of explanation, one relating to that given by Plato which was more inclusive and linked to the problem of mimesis. Those traditions require examining in terms of the cognitive tensions which lie behind mimetic performance.

In the secular Western tradition, the case against 'performance' and art as distinct from ritual was most comprehensively developed by Plato in Book X of *The Republic*. A creative force, perhaps God, created the idea of, say, a chair, the 'real' chair from the standpoint of Platonic idealism, one form of which a carpenter can produce. What the painter then creates is removed from reality at the third level. It was the same with poetry, even with Homer, for a poet is a 'creator of phantoms who we defined as the imitator' (599D). Such individuals 'do not lay hold on truth; (600E), for they are dealing in appearances rather than in reality. That is the reason why all poetry has to be excluded from the Republic, 'save only hymns to the gods and the praises of good men' (607A). In other words, Plato makes a distinction between what is ritual (and moral) on the one hand and what is frivolous on the other. Representation, mimesis or theatre has to be set aside from the real thing. Despite the importance of the theatre in Greek life, it was open to grave objections.

In Rome the theatre also aroused some antipathy from its earliest days, partly perhaps because it had become quite separated from cult. At the same time it achieved a wide popularity, though the actors sank deeper in the social scale.[8] The low status generally accorded the profession in earlier times and the lavish rewards given to some performers is part of this ambivalence. That element of low status virtually disappears in contemporary cultures, addicted as they are to performance and to lavishing praise on actors and acting. The earlier objections continued, from pagans as well as from Christians who were particularly uncomfortable with those performances that parodied the sacraments on the stage as well as those exhibitions that forced them into mortal combat. As a result many Fathers of the Church advocated the complete suppression of drama and circuses. Their reasons sometimes included the more general grounds that harked back to Plato. The earliest commentator, Tatian (*c.* 160 CE), declaimed against the actor who 'outwardly counterfeits what he is not'.[9] Here it is not the licentiousness or blasphemy of the performance, nor even the worship of false gods of which Tertullian later complains, but 'impersonation', mimesis itself, the *re*-presentation of reality.[10]

The decay of the theatre in early medieval Europe was not due to Christianity alone, nor yet to more general Platonic doubts. The economy had declined drastically, above all in the towns. That 'collapse' did not come about just because of the arrival of the barbarians. Pirenne argues, indeed, that the decline had already begun by the third century, long before the Germanic invasions.[11] But even at that period the economy was influenced by changes which were related to cult and belief. I have elsewhere suggested that the substantial expenditure which the Church required to create a 'great organization' involved the substantial shift of existing resources from the family and therefore entailed changes in the kinship system.[12] We can extend this argument to 'culture' (in the more restricted sense of the term as high, artistic culture), as Spieser does to the decay of towns. He maintains that while

[8] Barish 1981:38–9.
[9] Tatian, *To the Greeks*, ch. 22.
[10] Tertullian, *On Idolatry*.
[11] Pirenne 1955.
[12] J. Goody 1983.

towns in the eastern Empire were still rich and active at the beginning of the fourth century, by the seventh decay had taken place to such an extent that, apart from a few exceptional cases, some archaeologists and historians see an almost complete disappearance of urban life.[13] This development took place during the period following the reign of Constantine, when the building of churches was permitted and encouraged. Major resources were needed for their construction and for the subsequent maintenance of plant and personnel. As Brown remarks: 'In the second century, the tide of surplus income had poured into public buildings; in the fourth, into the glorification of the emperor and the magnates; from the fifth century onwards, this rich flood welled into the Christian Church "for the remission of sins".'[14] It was of course this wealth that made possible 'the amazing artistic achievements . . . the vast basilicas, covered with mosaic, hung with silk-embroidered tapestries, and lit by thousands of oil lamps in massive silver candelabra . . .'

Accounts of the early lives of saints give some idea of this process of accumulation, which represented a spiritual as well as a material investment on the part of individuals.[15] Such major material transfers to the church were made partly at the expense of the towns whose endowments and commercial receipts suffered accordingly. In late Antiquity rich individuals had lent money to municipalities, receiving interest which was partly financial, partly social. In the third century, inflation destroyed the value of the fixed incomes of the towns which depended upon rents from civic lands, interest on money endowments and the *munera* given by councillors to those that had elected them – an obligation that attracted increasing disfavour. But the main problem for the maintenance of public buildings arose because in the last decade of his reign Constantine

---

[13] Spieser 1985:50. In Britain the larger towns continued to exist (Wright 1861:i, 77), but in a much less prosperous state. On the West more generally, see Hodges and Whitehouse 1983.

[14] Brown 1971:108–9. He goes on to say: 'the rise of the economic position of the Christian Church was sudden and dramatic . . . By the sixth century, the income of the Bishop of Ravenna was twelve thousand gold pieces'.

[15] For example, the Life of St John the Almoner.

confiscated these rents and dues, as well as seizing temple treasures and estates. That expropriation, which was confirmed by his son, Constantine II, had a disastrous effect on public buildings and on the nature of urban life. In general endowments now began to go to the church rather than to the municipality. In other words, there was an explicit shift from theatre to church, from mimesis to rite, from 'play' to work, underneath which lay an implicit conflict between them.

That trend was reinforced by an ideological one. The prohibition of Deuteronomy (xxiii:20) upon lending to 'brothers' at interest was interpreted by St Jerome (340–420) and St Ambrose of Milan (340–397) as a condemnation of lending at interest to any Christian, since all men (at least all Christian men) are 'brothers'. As a result of this universalization of morality in the early persecuted Church, all such lending became a sin and the Carolingian Age saw 'the promulgation of a general prohibition of usury among Christians, whether lay or ecclesiastical;.[16] That injunction struck at all types of commercial investment. There were of course ways of circumventing the provision in Christianity as there were in Judaism and later in Islam. But the effect of the ban was to encourage charity, that is, ecclesiastical donations, rather than commercial or municipal investment; charity meant gifts to the Church (sometimes on a temporary basis), not loans on interest to the township.

The contributions to the construction of new churches, the shift of funds, including a transfer from west to east, that is, to the Holy Lands, expanded the building trades. The magnificent results constituted a powerful attraction for pilgrims, worshippers and visitors alike.[17] But along with the prohibition on usury, such expenditure meant a decrease in investment in commerce and above all, as Spieser suggests, in towns and in the facilities they provided for their citizens, namely, baths, fountains, archways, squares, gymnasia and public buildings, including theatres. Imperial ceremony continued with *'la fuite vers le haut'*, as a result

---

[16] Nelson 1969:5.
[17] Heim 1985:208.

the towns were in difficulties despite the efforts of Justinian, for there was also a vast movement of resources towards the Church. Amenities suffered and the ideology of the town disintegrated, for the city depended upon patronage, charity and social investment. This was especially true of the theatre, which has rarely been able to maintain itself without patronage of some kind. In any case, it could hardly have continued to put on classical drama (though this was still read for the purpose of learning the language) since this was so heavily impregnated with pagan, that is, non-Christian themes.

For the history of Western culture the results were dramatic. During the Roman occupation, until the late fourth century at least, Britain had conventional theatres in six towns: St Albans (or Verulamium), Brough-on-Humber, Canterbury, Catterick, Cirencester and Colchester; if amphitheatres are counted, then another twelve centres should be added. All disappeared and no structure of this kind was built again until 1576, over 1000 years later.[18] The theatre at Verulamium was erected around 155 CE and continued in use until about the year 395. It possessed a stage with a wooden floor and, after about 200, a curtain slot, proscenium and stage buildings. At first, performances took place in the central arena, then on the stage, later returning to the centre.[19] What has to be noted is that this theatre did not simply decay. It was 'deliberately filled with rubbish', possibly about 400 CE.[20] In other words, its disappearance was not only the result of economic collapse, but was in some degree intentional.

The general decline struck at most of the Roman public buildings, including baths, the only exception being the churches which all major towns seemed to have possessed at this time and some of which continued in use until the ninth century. As the major continuing public institution in a community, the Church

---

[18] I refer to specialist theatres. There were purpose-built earthwork 'amphitheatres' in Cornwall and East Anglia in the fourteenth century and indoor productions in great halls in the early fifteenth (Tydeman in Beadle 1994:3).
[19] See K. M. Kenyon and Frere *ca.* 1963; K. M. Kenyon 1935.
[20] Mackreth 1987:138.

inevitably took on some of the civic or municipal functions, or else promoted their equivalents. Verulamium, the capital of Roman Britain, was plundered to build a church on the top of the nearby hill where the Roman soldier, Albanus, had been martyred as a Christian in about the year 304.[21] It was around this building that the new town of St Albans grew up; but while both the Saxon Abbey church (said to have been built by Offa, King of Mercia, in the eighth century) and the later abbey (of the eleventh century, constructed by the Normans to establish the dominance of Latin civilization over northern peoples) were great centres of learning, there was neither public theatre nor baths. Written plays in Latin continued to be used for instruction in the classical language, possibly even for reading aloud in the cathedral school; the library of the Benedictine Abbey owned a twelfth century manuscript of Terence which was illustrated with ink-drawings of masked actors.[22] But there was no permanent theatre nor any public performance of these plays.

For the outside observer there is a sense in which the Mass became the functional equivalent of the drama, and the clergy the actors. Yet for the participants themselves these rites were explicitly not theatre, the clergy not actors. These had disappeared, not only through lack of financial support, but because theatre was deliberately rejected like icons, for secular drama was both pagan and sacrilegious. Moreover, for some it was a re-presentation and hence in itself a lie. So although for limited analytical purposes the ecclesiastical celebration may be taken as an equivalent, for the participants the distinction between different types of performance, between rite and theatre, between work and play, was highly significant. It related to the desirability of the one and the objectionable or ambiguous character of the other.

The effects on cultural activity were radical in another way. Not only were libraries, and major performances, shifted away from the town and placed inside the church, physically and spiritually, but an outcome of the decay of the old centres was the re-siting of

---

[21] Verulamium, in the valley of the Ver, was originally a Belgic town.
[22] Bodl. ms Auct. F. 2. 13. See Lancashire 1984:258.

places of learning, sometimes in out-of-the-way parts much further than St Albans lay from Verulamium, in hilltop monasteries such as Monte Cassino in Italy, or in deserts, such as Saint Catherine in the Sinai. Contrast the great Hellenistic library of Alexandria, situated in a major Mediterranean port, with that of the monastery of Saint Catherine, which lay at a distance of several days of parched travel away from any settlement, let alone a town, yet it possessed one of the great ecclesiastical libraries of early Christendom. Here learning had moved from the town to the desert, with important implications for its status, content, access and consequently for the nature and practice of learning. Even when a library was housed in a church around which a town developed, it remained enclosed in ecclesiastical space.

Of course, the lack of theatres or of public performances of classical plays did not mean that there was no drama outside the Church. There were certainly 'games' (*ludi*) which are also 'plays', some, including wrestling matches, resembling those at which earlier Christians had suffered so grievously, as well as others closer to folk drama and to ceremonies that adapted earlier forms to a new dispensation. Nevertheless, these popular performances did not escape censure. Axton sees the anti-theatrical writings of Tertullian, Jerome and other early Fathers of the Church as a response to 'the scurrilous pantomime theatre of the late Roman Empire'.[23] But the net was cast more widely. Objections were made by medieval churchmen to *spectacula* and to *ludi*, to mimicry, 'folk pastimes, "disguisings", dramatic dances, contests and games of all sorts', including 'clerical unruliness' and revels like the 'Feast of Fools' on the Twelfth Night. In 679 the Council of Rome ordered the English bishops and clerics not to countenance '*jocos vel ludos*'.[24] The existence of the order itself indicates that theatrical and dramatic representations were banished not only because of barbarians, who with the passage of time are easily accustomed to luxury, nor only because of a radical shift of expenditure from town

---

[23] Axton 1974:31.
[24] These *ludi* may have been spectator sports like wrestling, related to tourneying and courtly feats at arms (Lancashire 1984:xiii).

to Church, nor yet because the Mass in the church replaced drama in the theatre. all that did happen. But there were also deliberate objections to dramatic activity on the part of the Church.

Despite these attempts to suppress such performances, they continued, or were revived, in some popular forms outside the church and the tendency to elaborate and enact, especially for the benefit of the populace, brought about the growth of extra-liturgical dramatic elements inside. Folk performances were condemned as early as the Council of Rome (in CE 826) and that continued right down to fourteenth-century Wells, where the objections show how often ring dances took place in church or churchyard. About the year 1250 Oxford students were reported using masks; along with 'wrestling and other dishonest plays in cemeteries, theatrical plays and filthy spectacles', *chorae* were prohibited by a Synod of Exeter in 1287.[25] The scope of the objections to popular *ludi* was very wide and included the fact that they mimicked and criticized the behaviour of courtiers (under Louis the Pious 778–840) or clergy (under King Edgar, 959–75).[26] But there was also the puritanical argument of Agobard of Lyons (823–24); he castigated clergymen who gave lavish hospitality to mimes, players and buffoons while the poor were left to perish of hunger.

The first English evidence of the ecclesiastical tropes appears in the Winchester '*Quem Quaeritis*' (*c.* 970), also known as the *Visitatio Sepulchri*, the text of which has rubrics for performance. Significantly, like early icons in the Eastern Church, it was in some ways almost deliberately non-representational. Nothing about the garments, the properties, the construction is 'realistic', according to Axton, exemplified by the fact that three male clerics play the parts of the three Marys.[27] This text, in which Easter is anticipated, was used throughout Europe and was consistent with liturgical customs across the continent; it could therefore be 'readily adapted and persisted, in many places unchanged, for centuries'. Later

---

[25] Axton 1974:55.
[26] Tydeman in Beadle 1994:11.
[27] Axton 1974:65, 67.

texts from the twelfth century show 'a new and possibly unrelated tradition' of extra-liturgical scriptural plays growing up beside the tropes, sometimes performed outside the church buildings.[28]

Nevertheless, from the second half of the twelfth century, objections were still occasionally made, even to church drama, though not as frequently as to secular varieties. About 1160 Gerhoh of Reichersberg attacked ecclesiastical plays, voicing a deep-seated suspicion of the 'illusionary power of drama'. Nor was ritual altogether immune. Some even objected to the way the Mass itself was celebrated and in the twelfth century, the Cistercian, Aelred of Rievaulx, condemned English priests for using 'histrionic gestures and emotive pauses, for pulling faces and singing expressively', a fashion more appropriate to the *theatrum* than to the church.

This 'theatre' continued at a popular level as a separate tradition. In the secular tradition there has been a strong tendency to see folk plays as related to 'primitive' ceremonies. Early in this century Jane Harrison noted a type of combat drama in Thrace which was described in terms of 'sympathetic magic' of a primitive kind.[29] Building on the traditions of 'Cambridge anthropology' in the manner of E. K. Chambers, modern English mumming has been regarded as a survival of fertility plays whose 'original shape and magical purpose have become confused'.[30] These performances clearly have a morphological resemblance and possibly a historical connection. But folk drama of this type, which also had its links with the urban games promoted in Rome, displays one profound difference from so-called primitive rituals. It is play rather than religious rite. Mumming cannot simply be counted as a survival bearing the same traits as the original; the tradition has been marginalized, as a result of which both meaning and form have changed. The appearance of a dominant religious tradition of the written word which institutionalized its own rites, may have left others as games (plays) or as magic. So there are dangers in taking mumming as representative of the forms of earlier, purely oral

---

[28] Lancashire 1984:xii.
[29] Axton 1974:35.
[30] Axton 1974:37.

cultures, just as there is in the case of Yugoslav songs or even German 'fairy tales'. For the commanding heights in all these cases have been occupied by the written culture of the 'elites', leaving the folk to fill in the gaps. That is one reason why we have to be careful in comparing Homer with later singers of tales.[31]

A recent collection of essays on medieval drama rejects its origin in pre-Christian ritual (which is rightly recognized as a different form of social action) in favour of the notion that 'drama has always been a crucial force for encouraging communal integration and for expressing a sense of corporate identity'.[32] Such a suggestion substitutes a loose functionalism for an unsatisfactory evolutionism. There is no evidence that drama has *always* been around; as theatre it is an intermittent phenomenon, often fraught with ambivalence. And the assumption that it encourages communal integration and corporate unity is a construct of the observer, rarely reflected in the intention of the participants, whose activities have at times been looked on critically by part of the community.

Despite condemnations, folk plays continued to be created and performed while religious drama grew up first inside, then outside the walls of the church. The impulse to play, to elaborate and to educate took a variety of forms. The opposition to plays, and indeed the whole notion that representative art was a dangerous illusion, gradually became less important with the twelfth and thirteenth centuries and a theatrical tradition began to be reborn.[33] By the thirteenth century religious plays were performed in towns throughout the provinces where there were major religious buildings. There is also evidence that some people knew of Terence's plays and even imitated them, in England as in continental Europe. Furthermore, in the course of the thirteenth century, from the reign of Edward I to that of Edward III, drama became increasingly legitimate partly because of Court and ecclesiastical

---

[31] J. Goody 1987; Lord 1960. The 'fairy tale' presents a different problem that I discuss later.

[32] Tydeman in Beadle 1994:13.

[33] We may see a parallel development of representation in the naturalistic relief of Gothic cathedrals and in the realistic poetry of Chaucer's *Canterbury Tales* and, very differently, Langland's *Piers Plowman*.

patronage. Secular plays ('spel') appeared at the marriage of Edward I to Margaret of France in 1299, although in the previous century it was said that London 'in place of shows in the theatre and stage plays [as at Rome] has holier plays, wherein are shown forth the miracles wrought by Holy Confessors . . .' In England the first extant secular play, *Interludium de Clerico et Puella*, dates from that period; Christmas disguisings are reported from London by 1334. Other 'clerks' plays' were performed outside the church. The great pageant cycles of the Corpus Christi plays emerge a little later. In towns the market-place and the streets became the scenes for such performances with control passing to the city authorities and to the craft guilds. A lay tradition emerged, though one that still employed religious themes.

Clerks' plays are reported elsewhere in Europe at a yet earlier date. The life of St Nicholas, the patron of scholars, is known to have been dramatized from about the year 1100. From Arras, Jehan Bodel's play on the subject was one of the first 'urban' dramas of the medieval period and showed complete indifference to the liturgical tradition. The plot turns around an icon of the saint which was captured by the Saracen ruler during the crusades. To test its power, the king places his treasure under its protection. When the icon is stolen and then returned through the intervention of St Nicholas, the king is converted to Christianity.

This 'urban' drama is characterized by a measure of 'realism'. In the same town of Arras there were several charitable guilds dedicated to St Nicholas, whose festivities began on the Eve of December 5th. The *Confrérie des clercs de Saint-Nicholas* attended Mass on that day and later feasted while the Life of the Saint was read aloud. On such occasions the story was sometimes brought to life by its re-presentation in a play. On St Nicholas' Day 1417, two centuries after Bodel's death, his play was revived by the scholars of Notre-Dame de Saint Omer, after which the actors went to nearby taverns where they diced and drank heavily (an activity normally forbidden to them but occurring in the play), 'apparently in imitation of the play'.[34] The spectacle rebounded on life in a

---

[34] Axton 1974:132.

complex way, encouraging temporary participation in behaviour which was disapproved of over the longer term. That was believed to be one of the recurrent dangers of representation, that it would promote undesirable or immoral acts by displaying them on the stage.

Despite the revival, opposition did not altogether disappear. In 1303 Robert of Brunne condemned '*clerkes plei*' (that is, performances outside the liturgy) although he defended Nativity and Resurrection tropes. In St Albans the constitution of the Abbey in 1328–49 prevented the clergy from attending '*illicita spectacula*' or being '*aliis ludentibus*'.[35] Not until 30 June 1444, do we hear of a secular play in the town itself, that of *Eglemour and Degrebelle*. In his magisterial account of *The Anti-theatrical Prejudice* (1981), Jonas Barish often speaks of pathology, of extremes, likening fundamentalist anti-theatricalism to old-style anti-semitism. From the contemporary perspective, especially that of a liberal-minded teacher of literature, it is difficult to appreciate that there are other, more substantial, foundations for objections to theatre. One of these was the supposedly licentious lives of the players; in medieval Europe the word *theatrum* was understood to mean a tavern-cum-brothel with a floorshow provided by *mimi*, by mimics.[36] Those objections have a link with the problem of men dressing up as women, which was forbidden as long ago as *Deuteronomy*. Why? To prevent a confusion of identities? Because of fears about one's dominant sexuality?[37] Possibly. It was also a matter of going against what God had created. In addition to religious objections, there was more generally a question of the fundamental illusion of representation, which involves 'mimicry' and, therefore (in the short term at least), untruth, a lie.

---

[35] *Gesta Abbatum* (ed. T. H. Riley, 3 vols, 1867–69), II, 469. As at St Albans, the Winchester clergy were forbidden from participating in '*ludibrorum spectacula*' or '*ludos inhonestos*' in 1384, as indeed were scholars, an indication that such spectacles were then being performed.

[36] Axton 1974:18.

[37] For a Renaissance discussion of anti-theatrical objections to males being effeminized by dressing up in women's clothing, see Levine 1994. Also Orgel 1996.

On the religious level this argument parallels the debate between the Cistercian father, Bernard of Clairvaux, and the Abbot Suger, builder of St Denis in Paris, the first great Gothic church, about the merits of plain and stained glass. For Suger, the beauty of the glass pointed the way to God; for the more puritanical, it obscured His true light and was at best a distraction, at worst an illusion. Hence the seventeenth-century campaign in East Anglia where Dowling reports the mass destruction in one day of 1000 pictures (actually panes of stained glass) at the parish church of Clare in Suffolk. King's College in nearby Cambridge escaped only by a hair's breadth, because of powerful patrons. Meanwhile, Puritan and non-conformist churches were built without stained glass and without images, and their congregations practised thin rather than thick rituals. That remained true in much of the Church of England until the revival of ritual under Newman and others in the second half of the nineteenth century. Nor was this movement towards thicker rituals confined to the Church of England. It is equally noticeable among Baptist and Methodist churches in the south of the United States, where some branches have recently thickened both their rituals and their iconography; although the stained glass introduced into their hitherto plain windows is generally abstract in design, this development represents a move towards the elaboration of the decorative schema, towards the values of secular society and perhaps towards those of 'established' churches.

As we have seen earlier, similar sentiments about drama were expressed by those proto-Protestants, the Lollards. The followers of John Wycliffe (c.1330–84) saw even miracle plays as false images. While this movement did not greatly affect the provinces, the religious drama of London, now a great financial centre, all but disappeared except for some plays performed under local auspices. The Lollards of London objected to its presence, and for their annual feasts the guilds had to import players from the small professional troupes touring the country at this time (1426). Even a century-and-a-half later Elizabethan players avoided the puritan City by settling on the south bank. Drama at the Court also suffered under the Lancastrian kings, especially Henry IV; both he and his son claimed to have uncovered Lollard assassination plots where the traitors were to be disguised as Christmas mummers.

The Lollard theme was taken up by certain Protestants and especially by the Puritans. The Feast of Corpus Christi, the occasion when mystery plays were performed, was suppressed in 1548 during the reign of Edward VI; the Protestants obviously purged what they regarded as papist pageants just as they did papist rituals. In the secular world new plays were composed for the king, but any play whose theme ran counter to the Act of Uniformity incurred a penalty under a statute of 1549. At roughly the same time the Scottish Kirk tried to stop the Robin Hood plays in 1555, and all scriptural plays in 1574. The main secular theatre was again affected: Lindsay's *Thrie Estaitis* was performed in 1552, following which there was an absence of theatrical performances in Edinburgh until the second half of the eighteenth century, mainly due to dogma but partly to the incidence of wars and the disappearance of the Court to London. In Elizabethan England there was greater freedom than in Scotland for local custom to flourish, but the town mystery plays tended to disappear, partly for financial reasons which were probably related to religious ones. The potential audience was certainly divided about the merits of religious plays, if only because it was divided on religious affiliation; it was split about the very idea of imaging and representation, some allowing, some disallowing.

The rejection that occurred in this period was not only a matter of fiat from above nor yet of tradition from the past; some widespread cognitive tensions and contradictions existed about forms of mimesis as we see from the persistence of anti-theatrical reactions. On the one hand, there was the pressure to enact, to elaborate, and on the other there were doubts about doing so. Ecclesiastical promptings could elicit a ready response to the suppression of the theatre, since the potential for its denial was already there within the minds of people, within the 'culture' (though such ambivalence, I argue is transcultural, transversal). It was not Cromwell or the Puritans alone who banished drama from the English stage; we can only understand the changing popular attitudes by assuming a degree of ambivalence as the result of which members of a society may subscribe to opposing views over time.

Even with the rebirth of lay theatre under Elizabeth, criticism continued. Each company needed the protection as well as the patronage of the armed, wealthy and prestigious nobility. Shakespeare's first known play was produced in 1591 in a period when other forms of drama were being attacked. The biblical cycles of Coventry, Chester and York were suppressed between 1575 and 1580, and the playbooks of the York cycle were confiscated. Towards the end of Elizabeth's reign the performing of what was seen as Catholic drama came close to treason. But attacks were not only directed against the wrong use of theatre. General prohibitions against all local drama were issued by the civil and ecclesiastical authorities alike.[38] Mimetic activity became the subject of litigation, especially if this took place on the sabbath; the same was true of dancing or music. Even the Protestant 'comedie' of John Bale, *The Three Laws*, was criticized; and Bale himself was led to accuse actors 'of mocking Protestant preachers with May games'. So these attacks involved more than the censorship of the works of opponents which had been introduced in 1549 by the London council. For extreme Protestants, all acting, drama, mimesis was wrong; for re-presentation itself was false. Imitation was seen as having the power to corrupt, a position that had earlier been taken by St John Chrysostom and, outside the Christian tradition, by Plato himself. Now it became a critical feature of the anti-theatrical prejudice again, for example, in the idea that men might be corrupted, effeminized, by dressing up as women, or in other ways.[39] The late medieval stage had a background in university productions and craft guilds, which were all male. Actresses appeared in continental Europe in the middle of the sixteenth century but not in England. That was also true in the Netherlands and in certain areas of Protestant Germany, but there it was the theatre itself that was felt to be morally dangerous. The public stage was entirely dispensed with.[40] Does Shakespeare express something of the same

---

[38] Johnston 1991:121–2, from which this paragraph is largely drawn.
[39] Levine 1994.
[40] Orgel 1996:2.

doubts about mimesis rather than morality when he offers his audience a play within a play? In a sense that insertion, in *Hamlet* and *A Midsummer Night's Dream*, challenges the theatrical illusion itself. At the same time such an interlude can be more intense than the play itself, arousing Hamlet's emotions more dramatically than in real life, though the intention was to catch the conscience of the king. In *A Midsummer Night's Dream*, the use of fairy potions attacks the very notions of love while the play of the rude mechanicals seems to subvert the idea of acting itself. Certainly at other times the playwright deliberately breaks the illusion regarding the sexuality of actors as when Cleopatra exclaims:

> . . . and I shall see
> Some squeaking Cleopatra boy my greatness
> I 'th' posture of a whore.[41]

Deliberately provocative, the tactic is also dangerous, since it reminds the audience that Cleopatra is not the Queen of Egypt but a boy playing the part on a London stage and the suspension of disbelief is directly challenged, as in the Brechtian notion of alienation.

In some cases such objections extended from drama even to ecclesiastical ceremonies, to all rites of a formal kind. It was understandable that May follies were regarded as the devil's work. But in New England objections went further; 'sabbatarianism was antithetical to traditional religious observances, and averse to the distinction of commemorative days'.[42] May Day, April Fool's Day, Christmas, all were suppressed, at least in public, the latter by an ordinance of 1658, though Anglicans continued to celebrate the occasion. Even the sectarian Protestant celebration of Guy Fawkes on 5 November, which celebrated God's vigilance against Catholic conspirators, replacing All Souls' Day, and which finally disappeared in the United States with the Revolution, was regarded by some New Englanders as a sign of unreformed superstition, for the

---

[41] *Antony and Cleopatra* V, ii, 215–17.
[42] Cressy 1989:197.
[43] Cressy 1989:203.

elect had other, more substantial, witnesses to providence.[43]

Within Christianity anti-theatricality was not confined to England nor yet to the Puritans. This situation was paralleled in France in the following century, '... the century that saw the most brilliant single period of theatrical activity in French history ... should at the same time have been the target of a sustained and unrelenting attack from all quarters of the French Churches' – Jansenist, Jesuit as well as Protestant.[44] The Jansenists in Catholic France were equally severe, as they were with icons, resting their objections firmly on the views of St Augustine and showing the same aversion to earthly pleasures.

In seventeenth-century France there was a continuing dispute (the *querelle du théâtre*) over the moral worth of the theatre (*la poésie représentative*) between theologians and dramatic theorists. In particular the atmosphere of physical austerity around Jansenism (and Protestantism) led to a domestic crusade against un-Christian behaviour, which included theatre-going.[45] There was even an active discussion after 1680 about closing the Paris theatres, while the Church's harassment of actors and playwrights like Molière is well known. Religious writers objected particularly to the illusionist theatre with its creation of imaginary worlds, offering the vision of an alternative creation.[46] In a more concrete way the theatre offered an alternative to the ritual and instruction of the Church, the more so when it insisted on its didactic role.

The best known protest lay, however, in the more secular tradition of Plato and appeared in the following century. In his *Lettre d'Alembert sur les Spectacles* (1758), which arose out of a contribution to the *Encyclopédie*, Rousseau engaged in a vigorous polemic denying not the failure of the theatre in its service to God but to men themselves, especially in the effects of mimesis on morality. It was but part of his general attack on the arts which, like luxury, debilitate civilizations.[47]

---

[44] Phillips 1980:3.
[45] Phillips 1980:11.
[46] Phillips 1980:248.
[47] The evil effects of luxury is much to the fore in another important eighteenth-century work, *The Spirit of the Laws* of Montesquieu.

Interestingly, Rousseau, like Plato, Augustine and Tertullian, is said to have greatly enjoyed the theatre in his youth. According to one commentator, Tertullian 'seems merely to have traded one extremism for another, a frenetic licentiousness for an exaggerated asceticism'.[48] Could that not be because of problems inherent in that type of performance? In a theocentric world, which is also a world of uncertainty, God's uniqueness may be a matter not only of belief but of salvation and survival; it is fundamentally wrong to imitate his works. In the secular tradition of Rousseau, what is imitated is often seen as a lie, or at least as second best, or as distracting from more serious, less luxurious, pursuits.[49]

Rousseau may have looked back to Plato, just as the French Revolutionaries later did to Rousseau, the Puritans to the Lollards and the Jansenists to the early Fathers of the Church. However, we are not simply dealing with imitative behaviour, with an inert tradition. What emerges relates to deep-seated worries about the relation of representation to reality and about the luxury and dispensability of drama and to some extent of rite. In the eighteenth century it was not only Rousseau who rejected festivals; so too did other *philosophes* of the Enlightenment. Royal rituals, ecclesiastical ceremonies, even the theatre itself were attacked by Diderot and others as the perpetuators of privilege; there were too many festivals which distracted the masses from work.

The arts were also a problem because they were seen as necessarily political; there was no question of art for art's sake. In his article on painting in the *Encyclopédie*, Diderot had announced that 'the governors of men have always made use of painting and sculpture in order to inspire in their subjects the religious and political sentiments they desire them to hold'.[50] With the Revolution, art of the old order was held to carry the wrong message, but it was at first agreed that the *Commission de monuments* should preserve the

---

[48] Barish 1981:54. Burwick 1991:22–6. In England a Christian view at that period was put forward by J. Collier, *Short View of the Immorality and Profanity of the English Stage* (1698) and a century later by J. Styles in *An Essay on the Character, Immoral, and Antichristian Tendency of the Stage* (1806).
[49] Burwick 1991:22–6.
[50] 1751–65, vol. XII, 267; see Izerda 1954:13.

best. As early as 1790, however, one group of artists requested the king to 'order the destruction of all monuments created during the feudal regime'.[51] The collapse of the monarchy in 1792 saw the beginning of 'a torrent of iconoclasm' that lasted three years. Statues came crashing down; pictures at Fontainebleau were burnt to appease the spirit of the murdered Marat. In 1794 members of the Commune of Arts planned a ceremony in which a portrait of the Dauphin was to be dragged to the foot of a liberty tree, mutilated and burnt. Religion was a particular target; all 'religious effigies' were ordered to be destroyed by the Paris Commune.

Some went even further and objected not only to relics of the *ancien régime* but to all art. Rousseau and others had encouraged the idea that the arts were the product of luxury and vice, of over-civilized societies. With the Revolution there were some who wanted to get rid of any distinction between 'royal' and 'republican' art; all should go. The same sentiments were even expressed about books. But that attitude was far from universal nor did it last; attempts were soon made to draw a line between 'luxury' and 'art'. While the painter Jacques-Louis David took up the idea of iconoclasm, he also looked forward to a purer art.[52] The statue of Louis XIV in the Place des Victoires was destroyed and a statue of liberty raised in its stead. In the end even much old art was preserved and placed in the great Louvre Museum, opened to the public in 1793, with objects 'torn out of their cultural context and regarded as "art"'.[53] The public museum neutralized the politics of private art and at the same time resolved the problem of luxury and to a large extent of iconoclasm.

The French Revolution created an equally important divide between the new order and earlier theatre and ceremony. That gap was to be resolved by the establishment of new festivals and a new calendar. Previous performances were tainted by royalty, by the Church or regarded, like the maypole, as 'insignificant childish

[51] Izerda 1954:15.
[52] On David and iconoclasm, see Besançon 1994.
[53] Izerda 1954:21,224.

games'.[54] Once again there were more general objections, for the power of images in themselves was suspect. Nevertheless, as in early Christianity and Buddhism, these were recognized as having some potential for good as a means of educating adults. That excuse did not apply to traditional theatre with its mimicry, its confined space and artificial spectacle but rather to the open-air festival in which simulacrum and symbol were played down in favour of allegory, 'an imitation that is to a certain extent non-imitative'.[55] Allegory, comments the French historian Ozouf, is allusion rather than illusion, a word that embodies both the delights and fears aroused by the theatre. In other words, the authorities wanted both to employ and to guard against the power of re-presentations. As in later revolutions, realism was preferred for it partially cleansed the artifice. In other contexts realism could be rejected for that very reason; it was too representational. But here sculpture won over painting, complete figures over busts, since they had greater verisimilitude, while cardboard rocks and trees fell into disfavour in face of the 'real' thing which it was possible to utilize in open-air performances. Indeed, many revolutionaries remained 'obstinately convinced . . . that everything that is figurative is false'.[56] Even local ceremonies had to be done away with because they tricked the audience. Instead of ceremony, the commissioners dispatched by the Directoire saw only spectacles, 'a reduction of traditional life to the theatre', of rite to drama.[57] Revolutionary societies have often felt this need to crush performances, even at the popular level. Their opposition to theatre stems firstly from the fact that it expresses the view of the previous ruling class or the *ancien régime*, and secondly, because in many forms it is itself elitist; thirdly a more widely-based rejection may derive from the very notion that mimesis is false, unreal, that even rites can mislead.

From the standpoint of cultural history the very early collapse of

---

[54] Ozouf 1988:340.
[55] Quatremere de Quincy 1801, quoted by Ozouf 1988:211.
[56] Ozouf 1988:205.
[57] Ozouf 1988:223.

the classical theatre in Europe was as remarkable as the virtual disappearance of the three-dimensional (classical) icon. Both had been among the artistic glories of the ancient world. Obviously much of the content would have had to be changed to fit the new dispensation. But there was more to this rejection than the obsolete religious content or even the antipathy of Christianity itself. It was a question of the nature of the activity and the associated ideology, which also raised problems for the theatre in other traditions dominated by the Near Eastern religions.

In the Judaic context this is clear; there is nothing in biblical or Talmudic writing that can be characterized as 'drama' or 'theatre'. While there are a few post-biblical examples of dramatic works written by Jews, the rabbis generally disapproved of the theatres, amphitheatres and circuses of the Hellenistic–Roman world. Attendance was discouraged, partly because sacrifices were offered at the performances but also because spectators would be sitting in 'the seat of the scornful' (*Psalms* 1:1), a generalized version of one of the Christian objections. Indeed, the Mishna on idolatry reads like Tertullian's *De Idololatria* and *De Spectaculis* which were approximately of the same date. In a passage of the Midrash (*Ruth* 2:22) Naomi tells Ruth that if she converts to Judaism she will deny herself certain pleasures for 'it is not the custom of the daughters of Israel to frequent theatres and circuses'. The theatres that were built in Palestine during the Hellenistic period were destroyed at the time of the Maccabean War (167 BCE). In popular entertainment Jews, like Christians, were often ridiculed (Jewish women were forced to eat pork on stage) so that the rabbis were led to forbid their workmen even to construct a stadium or amphitheatre.[58] For those were the places of their torment; Vespasian, on one occasion, slaughtered 1200 Jews in the stadium at Tiberias. Some Jews did appear on the Roman stage, some rabbis condoned attendance, but it was not until the mystery plays of the early Renaissance began to influence life in the ghetto that forms of drama emerged and the

---

[58] Elmslie 1911:26–7; 'Aboda Zara 1,7.

Purim play gradually became a counterpart of the Christian carnival.[59] While Jewish communities sometimes contributed to local celebrations, their participation in other theatrical productions remained 'at best insignificant' until the nineteenth century.[60]

In the Near East such objections extended well beyond drama. Islam, according to Grabar, was 'not conducive to fine arts', a feature he claimed to be a characteristic of the prophetic religions as a whole. Representation of living beings was prohibited in the later tradition, as a result of which the graphic arts placed their emphasis on calligraphy and on the arabesque, that is on the abstract. Some figurative art did make an appearance in early palaces and 'at the doors of the bath-houses' – that is, in private, courtly space. After the thirteenth century the non-Arab countries of Islam saw the development of the miniature under Chinese influence, but it rarely dealt with religious subjects. Mosques continued to be largely bare of pictorial decoration, concentrating attention upon the word of God.

As in the *Republic*, even poetry did not altogether escape. The Qur'an sees poets as roving around without ethical purpose; for many pious Muslims 'poetry was something suspect, opposed to divine law, especially as it sang mostly of forbidden wine and free love'.[61] Since music might be connected with such dubious activities, it too was often condemned by religious leaders, and was rarely used for sacred purposes except by dervish brotherhoods. It is not surprising that opera never developed. Drama too was rejected, for God was the only possible actor. One major exception was the 'passion play' (*ta'ziyah*), enacting the martyrdom of Husayn and other descendants of Ali, that is performed today among the Shi'ites of Iran and Lebanon.[62]

---

[59] See for example Kirshenblatt-Gimblett 1990.
[60] L. Sowden, art. 'Theater', *Encyclopaedia Judaica*, Jerusalem, 1972, 15:1050–51.
[61] O. Grabar, art. 'Arts of the Islamic Peoples', *The New Encyclopaedia Britannica*, Chicago, 1978, 9:952–1011.
[62] Peters 1956.

Although there was little theatre outside the later Ottoman court, which had its own troupe (once again the court excused itself), we do find mime associated with story tellers, the marionette theatre and shadow puppets, which were probably of Eastern origin.[63] In medieval times, the only extant plays were the shadow plays of Ibn Daniyel.[64] But, by and large, the performing arts received little official attention because of the questions of idolatry and of human portrayal. When the western theatre was introduced to Damascus in the 1870s problems arose. Objectors employed arguments from traditional discussions of what would, nowadays, be thought of as fundamentalist puritanism (for example, relating to the whole question of gender). Any representation of a living thing challenged the uniqueness and omnipotence of God, who alone can create life.

Islamic attitudes influenced the development of theatre on the wider Asian scene. For India, too, experienced swings in the presence of drama. The Sanskritic theatre, of Kalidas for example, developed in the first century CE, possibly influenced by the performance of Greek plays in north Indian cities.[65] Performance stopped abruptly with the Muslim invasions, beginning in the tenth century. Nor were these swings confined to the theatre, though there they were more pronounced. Rituals too gave birth to quite contrary trends, in India and in China as well as in Europe. Brahmin ritual bred its radical opposite in various ways. A materialist school arose that denied life after death and the existence of 'immaterial categories'. They objected to 'the senseless ritual and ceremonial on which the priests insisted, and which was their livelihood'.[66] In fact, 'throughout the Vedic literature consisting of the Samhitās, the Brāhmaṇas and the Upaniṣads, we find two opposed currents of thought running parallel, sometimes one becoming dominant, sometimes the other, the one enjoining animal sacrifice

---

[63] See Mair 1988.
[64] Edited by Mustafa Badawi.
[65] See also V. Rhagavan, *Some old Lost Rāna Plays* (Annamalainagar, 1961).
[66] Thapar 1966:64.

in the *Yajñas*, and the other condemning it.[67] The condemnation of such rituals led to a rejection of sacrifice, at least among the dominant Brahmins. Nowhere is the resistance to ritual more clearly expressed than in the Edicts of the Emperor Aśoka of the third century BCE. The version from Girnar, Gujarat, reads:

> 1  No living being may be slaughtered for sacrifice, no festival gatherings may be held.

While that statement might be read as expressing attachment to a new religion (Buddhism) the fourth edict shows a wider resistance to rituals in general:

> 4  Pryardarsi provides Dharma by proclaiming it by beat of drum, which has achieved more in this way than has been accomplished in many hundred years by providing spectacles of celestial cars, elephants, hell fire and so forth to the people.

Moreover, those rituals carried out at weddings and other stages in the life cycle are considered 'trivial'. Attention should rather be paid to gifts to Brahmins and to holy men as well as to the pilgrimage; in other words, even familistic rituals are out, for there is 'no kinship like the kinship of dharma'.[68]

In China, too, we find an important theatrical tradition centring upon highly formalized opera. As spectacle, however, this carried certain dangers for the participants and was largely rejected by later revolutionary regimes. The court, in the shape of a Tang empress, is specifically credited with founding the first drama school, the 'Pear Garden' in 720 CE. Singing and dancing were combined with story telling; masks were adapted to the new art form. In the Yuan dynasty (1279–1368) the plays were used to popularize Daoism. Nevertheless, a clear distinction was maintained between rite and

---

[67] Sangave 1959:378. The author continues the sentence '. . . and the latter thought was always held and propagated for the first time by the Jainas'. The reference is to A. Chakravarti, 'Jainism', *Culture of Hindu India*, i, 185–8. On Indian materialism and atheism see Thrower 1980 and Chattopadhyaya 1959.

[68] This version and its translation appear outside the National Museum of India, Delhi.

theatrical performance. Chinese drama is secular as far back as we can trace it – 'to the masques and buffooneries with which Han emperors were entertained two thousand years ago'.[69] These plays were the predecessors of the formal operas and while religion and rite were one source of subsequent developments, they were by no means the only one. Some of these antecedents were secular, involving dance, song, music and costumes.[70] One such predecessor was the Great Warrior Dance, described by Sima Qian (145–86 BCE), that enacted King Mu's overthrow of the Shang Dynasty to found the Zhou. Also there were jesters and acrobats at both court and popular levels, and, in addition, the mimicry of the hunt.

Thirty plays were published during the Yuan period when 'theatres were often large, fairly permanent and fairly substantial structures'. This secular drama was performed by professional family troupes. In the early days women acted not only female but also male parts; there seemed to be 'little general distinction made between the career of an actress and that of a harlot', so that once again players in the theatre were involved in cross-dressing and were seen as immoral creatures.[71] Their performances took place at court or in the entertainment district of the town.[72] In a play of Du Renjie a farmer comes to town and is enticed into the theatre, which he has never seen before, and made to pay an entrance fee of 300 cash. There he discovers an orchestra of girls facing the stage:

> Not calling the spirits down like they do in our country gambols,
> But ceaselessly banging of drums and clashing of cymbals.[73]

[69] Hawkes 1989 (1964):74. The notion of a sacred/secular divide may not be all that useful in China, at least in late-Imperial times. Plays would often be held in temples, often with religious themes, but the temple is not always regarded as sacred space in a religious sense.
[70] Zeami (1363–1443), who was the 'father' of Japanese Nō drama, traced its origins to dances associated with the gods.
[71] Dolby 1983:52.
[72] There is also evidence of amateur dramatics (Hawkes 1989:163).
[73] Hawkes 1989:150

This implicit contrast between rite and theatre (country and town) also emerges in the account of national mourning in the famous novel, *The Dream of the Red Chamber*, where 'for a whole year an interdict is placed on all kinds of musical and theatrical entertainments';[74] there was a kind of aesthetic fast. So the 'play' was quite a different activity from ritual, although it might be embodied in festivals. Since the Yuan, drama had taken the form of opera which ran into many local varieties. For example, Cantonese opera was one of fourteen theatrical genres performed in the province of Guangdong, excluding the puppet ones; about 365 regional types of opera have been noted in China.[75]

Literature too developed a secular genre of its own. A 'half-educated' urban reading public for cheap popular fiction developed centuries earlier than in the west. Objections arose, however, to fiction and to drama as fare for the young. For junior members of a noble household in eighteenth-century China 'fiction or drama of any kind was forbidden reading'.[76] Hence the precautions taken by the adolescent hero of *The Dream of the Red Chamber*, Baoyu, to prevent anyone seeing him read the play *Xixiangji* which had been written at the end of the thirteenth century on the basis of much earlier prototypes.

As a public spectacle, opera had its own more explicit dangers of a different kind. In the Cantonese variety, sacrificial offerings to the White Tiger were performed partly to keep the audience out of trouble but also 'for protecting the actors from harming the local people when they "opened their mouths" during the performance'.[77] This was an act of exorcism that was connected, as are Chinese operas in general, with the practice of Daoism. After the 1911 revolution against the Qing dynasty (1644–1911), 'talking plays' of a Western kind made their appearance. Due to the literary and political impact of the May Fourth Movement of 1919 the supplanting of literary Chinese as a medium of written communi-

---

[74] Hawkes 1989:161.
[75] Chan 1991:1.
[76] Hawkes 1989:17.
[77] Chan 1991:76.

cation meant that the living language of speech gained cultural legitimacy even among the elite. 'Literary Chinese is as remote from the colloquial language as Anglo-Saxon from English': while it was used, literacy was unattainable by the great mass of the people, who had neither the time nor the means to obtain a classical education. That is the problem with all classical or literary languages, as Wordsworth recognized in the introduction to *Lyrical Ballads* (1798). Its disappearance made literacy easier of attainment, but it also left the door to the storehouse of Chinese literature firmly locked, and 'cut the reader adrift from a literary tradition which had lasted through two millennia'.[78] The time was ripe for new literary and artistic forms.

The later Cultural Revolution had a more radical effect, even on other less formal genres. A type of picture recitation (*banzuan*), one of a variety originating in India and extending to the Near East, was highly popular in western Kansu province until the Cultural Revolution of the late 1960s and early '70s 'when its practitioners were ruthlessly persecuted and their texts confiscated and destroyed'.[79] That rejection was partly a consequence of the religious, or 'feudal', aspects of their content; but, during the Cultural Revolution, it was also art itself that attracted adverse attention. The Red Guards damaged paintings and broke porcelain in people's homes, seeing in them only luxury and feudalism. To those reformers traditional genres seemed stilted, artificial and were identified with a dying society, with the *ancien régime*. In her widely-read family history, *Wild Swans*, Jung Chang writes that after June 1966 when schooling stopped, 'There were virtually no books, no music, no films, no theater, no museums, no teahouses, almost no way of keeping oneself occupied – except cards, which, though not officially sanctioned, made a stealthy comeback.'[80] Elsewhere she writes:

> 'Relaxation' had become an obsolete concept: books, paintings, musical instruments, sports, cards, chess, teahouses, bars – all had

[78] Hawkes 1991:237.
[79] Mair 1988:9.
[80] Jung Chang 1991:482.

disappeared. The parks were desolate, vandalized wastelands in which the flowers and the grass had been uprooted and the tame birds and the goldfish killed. Films, plays, and concerts had all been banned: Mme Mao had cleared the stages and the screens for the eight 'revolutionary operas' which she had had a hand in producing, and which were all anyone was allowed to put on. In the provinces, people did not dare to perform even these. One director had been condemned because the make-up he had put on the tortured hero of one of the operas was considered by Mme Mao to be excessive. He was thrown into prison for 'exaggerating the hardship in the revolutionary struggle'.[81]

As in the French Revolution, a clean sweep was made of all earlier elite forms, but even revolutionary art had its dangers.

China was part of a much wider area in east and south Asia that developed dramatic forms distinct from rites, even though they sometimes used mythical themes and were offered to the gods. The area extended through the Indianized states of south-east Asia where versions of the Indian *Mahābārata* and *Rāmāyana* epics are presented by shadow puppets. In Indonesia, the *wayang kulit* was only one form, the best known, of *wayang* performances;[82] the others included the *ktlitik* or puppet plays, the *wong* or dance dramas and the *topeng*, dance dramas using masks. While these performances often took place at temple festivals, and were based on Indian epics, they also included many contemporary references, political, social and personal. Parallels to this hierarchy – in the range of theatrical performances found in other parts of the world such as India, China and Europe – are striking. In addition, there were the *ludruk* performances analysed by the anthropologist, Peacock, 'a secular, proletarian drama' involving fantasy and mockery, played by a male cast of characters that we find again in West African 'concert parties'. But while these performances may have started only in the early nineteenth century, the older varieties were surrounded with offerings to spirits (as in puppet plays)

---

[81] Jung Chang 1991:441.

[82] Anderson (1965) for the political uses of these performances, discussed for *ludruk* by Peacock (1987).

designed to protect the participants.[83] Peacock speaks of these dramas as 'rites of modernisation' since they orient the inhabitants of Indonesia in that direction, but the usage seems to erode the distinction made by the actors between *ludruk* (anyhow as commercial drama) and the traditional religious offering of *slametan*, which he sees as playing complementary roles.[84] Although for the anthropologist, Geertz, the Balinese *negara* were theatre states, statecraft was more than the thespian art.[85] 'The dramas of the theatre state, mimetic of themselves, were ... neither illusions nor lies ... They were what there was.'

Despite this distinction of the actors there is a current tendency to follow the producer, Schechner, and the anthropologist, Turner, in overriding any distinction between theatre and ritual under the blanket term 'performance'. Turner divided performance into social (social drama) and cultural (aesthetic drama) variations.[86] His collaborator, Schechner, regarded the field of performance studies as embracing 'performance behaviour of all kinds and in all contexts, from everyday life to high ceremony', consisting of actions 'rehearsed, prepared, and presented'. Performance theory (or often theories) consists in looking at human behaviour – individual and social – as a genre of performance. And vice versa. While this notion adds some topics to investigate and some propositions to follow up, it hardly constitutes 'theory' in any usual sense. Schechner quotes approvingly Turner's comment:

> Cultures are most fully expressed in and made conscious of themselves in their ritual and theatrical performances. A performance is a dialectic of 'flow', that is, spontaneous movement in which action and awareness are one; and 'reflexivity', in which the central meanings, values and goals of a culture are seen 'in action', as they shape and explain behavior.[87]

[83] Peacock 1987:36.
[84] Peacock 1987:218; Geertz 1976:11.
[85] Geertz 1980:120,136.
[86] Turner 1979:72.
[87] Schechner and Appel 1990:1.

There are two problems in Turner's statement. Firstly, there is the reification of culture which is seen as having 'central meanings, values and goals'. But does it? Can we define even in imprecise terms these features for any 'culture' we know? How long do they persist? The approach inevitably stresses the homogeneity of human life, whereas an alternative, more realistic view would emphasize the conflicts and contradictions that inhere in it. Turner allows for conflict but only in the redressive phase of the social drama. That consideration leads to a second point. If theatre constitutes the fullest expression of a culture, what leads to its rejection? Ritual is rarely rejected in the same general way partly because its definition is often so broad, like performance, that it is virtually all-inclusive of repeated speech and actions. Turner sees theatre as being the industrial equivalent of ritual in non-industrial societies, a dominant form of cultural–aesthetic 'mirror' in which it achieves a certain degree of self-reflexivity.[88]

But despite the distinction between drama and rites in China, for example, objections were sometimes raised to both, not only to dramatic performance but even to elaborate rites themselves. Chinese culture was far from unitary in this respect, even about some basic issues. In written discussions of morality, similar kinds of disagreement arose as in Christianity. The conservatism of the sayings of Confucius is well known; he was committed to the rites (*li*), especially those directed to piety towards parents and respect for the ruler, all in the interest of harmony. At the same time benevolence (*ren*) was the basis for a wider morality: 'What you do not like yourself do not do unto others.'[89] In other words: universalism of a sort was found in harness with particularism. The second component was developed by the rivals of the Confucians, the Mohists, founded by Moze (*c.*480–*c.*390 BCE), who were accused of outraging filial piety by teaching sons to love other people's parents as much as their own. Whether or not they intended this, they expressed doubts about some rites. The Mohist

---

[88] Turner in Schechner and Appel 1990:8.
[89] *Analects* 3, XII. 22.

*Economy in Funerals* is sceptical about the value of 'fine funerals and prolonged mourning'. If these '"can really enrich the poor, increase population, replace peril and disorder by safety and order, then they are good and right, and a duty for loyal sons", but otherwise they were not. Since extravagance in mourning wastes goods, interferes with productive work, and damages the health of mourners, this test is sufficient to discredit it.'[90] Similar sentiments are found in the essay of the first-century writer, Wang Chong (also romanized as Wang Ch'ung), on 'Simplicity in Funerals' as well as in other sources.[91] Wang Chong criticizes the 'general craving for luxury' combined with the belief that the dead are like the living, which leads the latter 'to make dummies to serve the corpses in their coffins, and fill the latter with eatables, to gratify their spirits'. Very often mourners will ruin their families with the expense and even acquire slaves to kill to follow the deceased to the grave. 'They ignore that in reality it is of no use, but their extravagance is eagerly imitated by others', even though Confucius condemned these practices.[92] The critical comment of Wang Chong about dummies is clearly directed to the performances and the representations that accompanied and followed the burial of emperors, as in the tomb of Qin Shi Huangdi who was interred with the well-known army of clay soldiers (which replaced and represented living people formerly interred in their master's grave). Wang himself did not reject the arts but he wanted them to provide moral instruction:

> when later generations composed music they merely wrote some verses for certain tunes without any relation to social mores or customs at all. . . . If we want to return people's customs to simplicity and purity, we must take the theatrical music of today, eliminate all the depraved and licentious words and tunes, and keep only the stories about loyal ministers and filial sons, so that everyone among the simple folk can easily understand, and their innate knowledge can unconsciously be stimulated into operation.[93]

---

[90] Graham 1964:31–3.
[91] Wang Ch'ung 1911:II, 375; De Groot 1910:II,659.9.
[92] Wang Ch'ung 1911:369–70.
[93] Chan 1991:233.

That offered a recipe for noble if boring art, closer to instruction than entertainment.

The problems of representation also arise in a pronounced way in the literary traditions of Zen Buddhism and in neo-Confucianism of the Wang Yang-ming persuasion, neither of which placed much emphasis on that process, rather directing their efforts to the transmission of teaching by direct means. A well-known story tells of a group of Zen monks who chop up a statue of Buddha on a cold night to get fuel for their fire.[94] As with figurative representation in sculpture, there is an ecclesiastical, a theological, objection to religious action on stage. God does not appear in 'plays', while mimesis itself may be seen as an attempt to recreate the creation as well as the Creator, in other words, any living thing.

As Wang Chong implies there are other problems with mimesis, apart from mimicking the holy. Firstly, it is re-presentation; what it presents is not the original. It is something 'rehearsed', 'played' by 'actors'. In his work on 'The Anti-theatrical Prejudice', the literary critic Barish suspects a general explanation is necessary: 'The fact that the disapproval of the theater is capable of persisting through so many transformations of culture, so many dislocations of time and space, suggests a permanent kernel of distrust waiting to be activated by the more superficial irritants.'[95]

Stephen Greenblatt, often regarded as the progenitor of the new historicist school of literary criticism, has been criticized for the 'casual lumping of saints, shamans and Jesuits' together. He in turn has objected to Barish for thinking that 'the anti-theatrical prejudice . . . reflects a fear or distrust innate to or inherent in the human mind'. That is to say, Barish

> does not really entertain the possibility that a phenomenon in one period, which *seems* analogous to a phenomenon in another, may arise amid such different social conditions and play such a different

---

[94] I am indebted to Jan van Bremen for these references.
[95] Barish 1981:4. On page 79 he attributes anti-theatricality to 'the life-like immediacy of the theater, which puts it into unwelcome competition with the everyday realm and with doctrines espoused in schools and churches'.

role in a culture's power relations and discursive systems that the two phenomena cannot be seen as continuous with one another or as products of an underlying human nature.

Both objections seem to neglect the contexts of enquiry (not all are identical) and hence are unsustainable. In Barish's study of antitheatricality the actors themselves often recognize the kind of long-term continuities of reference that writing greatly facilitates. But even if specific continuities were not present, the observer is at perfect liberty to extract from the particular historical context trends that are perceived to be interesting, comparable, and possibly related to some general factors – general but not, of course, necessarily universal. We do not have to find the practice located 'in an underlying human nature', nor in any feature that is 'innate to or inherent in the human mind'. That is to take an overly psycho-genetic view of human thought. But we need to see certain trends as related to aspects of human situations that are not unique in a historicist sense but are widespread; for example, within certain modes of production or of communication, in this case the reference is to particular cognitive tensions. To make such a statement is to take a stance which for some phenomena offers a more satisfactory explanation than Greenblatt's particularism or than the universalism attributed to Barish. From my point of view both are excessive since Greenblatt denies an interest in anything but local knowledge (though this at once threatens his analytic endeavour since he is not himself part of the local scene), while universalism seems to go beyond the intermittent evidence; a feature such as transvestism is not so much inherent as recurrent. Barish does not attempt to explain the swings of the pendulum, let alone the disappearance or dimunition of objections in recent times. For that we need to turn to the growth of secularism and of consumer cultures.

Secondly, imitation of elders by children is, as Tarde argues, essential to the learning process, but when adults copy adults, it threatens their identity, their individuality, their status, their idiosyncracies. The actual mimicking of an individual parodies his actions; it is a kind of caricature, amusing when she or he is not there, but often deeply offensive when she or he is. Such mimicry may be allowed during periods of 'reversal' or 'liminality', Twelfth Night occasions, the Carnival, the village fête, but only within limits. Even the Shakespearean fool could overstep the mark, privileged though he was by his royal masters. It is easy to 'go too far' and this is partly a question of audience. *The Merchant of Venice* was successful with a Christian audience in a way that it would never have been with a Jewish one. Ben Jonson's *Bartholomew's Fair* was directed to the Laudians rather than to the Puritans, though the latter would have found not only this but all forms of mimesis objectionable. One element in earlier Jewish and Christian objections to the theatre had been that these groups were mocked by the dominant theatrical cultures. For the population at large, mimicry may be more acceptable in the secular theatre, where it is 'framed' by the dramatic space, the stage, the set, the proscenium arch, and set aside from life itself. Thirdly, there is the aspect of privileged performance, of luxury and of wasteful expenditure that we have seen expressed in the eighteenth century, as well as in the comments on elaborate rites, especially for the dead. Funerals are a particular target, since the dead may be seen by some as no longer able to enjoy the things of this world, especially in a mocked-up form.

How do these considerations, drawn from religious and secular performances in Eurasia, bear upon the situation in Black Africa and in similar societies? That is, upon the relative absence of theatre in oral cultures (though not, of course, of rite) and upon the distinction between the two. Clearly developmental factors restricting the creation of wealth, of techniques and of social differentiation meant the absence of highly elaborated court and urban cultures that could produce theatre in the sense of distinct physical structures, specialist performances, performers and written plays. Moreover, in the virtual absence of writing in local languages, the objections we have found in Eurasia could not be made explicit in the same way, much less embodied in an 'antitheatrical tradition'. But can we detect evidence of resistance to dramatic representation?

In Africa, performance in the wider sense of rites and ceremonies abounds, but secular theatre is rare and the two need to be firmly distinguished. This conclusion is not mine alone. In his book, *L'Invention du théâtre*, which discusses West Africa in depth, Alain Ricard draws a clear distinction between rite and theatre, which '*n'est pas de l'ordre du donné anthropologique, en Afrique ou ailleurs: elle est le produit d'une élaboration poetique*'.[96] While I would not make the distinction in precisely these terms, his meaning is sufficiently clear. He even plays down the role of the rituals of Dionysus in the origin of the Greek theatre. '*Le théâtre pour Aristote commence avec le texte.* . . . *Ces textes mettent en scène la représentation d'une action; ils en font un spectacle* (opsis): *c'est là le trait fondamental du théâtre*', that is, mimesis. For the theatre, he argues, we need not simply participants ('actors' in the sociological sense), but '*comédiens*' (professional players), who follow a text (a play).

Concert parties, trance performances such as Jean Rouch's *Les Maîtres fous*, puppets, are mostly either recent imports or else small beer.[97] To many observers, drama in oral cultures exists only in the form of religious ceremonies ('ritual drama') and the formal recitation of prose narrative ('secular drama'), or even the social dramas (narrated incidents) of V. Turner. 'Theatre in one sense', writes Messenger, 'appears to be more rare in the non-literate world.'[98] However, even narrowly defined, it does exist, although very unevenly distributed, being found in a few groups but not at all in most. In West Africa it appears in south-eastern Nigeria among the Ibibio as well as in Mali among the Bamana (or Bambara, Mandingo). In both areas it is associated with the use not only of masks but of puppets; and in both areas it is undertaken by male members of special associations. There were also masked

---

[96] Ricard 1986:24.
[97] In *Life in Southern Nigeria* (1923), P. A. Talbot describes puppet plays among the Ibibio with plots of an apparently similar kind which are rehearsed for seven seasons and shown publically. See also Labouret and Travélé (1928) for reference to Hausa puppets, and Arnoldi 1988. For further references see her work on Mali. *Les Maîtres fous* is the title of a film by Jean Rouch about Songhai migrants to Ghana who meet on Sundays to dress up for a performance that is somewhere between trance, rite and a play or skit.
[98] Messenger 1971; Herskovits 1944.

performances specifically for entertainment among the Lorhon and Baule of the Ivory Coast.[99] In most other parts there is nothing at all of this kind.[100] An interesting reference in the early administrative documents on the LoDagaa area refers to a complaint of the French authorities about a disruptive visit by a group from the Northern Territories of the Gold Coast (Ghana). The District Commissioner at Lawra noted that this appeared to be a wandering dance troupe. I have never encountered such a troupe in that area, although at the end of the farming season, dancers do go from one market to another to perform kɔbine, the farming dance.[101] That seems the most likely possibility, for this is an area where there are no theatrical organizations of the Ibibio–Bamana kind.

The Ibibio make a clear distinction between two kinds of performance enacted by what have been called 'secular' associations (ɔf:ɔŋ) and 'sacred' ones (ɛkɔŋ).[102] These cater for different audiences; the first appear at social events such as 'fattenings', weddings, burials, funerals, while the second perform in village squares before the whole populace. In the latter case the plays are performed only every seven years when the actors travel around neighbouring villages. Each lasts between fifteen and forty-five minutes and are rehearsed over the six-year period between

---

[99] T. Phillips 1995:455; Vogel 1977.

[100] Chief Gandah, founder of the chiefly dynasty at Birifu (LoDagaa), did have a male and female puppet on a string which he made copulate with one another by manipulating his big toes; these were referred to as little beings of the wild (*kontomble*). Puppets were not local; his son thinks that he either acquired them in Tamale, the main town in northern Ghana, or else from Muslims from Mali who occasionally visited the area. The nearest local equivalent are the *batibe* (the wooden shrines, carved figures) also connected with the beings of the wild, which were associated with performances during funerals, especially in Lawra and Nandom; in Birifu these were carried out by the Selayiili clan. Such performances might take the form of putting a knife through the nose, or carrying pots by holding the rim under the lower lip.

[101] See Goody 1956.

[102] On this widespread distinction in performance which is basic to rites and theatre, see Peacock 1990. Gluckman (1974) discusses the distinction between 'ritual' and 'secular' masks in Southern Africa; the latter are sometimes used for entertainment.

appearances. As distinct from rituals in my experience, such performances are rehearsed, though secretly in the case of satirical items. The whole performance includes not only plays but music, dance and sometimes acrobatics and sleight of hand. Beforehand the players have to refrain from sexual intercourse and observe some other taboos, as is the case with other dangerous activities such as hunting.[103]

At the performance witnessed by the Messengers in the 1950s, about a thousand spectators were present. The plays were presented first, with the various skits being separated by a dance, by music or by stilt-dancers. Late in the afternoon a puppet play was staged and at dusk the whole performance ended. Like the troupe, the leaders of the dancers wore raffia skirts and headbands stuck with feathers, but they also had birds' wings over the ears and carried mirrors and rattles in their hands, as well as whistles in their mouths. Some solo dancers wore masks and would engage in satire and ridicule, alternately mimicking, singing, dancing and running. Individuals were singled out for attack, which was also the case with the performances reported by the British administrator Jeffreys in the 1930s when he saw 'a number of disconnected satires on current subjects' performed by 'seven male dancers and a number of men dressed as "women"'.

The satire of the 'sacred' associations can be either specific or general. Particular individuals and groups are named, such as Hausa traders, indigenous courts, colonial administrators, and missionaries. 'The general types of behaviour ridiculed were: domineering wives, promiscuity, corruption, theft, stupidity, lack of skill, mistreatment of kin, breaking the subtribal food taboo, imitating Europeans, drunkenness, sterility, sexual jealousy, suicide, and failure to conform to the mores of institutionalised friendship. Physical ugliness, mental illness and poverty were conditions singled out for attack.' Hence the role of this drama is 'to amuse audiences by ridiculing the motives and actions of well-known individuals'.[104]

---

[103] On concert parties in West Africa, see Collins 1985.
[104] Messenger 1962:29.

In Mali, a rather similar performance, the *koteba*, occurs in the countryside, though it has also migrated to the town.[105] As Labouret and his local collaborator described these performances, they had nothing to do with 'banal exhibitions of puppets, of sleight-of-hand, of magicians, of animal charmers, such as are found in certain parts of Africa, but are real plays well organised, aimed at portraying a specific incident and employing human actors'.[106] The plays were comic, with no tragic element or moral aim, intended solely for entertainment by showing on the stage characters, faults and vices which have been carefully observed in daily life and presented, they claimed, with much truthfulness.

According to a more recent account of the Bamana, these plays are performed by the young men's *ton* or 'age-grade association' which organizes all the activities of the initiated between roughly ten and thirty years of age. The association acts as a work group (when it is known as *ngonson ton*) and as an entertainment society (when it is known as *koteba ton*). In the second case it arranges entertainments together with the associations of neighbouring villages, especially in the form of song, dance and theatrical competitions held during the dry season when there is no farm work to be done. During this period it performs at marriages, for official delegations, at the death of a village elder, but most commonly 'to make the village glad'. The performances begin after dark with boys and girls dancing in separate circles for about two hours. The boys follow this with acrobatic dancing, then before midnight the plays begin. When the actors have finished their preparation four or five boys run on to the public place and do a short dance known as *kaka* which is said to convince the spirits of 'the playful, non-serious intent of the plays that will follow'.[107] There is danger in dramatic representation, even in skits on people and mores, especially when these may be taken too seriously. The evening's performance consists of eight to thirty short sketches performed at a rapid pace but having no thematic continuity.

---

[105] Meillassoux 1964.
[106] Labouret and Travélé 1928:74.
[107] Brink 1977:62.

'Paraded in rapid succession onto the moonlit village square for a night's *kote-tlon* performance are such characters as the debtor, the wicked millet farmer, the unfaithful wife, the man who marries his mother-in-law, the man with a long penis, the lazy son, the sorceress who eats children, the wife who beats her husband, and the woman who loses her vagina in the river.' Humour is said to be one aim, though another is 'to educate and moralize about culturally desired beliefs and behavior'.[108]

In Africa then drama also has its dangers as well as its delights, especially for the participants. At the sacrifice initiating a youth's entry into the Ibibio association, a prayer is offered: 'Let us perform freely and have no trouble. Do not permit our enemies to poison to us. Let us come and go freely.'[109] There is also a universal danger in playing a public role of this kind, a danger of sorcery.

Similar dangers exist for Bamana players and for the audience. 'Sacred articles' are buried to encourage peace among the participants (including the spirits), for malevolent forces threaten disruption. Beings of the wild are especially dangerous since they are jealous on account of their own parallel performances. As a result they may try to kill a well-known player and his group. Members of the village may also use secret powers against players they believe are criticizing them personally.[110] These actions 'discourage theater performance' and force the troupe to make annual sacrifices to the 'sacred articles' and to wear amulets to ward off evil powers. Here is a clear case where both the public appearance of the players in itself as well as their critique of members of the public are likely to bring trouble which has to be warded off.

In other parts of the Bamana region around the Malian town of Segu, a similar type of theatrical performance is carried out with puppets under the auspices of the village youth associations, the *kamalen ton*. These groups, consisting of young men and unmarried women, engage in public works and communal agriculture

---
[108] Brink 1977:62.
[109] Messenger 1971:210.
[110] Brink 1977:63.

or fishing. In the village of Kiranko performances take place twice a year, in late May before the rainy season or in October at harvest time. Puppets and masks are used and both, whether they take an animal or human form, are known as *sogo* or 'animal'. Arnoldi writes of these performances in terms of entertainment and distinguishes between a play (*tlon*) and a ritual (or power) genre; the two forms are clearly separated by the actors, that is, plays are distinguished from masquerades.[111] Puppetry is performed on the public square and all can attend; ritual performances are carried out by 'secret' societies.

Neither the LoDagaa nor the Gonja of northern Ghana, among whom I worked, had theatre of this kind. On the other hand, they had 'play'. On moonlit nights, especially when farming was done, the LoDagaa would sometimes bring out the xylophones and dance. In addition there were other dances on ceremonial occasions such as funerals and performances like the Bagre. This 'ritual' activity was much less common in the Muslim-influenced Gonja state, but secular dances, some of which were constantly being adapted from ones brought up from the south, were a pervasive feature of small-town life. A group of women dancers might buy identical cloth to wear on these occasions. Some amongst them would be rewarded by admirers by having a coin or note pressed on their foreheads as they danced. Performance, however, especially in a largely secular context, also has its dangers. My LoDagaa friend, Kpaari Gandaa, who much enjoyed dancing 'the farming dance' (*kɔbine*) in the market-place at Birifu when the guinea corn was about to be cut, always wore a special amulet at this time because of the jealousy he thought his dancing might arouse, though this was also a way of attracting the attention of women.[112] A similar theme emerged in farming itself. One did not speak or ask about the state of a person's crops lest envy raise its head – and with envy came witchcraft. On the one hand, being a successful farmer was good, on the other it was dangerous. The

---

[111] Arnoldi 1988; 1986:131; 1995; Brink 1980.
[112] Xylophone players would also wear amulets but not during the Bagre performances where the association's deity would protect members from harm.

fear of standing out in a prominent role, however, was especially strong in competitive and other activities in which an element of choice entered into the picture; that was not the case when rites *had* to be performed, sacrifices made, prayer said, whereas in many dances participation was optional; one did not *have* to show off and expose oneself, though this might attract the attention of the opposite sex as well as jealousy and witchcraft.

There was little dramatic element in these dances, but there was more, and even some mimesis, at LoDagaa funerals which, as elsewhere in Africa, were the most elaborate of the rites of passage. We have seen that the elaboration of such ceremonies has elsewhere come under local criticism because of their luxury and waste, and because they are directed towards those who are no longer in a position to enjoy such offerings; continuing to treat the dead as if they were living contains within itself a possible rejection based on a rejection of such waste. In other cases, these ceremonies may be criticized because they offer to the dead what should be given to God, as was the case with the early Christians who cut down radically on Roman funeral practices. Gifts to accompany the dead were sacrilegious, even though a token penny dropped in the grave lived on in parts of Europe. The massive offerings which had previously accompanied some northern chieftains and southern kings were again open to doubts about the 'waste' involved. The Christian policy was to channel those resources to succouring the needy (as well as to contributing to the Church and its personnel) rather than burying valuable goods in the ground where they would not be used. There were also theological objections. Salvation lay solely in God's hands; one worshipped him, not the dead, and then only by prayer, as was also the case in other Near Eastern religions.

Among various rites of passage, funerals are most likely to attract criticism, though comments on the expenditure at marriages have also been a frequent feature of societies in Asia and Europe, well aired by the Christian Church.[113] In China, Wang Chong comments that the people of *Ch'i* erected 'enormous sepulchres, filled with heaps of valuables', as a consequence of which the

---

[113] J. Goody 1990:459.

state was ruined. That was a telling criticism of the royal burial chambers with their underground armies. In addition to extravagance, such offerings were based on a false premise, that the living could help the dead and vice versa. In the Bagre myth of the LoDagaa (see chapter 5) and in their funeral rituals, one also finds a measure of critical comment on the expenditures required, which raises the possible question of waste, especially for the kin of others.[114]

These funerals were certainly a performance, a major performance, with the burial alone lasting three full days and attended by many of those living within earshot of the xylophone the lugubrious chords of which announced that a death had taken place. Not to attend a local funeral would be to open up the suspicion that one had a part in the death itself. Neighbours and many others from more distant villages sat around partly as spectators, watching, as well as drinking beer and eating snacks, but participating when their turn came. All this took place near the house where the dead person had lived and was now propped up in a sitting position on the special funeral stand, arrayed in the best cloth his or her kin could produce. In a sense, the dead body constituted the main spectator. Many of the acts in the performance were directed at it from the open space in front of the stand around which the participants were gathered. It would be too one-dimensional to describe this as sacred space; it is performance space, action space, in a more general sense.

Heightening the comparison with drama, there is even a mimetic phase. In this, individuals repeat the acts, in re-presentation, which they had carried out in the company of the deceased. If they had often hunted or farmed with him, they would go through the motions of these activities to 'take out the dream'. This act of remembering represents a Freudian working through of the relationship. On one occasion a procession of young men wearily carried heavy boxes one behind the other, as if they were returning

---

[114] On the consciousness of the economic expenditure on Asante funerals, including the proposed restrictions of the Kumasi State Council, see Arhin 1994.

home with their goods after several months of migrant labour down the Asante goldmines. Such rites were not simply repetitive but generative in that new activities were included, although the participants certainly thought they were doing what their forefathers would have done in their place.

The distinction between the body of the funeral rites and these mimetic performances are clear to the LoDagaa who may describe one as work (*tomo*) and the other as play (*dieno*), the word they use for joking in funerals and elsewhere. These mimetic acts raise smiles as well as sympathies. That would also be the case, for example, with acts that imitate the gestures of a hunter. The LoDagaa would regard such performances as very different from rites such as sacrifice or divination. And there are limits to what they find acceptable. They would, I think, reject dances that mimic the movements of animals, ancestors or beings of the wild, certainly if these involved physical disguise. While the LoDagaa are aware that their neighbours use masks, and while they sometimes acquire them expressly to present to those visitors who expect such things, they would not be comfortable using such artefacts. Their use would arouse an element of disbelief, even approaching ridicule, which may be one reason for their absence. In other words their reactions would imply the rejection of mimesis in those cases as well as the limited acceptance of it in others. Some elements of this mode are certainly present in their ceremonies as well as in the activities of the occasional visiting entertainer. Moreover, their rituals do at times entertain them, though 'engage' would be a better word. On these occasions the dancing, the drinking of beer and the talking certainly fell into this category. But entertainment is not the aim of the ritual as it is with Ibibio or Bamana plays. The intentionality is not at all the same. While similarities may be recognized, deliberate mimetic activity is thought of differently from the main body of rites.

That seems to me to be a widespread tendency. And it is one reason that renders theatricality more open to objection, for it raises a moral issue. People may see mimesis as just that – as a copying, an imitation, a re-enactment, a re-presentation, even as an untruth. A potential for the questioning of mimesis results from the cognitive contradiction inherent in representation: it is essential for certain purposes (even for language) but is not the real thing. It is clear that different societies (at different times) are more or less tolerant of the conceptual shift involved in humans taking on animal roles or in men taking on women's ones, tolerant of the ambivalence that such shifts involve. Those possibilities may emerge as ambivalence on an individual level while on the societal one it may lead to different societies or groups making different evaluations over time as well as over space, raising problems that touch upon assumptions of deep-rooted cultural continuity itself. This alternation of views is potentially present in the human situation itself, in the way of understanding the world. Ambivalence is not always present in everybody's consciousness. Normally re-presentation is found to be acceptable, but its existence is potentially capable of calling forth what I call cognitive tensions or contradictions.

As I think of it here, ritual embodies a different kind of action which is not performance in the same sense as these other re-presentations. It is not 'acting' but participating, though it may involve some mimetic elements. As such it does not give rise to the same implicit objections in oral cultures as re-presentation nor yet to those openly expressed by Puritans, moralists and revolutionaries in literate ones. On the other hand there are some parallels across the board in the criticisms of wastefulness, of extravagance, of the neglect of alternative needs. The LoDagaa, especially those less closely bereaved, may mutter about expenditure on funerals, just as some complain about the amounts needed for the Bagre. Even 'essential' rituals may come under critical scrutiny on account of their costs. One version of the Bagre myth from Lawra explains how the forefathers of the clan had abandoned the whole performance, perhaps because of cost, perhaps because of its ineffectiveness. Indeed, both factors are included in an assessment of costs and benefits which may occur at any time such a performance takes place. For these performances are not pre-programmed calendrically; they do not have to take place at any specific time and may be postponed. Cost-cutting sentiments of husbanding resources are more explicit at funerals. One of the first professional African social scientists, Kofi Busia of Ghana, wrote about the waste involved in funeral ceremonies in Asante. Such sentiments were not only part of his Methodist upbringing (in a chiefly family) but emerged from this wider feeling, not necessarily against rituals as such, but against extravagant or elaborate ones. He was making them explicit, as was Wang Chong in China.

Referring back to the beginning of this discussion, there are two general points I want to make in connection with the largely oral cultures of Africa. Firstly, to merge rites and drama into a single category of 'performance' may lead to the exclusion of intentionality and to the omission of the people's own perspective which embraces distinction as well as similarity. Those distinctions may have significant consequences because other forms of dramatic activity may be given less weight (for example, the performances of concert parties and jugglers), and that, in itself, may contribute to the minimal development of a secular theatre in Africa, although there are obviously socio-economic reasons of a broad kind for its absence which also need to be taken into consideration.

Sociologists and anthropologists are partly responsible for this conflation of religious rite and secular drama, for they often talk about people in society filling roles as actors, for example, the role of father. Analytically, it is possible to take that stance. But there is an obvious difference between a Western actor taking on a role in a play by Dario Fo and a man becoming a father. In the first case he is taking on a role, a persona, in a temporary fashion to perform a play. From the standpoint of the participant, performing a funeral is a very different process. One is not mimicking, re-presenting; one is being rather than 'acting as', being someone else; or on a personal level one may be 'acting out', 'working through', 'enacting'.

Play is often specifically mimetic, but even within ritual, mimesis itself may be considered less serious, as play rather than work, a hierarchy that some such as Rousseau and Froebel have tried to overturn. The second point has to do with 'work' and 'play', between which a distinction is drawn in many African languages, contrary to the notions of some European scholars about 'earlier' societies. What is work and what is play differ from society to society, but the broad distinction remains; and play includes the less serious element. In some places it consists of drumming and dancing for fun, as when the Gonja bring out drums on a moonlit night and dance Simpa.[115] In a few places in West Africa we find dramatic performances of a theatrical (concert party) kind, clearly a form of folk theatre where speech, narrative and impersonation are developed in a much more elaborate way than in song and dance themselves. One reason why such performances are not more widespread (not as widespread as religious rituals) is partly because they are 'play' and hence dispensable, and partly because they are representing other human beings in a mimetic way and that may be seen as dangerous. For this, drama, as distinct from dance, comments continually on people in the neighbourhood, and it does so by mimicry. While such criticism gives pleasure to the many, it seriously discomforts the few. When the few are of another tribe, like Christians and Jews, that is one thing. However, the many may suffer from some of the same faults as those attacked so could be conscious of being the next victims. Satire, like gossip and witchcraft, can rebound upon the instigator.

The issue I am raising here is this. In Europe, and possibly in Asia, cognitive queries about representation were one reason why the theatre fluctuated in a temporal sense. The queries recur on different grounds and under different regimes. On the secular level, they turn around extravagance and privilege, around mockery, mimicry and mimesis. On the religious level, they turn around representation of the immaterial by the material, and more broadly representing any object created by the unique Creator God. That was the case with Christianity, Judaism and Islam.

These various factors had an effect on the temporal distribution of theatre in Europe and Asia. Apart from the early Sanskritic drama in India and the opera in China, theatre is not all that common as a developed art form even in Asia until we get to the *kabuki* of the late sixteenth-century merchant subcultures of Japan

---

[115] For Simpa among the neighbouring Dagomba, see Collins 1985.

and to the more heavily ritualized Nō plays. In the highly stylized Nō plays, the performers are essentially story tellers using their movements and appearance to suggest the kernel of the tale. They developed from festival drama at shrines and temples in the twelfth or thirteenth centuries and emerged as a distinctive form in the fourteenth century when they were performed at noble houses, largely for the warrior class. Tied to the 'feudal' order, the existence of Nō theatre was threatened by the Meiji Restoration (1868).

The other major theatrical form was Kabuki, dating from the late sixteenth century, when a former priestess assembled around her a troupe of men who danced as women and women who danced as men in her parodies of Buddhist prayers. This theatre was essentially for townspeople and farmers as distinct from Nō and Bukagu (a dance ceremony at the court). It is interesting that we find cross-dressing in so many instances of early theatre, as if to insist upon the fact that the illusion was false and should not be taken as reality. Cross-dressing became a cause of complaint against the stage but its widespread appearance seems to suggest that the theatre was itself offering a comment on the nature of the illusion of play.[116]

Kabuki gave birth to opposition as well as to support. In 1629 it was banned by the government because of its frivolous, bold and sensuous character. At that time young boys dressed as women performed the programmes, but this too was suppressed in 1652. As a result older men took over the roles and it has continued as an all-male performance to this day.

Public performances of this kind have their problems; either they dramatize religious themes in a largely secular context (as with the European mystery plays) or they may be seen as threatening the political and social order by re-presenting, mimicking, the behaviour of kings, chiefs and other power-holders (which was expressly forbidden in China).[117] The preferred alternative may be to stick to the religious context or to court performances that ally

---

[116] On examples of cross-dressing in Southern Africa, see Gluckman 1974.
[117] Scott 1983:137.

themselves with Church and State. The presence of Islam in Africa certainly played a part in the relative paucity of theatre, but can its uneven spatial distribution be attributed more widely to problems involved in mimetic performance of the same general kind as we found in Eurasia, raising queries about the nature of reality as well as about God's creation?

The problem of the separation between art and life, or acting and the actor, is dealt with interestingly by Schechner, who points out that the Yaqui (of Arizona) deer dancer is at once 'not himself' and 'not not himself', that he does not house his own identity.[118] That is true in Nō drama where the small mask never hides the actor's face; no attempt is made at complete illusion. Though this is an aim of the acting school of Stanislavsky, it is never actually realized. The Chinese film, *Farewell, My Concubine* (1985) is a fascinating account of the brutal progression through the harsh training of a boy, whose lone mother is unable to keep him herself, to be an opera performer; the central conflict is between the boy who 'becomes' the concubine, letting the illusion of the theatre take him over, and his friend who always insists upon the separation between opera and life.

There is some evidence of objections to elaborate ritual, especially at funerals. But there is no question of the absence of ritual, especially given the very general way in which it is defined.[119] In any case, rites have a different status from the secular performances we find unevenly distributed in Africa, which are intrinsically more dispensable, less entailed in daily life. The latter are also more subject to worries about mimesis, more prone to the potential ambivalence which arises from the cognitive tensions implicit in re-presentation. Is this part of the reason such performances are found in a few groups in Africa and not in others? And why, when they are present, they carry dangers as well as delights? *Explicit* rejection of the theatrical is characteristic of literate societies, as is the radical separation between both the participant and his roles, and the performer and the author. But following the

---

[118] Schechner 1985:4ff.
[119] See J. Goody 1961.

discussion of iconoclasm in Africa, I suggest that implicit distinctions of a similar kind are to be found in at least some of the oral cultures of that continent. Implicitly, at least, there is a problem about mimesis.

In looking at the absence of some art forms in certain societies and at certain periods, I am concerned with the largely explicit reasons for that absence in societies with writing and the largely implicit ones in oral cultures. Both rejections seem to be based on problems involved in the process of re-presentation itself. Anti-theatricality is not simply a feature of a particular intellectual or theological tradition. Theologically, re-presentation may clash with the uniqueness of God's creation or with notions about the possibility of presenting deity in material form. The objections extend beyond the Christian heritage, beyond the traditions deriving from the Near Eastern religions, into the more secular domain of Greek and Roman philosophers as well as further afield in Asia. In some extreme cases they may take the form of objections to rituals themselves, although ritual here often turns out to mean what other people perform, that is, over-elaborate and ineffectual rituals. Even Puritans had rituals, though these were 'thin' rather than 'thick'. Revolutionaries in England, France, Russia and China did away with the old varieties of performance although they established some new ones, few of which endured over time. In all periods formal theatre was more likely to be attacked than other types of performance because of its content, its association with class, its enclosed space and because of the ambivalences involved in notions of re-presenting what is presented elsewhere.

Do anti-theatrical sentiments continue down to the present? Not in the same form. As Benjamin argued for the icon, mechanized reproduction of drama in film and television has performed a democratic function, opening up the genre to the world, penetrating into each city and home, thus modifying objections even in Islamic lands. Doubts about performance persist, nevertheless, and are expressed theatrically, for instance, by Pirandello, by Brecht in his concept of alienation and by Artaud in his instistence on the theatre of cruelty. Much experimental theatre has been driven by a dissatisfaction not simply with contemporary drama but with the nature of theatre itself.[120]

A wariness about re-presentation, that, by definition, is not 'the real thing', is one element in the world-wide history of culture. I am not concerned with philosophical disputation, nor with any attempt to get at 'the truth' or at 'reality'; at one level the play is clearly real. But in dealing with cognitive processes we are dealing with the actor's perception of reality and representation. That is sometimes ambivalent and in any case subject to cognitive contradictions.

---

[120] Artaud 1964; Schechner 1985.

# 5

# Myth: Thoughts on its Uneven Distribution

All use of language involves re-presenting objects, experience, thought, though because of its centrality to human life language also plays a major role in their creation and conceptualization. Fictional and religious narratives are particularly subject to the problems of representation that I have raised as they have a special relationship to truth. In the next two chapters I want to discuss two genres, one oral and one written, in the shape of myth and the novel. These have the particular interest for me that marked icons, relics and theatre, in that they are unevenly distributed in human societies in ways that seem to go against many current assumptions about narrative; indeed, I have reservations in applying this term to myth. I do not propose to attempt any exhaustive treatment but to sample the evidence with a view to tracing doubts and objections to such genres. Once again I make no attempt to cover all that has been called 'myth' or novel. In the latter case I can focus on Europe, in the former on Africa, indeed upon my own material on oral genres among the LoDagaa, which I present in some detail as it is largely unpublished. For this reason I expand on the subject of genres more than is perhaps directly necessary for a discussion of myth and its absence.

In Africa there is really very little mythology about the gods. The Bagre myth of the LoDagaa includes an account of how God created not the first man but his first child (he was one of two) and his wife. I have also been told that God first created a woman.[1] In the myth God is described in words as an old man smoking a pipe, but he would never be figured pictorially in this way. Even so, the myth scarcely constitutes a narrative. Contrary to the expectation of Halbertal and Margalit (1992), there is little narrative centring on any gods, deities or supernatural agencies. Myth is seen by them as being 'the outstanding type of pagan representation'. 'Pagan mythology is in turn an expression of the limits of the gods, of their being part of primordial nature.' Whereas, the monotheistic beliefs of the Hebrews are 'free of pagan themes such as battles between the gods before creation'.[2] What is significant is 'God's absolute will', liberating the Bible from myth. Pagan ritual is a 'magical' attempt to compel the gods, whereas Hebrew ritual is the fulfilment of God's will. Halbertal and Margalit's account certainly exaggerates the difference between 'pagans' (polytheistic) and monotheistic actions and beliefs, between early mythical narrative and later religious views of the world; it suffers from too strong a focus on the literate Greeks, and the Eastern Mediterranean more generally. Narrative plays a much lesser role in most African cultures than is suggested. Why?

## *Myth and Mythology; Recitation and Sacred Knowledge*

Before approaching the question of the presence and absence of myth, we first need to make some attempt to circumscribe the boundaries of the concept we are using. The category 'myth' may seem self-evident and self-explanatory. In fact, the English language got along without the word until the nineteenth century. In Dr Johnson's great eighteenth-century dictionary, he includes only 'mythology', which he defined as 'a system of fables; explication of the fabulous history of the gods of the heathen world'.

---

[1] J. Goody, fieldnotes 1949–50, Bonyiiri, p. 658.
[2] Halbertal and Margalit 1992:68.

The situation in France was similar. *Mythologie* was used in much the same way, but *mythe*, defined as a 'traditional recitation that attributes to certain events and certain people a supernatural character', was only admitted by the Academy in 1835, nearly a century after *mythologie* (in 1740).[3] 'Myth' has since become a term with a plurality of references, a very powerful one like 'symbol', that everyone presumes to use in a similar way, whereas in fact they do so in very varied ones. It is a word that carries a great deal of emotive significance, for Yeats, for example, when he turned back to Cuchulain and the Celtic stories to provide him with the kind of certainty that his hesitant mind found so difficult to seize upon in Easter 1916.

The nineteenth-century usage made a clear dichotomy: they have myth, we have book. Myth is an attribute of non-literate societies that has been replaced by the rationality of the educated and the truth of the Bible. In many respects the situation has not greatly changed and usage harks back to the way the concept developed under Greek 'rationalism'. Earlier stories of the gods were rejected as *mythos*; current accounts of events were accepted is *istoria* or *logos*. This use of 'myth' emerged out an attempt to distinguish fact from fiction. What had been originally a term for 'narrative account' later came to take on the pejorative undertones of fiction, even of untruth. In this way Herodotus distanced himself from earlier storytellers such as Hecateus, just as Thucydides did from Herodotus. As Lloyd remarks, 'one after another, in the fifth and fourth centuries BC, Greek historians, philosophers, even medical writers, categorize what their rivals – predecessors or contemporaries – do as *myth*, while what they themselves offer are rational accounts, *logoi*.'[4] Watt and I (1963) argued that such a distinction becomes critical in literate societies when one continues to have to deal with earlier, no-longer appropriate, accounts, perhaps oral in origin, that one wants to modify or reject, though we were thinking of the work of predecessors

---

[3] *Dictionnaire de la langue française* (6th edn), A. Hatzfeld, A. Darmesteter and M. A. Thomas, Paris, 1920.
[4] Lloyd 1990:23.

rather than of contemporaries. Putting down oral forms in writing meant that one was faced with tales of the past, of the men of old, as well as those of the present, of today's generation, which otherwise would have been forgotten. These could now be physically set beside one another, raising in an acute form the question of truth or falsity. That is not to say that a difference between 'truth' and 'fiction' is absent from oral cultures, even though as the anthropologist Sperber has suggested, the boundaries may be differently drawn. Among the LoDagaa of northern Ghana there is a firm verbal distinction drawn between *yelmiong* ('proper affairs or true telling') and *ziri* (lies), though it is possible to argue that the LoDagaa concept of tales (*sũnsuolo*) represents a third category, approximating to that of fiction, where there is no intention to deceive.

There is no specific word for 'myth' among the LoDagaa. There are a number of related genres, however, the consideration of which will inevitably touch upon the nature of 'myth' and why I chose the term to describe the long recitation known as the Bagre.[5] We need to recognize two tendencies, not so much in the study of myth as in the direction to take before looking for something to study. The first treats myth as a sacred narrative, usually as a 'standard oral form' that incorporates supernatural beings, legendary humans and other living beings: in other words, gods, men and animals. This notion of 'sacred tale' is mainly what writers like Malinowski and Leach discuss under this rubric; even though such authors are often short on written *texts* of these oral forms, and their usage sometimes merges into that of mythology, they are generally referring to types of regulated utterance, standard oral forms.

The second trend treats myth as mythology, as sacred knowledge. Myth and mythology are firmly distinguished by Halbertal and Margalit. For them, myth 'is the characteristic expression of idolatrous thought'. Some consider it unique to paganism, others, like Buber, as contained in all religion.[6] Some

---

[5] J. Goody 1972; J. Goody and Gandah 1981.
[6] Halbertal and Margalit 1992:67, 264.

link it solely to 'they', others to 'we' as well. That is a perpetual dilemma for commentators.

Sacred knowledge is partly derived from the narratives that form the basis of Johnson's definition. These are 'the fables of the men of old', which later Greeks characterized as myth (*mythos*) but viewed as the source of the sacred knowledge of former times. Mythology, however, may include many other sources. In *Les Mythologiques*, Lévi-Strauss specifically claims the right to draw 'unhesitatingly on material provided by folk tales, legends and pseudo-historical traditions' as well as by 'ceremonies and rites'.[7] We are specifically dealing here with 'mythology', with 'the field of mythological thought', where our aim is the 'drawing up an inventory of mental patterns'.[8]

One problem here is the scope of cultural acts that one is examining in trying to arrive at these 'mental patterns'. There may be a case for limiting our analysis of the LoDagaa system of knowledge to that contained in the Bagre or other oral genres, but the full implications of this should be understood. Some would take in more in their analysis. Lévi-Strauss would include rituals. But we are reluctant to accept all the implications of the dichotomy insisted upon by Durkheim, between sacred (myth plus ritual) and secular action or knowledge, since the kind of evidence that myths, narratives or fables supply about the world at large is only part and parcel of the system of categories, of metaphors, polarities and analogies, that emerge from the total interaction among one people, say, the Nyoro (of East Africa), the Zuni (of the south-west United States), the Dogon (of Mali) or the Barasana (of Colombia). We may argue that myth as narrative, or ritual as ceremony, may have a privileged status, but that must be related to its locus relative to the local cultural system. While Zuni mythology is derived from specific vernacular recitations (myths), *le mythe Dogon* was constructed *inter alia* from a series of conversations of an anthropologist with a blind elder called Ogotemeli. The phrase,

---

[7] Lévi-Strauss 1970:4.
[8] Lévi-Strauss 1970:10.

*le mythe Dogon*, refers to a cosmology (or better perhaps a view of human/god relationships) that is not necessarily expressed in oral compositions at all; it is a text created by the enquirers (that is, not a vernacular text at all but an elicited text). If we look at 'symbolic systems' rather than myth, and the two are often seen as closely associated, then the knowledge represented by the much-discussed symbolic system of the Nyoro is built up from a study of a selection of all recorded activities.[9] Each account draws on a different universe. Its analysis is almost always observer-centred since a world view is constructed from a variety of sources and does not appear to the actor as a unity. Whereas the contents of 'an utterance-myth', a *récit* (or even a plurality of the same genre) do appear to the actor as a whole (of a more restricted kind) and need first to be analysed at the surface level before engaging in the more problematic search for a deep structure.

Another use of the term myth refers to those tales that centre upon a particular incident, deity or other focus, for example, the myth of Adonis. A closely-related area of analysis would clearly be not the narrative but the iconography centring upon this deity. The focus of such a study is a specific deity or character, and there is an assumption that one can aggregate all of these references into a whole as is done in many works on Greek mythology such as that of Robert Graves. But such an assumption is highly dubious. Who sees them as a whole except the observer? In fact, the references are drawn from different historical periods, from different social groups or actors, and from different contexts. What then is the justification for merging them into one continuous text?

The more restricted and 'literary' view of myth, then, refers to specific utterances, to '*le récit*', what I shall call an 'utterance-myth' as distinct from a 'cosmology'. The distinction relates to that offered by Lévi-Strauss between '*la mythologie explicite*' and '*la mythologie implicite*' at the end of *L'Homme nu*.[10] In the latter case, 'the mystical representations exist only in the form of notes, of sketches or of fragments . . .'. Both forms are seen as part of 'an

---

[9] On the Nyoro, see Beattie 1968, 1976; and Needham 1967, 1976.
[10] Lévi-Strauss 1971:598.

identical reality', they are '*deux modes d'existence de la mythologie*'. However, explicitness seems to me to be of great importance both in its composition and its consequences.

It is these differences in usages that partly explain the apparently contradictory assertions about the distribution of 'myth' in Africa and elsewhere. While some have remarked upon their absence, there is no shortage in Africa of the kind of utterances analysed in '*Les mythologiques*', though they often display some significant differences. What is in short supply in Africa (though not totally absent) is the long (partly narrative) texts of the kind recorded for the Pueblo of south-west USA and for the Murngin of Australia (to confine one's attention to non-literate societies). The Bagre is one of these extended oral compositions, one of the very few published African 'myths' (utterance-texts), at least if we are talking of '*récits*' comparable to Gilgamesh or to Homer. It is surely clear that Homer merits a different type of treatment than the other Greek 'tales' about gods that Graves or Kirk examine.

To take the first of these trends sketched out earlier, it has been argued by Paul Radin, the American anthropologist, that there are no myths in Africa and while one can disagree with him, one can also see what he meant. Ruth Finnegan, indeed, has written an entire book of 500 pages on 'oral literature' in Africa without ever mentioning the word myth except in inverted commas. When these authors avoid this term they do not mean there is no traditional knowledge (trend two) which is not tied up with, say, systems of categories, with supernatural agencies, with humans, even with the animal world. Nor do they mean there was no narrative, for that is contained in folk tales. They are referring to the absence of long sacred narratives of the kind reported from the Zuni of North America. In fact, neither author was altogether correct for we do find recitations of this kind in Africa, but they are few and far between. I did use the word 'myth' of the Bagre (found among the LoDagaa) because it was a long recitation, but as I have pointed out, it was not only secular as well as sacred, it was also deficient in narrative power. Hence my hesitation. For the term 'myth' may encourage us to think we are dealing not only with a special genre, but with a special form of thought, of thinking, even mentality.

That is a position we have to beware of. Finnegan makes the point by insisting on the term 'oral literature' for Africa, making explicit the comparison with the literature of our own society. In so doing she does I believe overlook some important differences between oral and written literature which are of considerable significance.[11] But these differences are not best expressed in terms of the problems concerning presence or absence of myth. In fact, with regard to forms like the Bagre, there is a whole series of possible axes of differentiation within the category of *le récit*.[12] Some would discrimate on the grounds of 'orality' (as distinct from written literature, the novel), of sacredness (as distinct from folk tale, animal stories), of seriousness (as embodying belief), of performance and audience (as distinct from epic), even of scope or length (in terms of comprehensiveness).

So I use the word 'myth' to refer to a genre, a long recitation deemed central to a particular society or group. Unlike 'mythology', such recitations are far from universal and have a very uneven distribution in human cultures, in America as in Africa. I am interested in enquiring into the reasons behind the presence and absence of myth in this sense, particularly in relation to Africa, and in seeing how this relates to the problems concerning presence and absence of other artistic genres that I have considered in the earlier chapters.

Unless one recognizes that some writers are talking about utterance-myths (or even text-myths) and others about mythologies, argument becomes futile and analysis slippery. The attachment to different usages makes nonsense of certain discussions, such as that between Lévi-Strauss and Turner on the relationship between myth and rite. When Richards says of the Bemba, and Turner of the Ndembu, that they have no myths,

---

[11] See *L'Homme nu* 1971:538.

[12] It is worth pointing out that there is really no English equivalent of '*récit*'; the words 'recital' and 'recitation' both refer predominantly to the act of performing a written text or written music, so that neither term is altogether correct for the Bagre. But I could think of nothing else except the French *récit*, which it seemed too precious to use throughout.

they are referring to oral *récit*, that is, to explicit utterance-myths, not to implicit ones (in Lévi-Strauss's terminology); that is, they are not referring to mythology. From their standpoint the apparent resolution (in the 'Finale' of *L'Homme nu*) is meaningless, that is, the injunction to separate all the exegesis from ritual and then count this as myth. The difference must be respected.

It is in the wider sense, of knowledge of the gods, sacred knowledge, that Wole Soyinka uses the term in his book *Myth, Literature and the African World* (Cambridge 1976); here he presses the gods into service and discusses the role of Yoruba deities, Ogun, Obatala, and Sango.

> They are represented here in drama by the passage-rites of the hero-gods, a projection of man's conflict with forces which challenge his efforts to harmonise with his environment, physical, social and psychological . . . their symbolic roles are identified by man as the role of an intermediary quester, an explorer into territories of 'essence-ideal' around whose edges man fearfully skirts.[13]

I earlier made the point that the analysis of 'mythologies' is usually observer-centred but in Soyinka's case the analytic frame is based on the surface structure, which is the level of understanding applied to a poem or a novel; the conflicts are present to the actor. Understanding is not achieved by reverting to an observer-level which probes into the transformations between different versions and between different cultures.

In no way do I underestimate the value of the other approach. It is one that is related to hidden, cryptophoric interpretations such as the psychoanalytical in which the actors can be brought to recognize unconscious meaning; this is an approach that can profitably be taken in looking at many types of human behaviour. But it is a different kind of enterprise, with different rules and different data and different results.

The sacred knowledge Soyinka is dealing with derives from tales; it is mythology in the original sense of Dr Johnson. As a writer, he

---

[13] Soyinka 1990:i.

tends to incorporate Yoruba mythology in rather the same way that Yeats did the stories of Cuchulain and the other resources of ancient Ireland. This is the way that recent writers such as T. S. Eliot tend to use the term myth. On the other hand, some employ the word for secular as well as for religious tales, for the outstanding narratives of an era, those that encapsulate the human condition at a particular time and a particular place, and so sacred in another sense, such as those of Oedipus, Don Quixote or Robinson Crusoe.[14]

There are two further aspects to the study of systems of knowledge, of cognitive structures, which are not strictly relevant to myth as representation but which prompt some comment at this point. One is the extent to which, whenever we are dealing in conscious or unconscious structures, the observer's analytical frame should be influenced or dominated by that of the actor. The second is whether we should view such a system of knowledge as a determined structure which individuals are seeking to express or interpret, or as the creation by particular individuals of systems of understanding out of a series of given building blocks that are both cultural and natural. The implications of these approaches (which I have set out as opposites in order to distinguish trends) are far-reaching. In the second case, the search for a determined structure will tend to stress constant features, the alternatives variants; and in treating variants the former will tend to treat them as transformations within a fixed frame, the latter as generative in an open-ended direction. The problem is clearly simplified when one is using as one's source the text of a recitation such as the Bagre; it is much more complicated if one is dealing with *Weltanschauung* (world view) or with symbolic classificatory systems. But in every case one is faced with finding a path between the two possibilities.

In dealing with representation it is in this context that the question of numbers arises. If one takes the view that the reproduction of systems of knowledge in general, or verbal forms in particular, is a quasi-automatic matter, the extent of the group involved and the number of versions collected makes no difference;

---

[14] See Watt 1996.

one significant individual, priest, or shaman may pass on this knowledge to his successor. But if you regard the process of reproduction as being generative rather than the precisely programmed reproduction of the genetic code, the question of the context and variants of performance becomes critical. In the first case, how is divergence prevented? If differentiation does occur, should it always be thought of as a transformation within a fixed frame? In that case we are obliged to bring some sort of intelligence to bear upon the problem of what transformation *outside* that frame would look like. We can demonstrate the fit only by showing the non-fit.

## *Genres of Verbal Art*

Let me turn back to the first tendency I pointed to in distinguishing the object of our study, that which starts with the idea of myth as a narrative genre, a verbal art form, a standardized utterance, oral literature, if you will. While distinctions of genre may be of less importance when dealing on the level of deep structures, it is of critical importance on that of manifest meaning, of cognitive significance. To make a point which is obvious once stated, Lévi-Strauss's comments about the manifest level of thought being unimportant might possibly be acceptable as applying to 'folk tales' but not at all to longer creations such as the Bagre.

In trying to indicate the categories of verbal art form used by the LoDagaa, I will first confine myself to the named genres. Of course, significant sub-categories may be distinguished by the actors through verbal elaboration or contextual placing, and, in any case, schema based on actor categories may be less important for analytical purposes than one based upon a distinctive set of observer categories. I make these points because the discussion of terminological sets, whether of kin, colour or animals, has tended to get bogged down by a failure to be clear about the difference between what, in the kinship sphere, I have tried to distinguish as roles and role-categories, the latter referring to actor-terms, the former to analytical concepts.

In 'prose' forms, the LoDagaa have a category of *sũnsuolo* (or *suolu*), which can best be translated as 'folk tales'; the word in Gonja is *aserkpang*. Both may include a song as well as prose. The general word for song is *yielu* (in Gonja, *icafa*), a term that refers not only to the songs interspersed in folk tales, but to those sung by shepherds, or sometimes played by them on pipes, to those sung by women as they grind millet or pound guinea corn, or by young girls as they enjoy their characteristic clapping and throwing game. However, songs sung at funerals were known as *lang*, and the singer as *lang-ŋmaara* or *langtfiere*; at the Harvest Dance or *k'obine* he was known as *yieltfiere*.[15] In general, these special songs have something of the character of the ballad or of *recitativo*, whereas the *yielu* is closer to the lyric. Both can touch upon sacred things; there are *yielu* in the Bagre, for example. But the *lang* deal in general with heavier topics, especially at funerals, where dirges are chanted in front of the dead body propped up on the funeral stand.

There are two further types of words and music. One comprises the kind of 'praise song' (*dano*) that a visiting musician will play in the hope of being rewarded by the recipient of his flattering address.[16] Such singing is rare in these stateless groups with their minimal hierarchies, being more characteristic of centralized peoples like the Gonja, where chiefs are frequently the objects of concentrated attention by professional singers and drummers, especially on ceremonial occasions. Then there is the singing of the xylophone player, of which it is said *o ŋmiera zukpɛ* – 'he beats out proverbs'. The word *zukpar* means both riddles (word games expecting an answer) and proverbs (which, in effect, close a discussion). In this case, it is the latter that are meant, proverb-like phrases being strung together in song.

Finally, there is the Bagre itself, which is chanted in a definite

---

[15] J. Goody 1962.

[16] An Atjate story tells of the boy who was very hungry, saw some fruit in an inaccessible part of the tree, sang the tree a song of praise and 'lo! the branches of the tree bent down to him and enabled him to climb up' (Cardinall 1931:229).

rhythm to a beaten accompaniment, and in a different manner from anything else. Reciting the White Bagre is known by the term *kaab* (*boor*), a term more generally used for the prayers made before a sacrifice is performed, which are chanted and accompanied in a similar way, with a knife or stick being beaten on a stone or gourd; the verb ŋmɛ is used of the Black Bagre. This long recitation-chant has no parallels among their neighbours and it is what I referred to as 'The myth of the Bagre'. The Bagre is not a category term; it is the name of a secret society and its recitation, though more generally it means 'mystical trouble', problems that only the supernatural can deal with.

There is no word in LoDagaa that we can translate as 'myth'. It is perhaps not surprising that we find no *generic* name for the Bagre, since it is unique. It is the Bagre; there is no other. However, there is also no term by which one can render 'epic' or any similar genre. On the other hand, the Bagre forms part of what is called *teŋkuri yele* (*teŋkor yel*), or traditional knowledge, touching upon the use of 'myth' as 'mythology'. Literally, the phrase means 'matters of the past' and includes all of that which we might refer to as mythology – knowledge about sacred things, supernatural events, the world of the past. The Bagre is only one element in what is an undefined corpus that includes not only 'sacred tales' about the supernatural but anything else handed from the past – history, kinship and most importantly for the actors, the technology transferred from one generation to the next. That body of knowledge provides answers in response to the recurrent question, 'Why do you do that?' Indeed, it is significant that the Bagre itself includes knowledge not only about rituals but also about productive processes which are described in some considerable detail.

It is this situation that leads me to claim that 'myth' (and I do *not* mean mythologies) may be culturally less significant than many have maintained. In the first place, not everybody in the society has access to the knowledge. In the second, long, elaborate, comprehensive, developed recitations of this kind have a discontinuous distribution; a few societies in the region have them (in fact they have only been recorded for the LoDagaa), many do not, even when we have adequate ethnographers (of the Tallensi, for example). Not all forms of Bagre performance (for instance, that among the LoWilisi or 'true Lobi') seem to have such a component.[17]

There is one further type of formal statement I would include, apart from prayer (*kaab*), and that is an unnamed category in LoDagaa that comprises legend or history. As far as I know this type of standard oral form remains undifferentiated from the body of spoken things, yet it takes a rather deliberate form. I refer, in particular, to clan histories which include not only accounts of the migration routes supposed to have been taken in arriving at their present location, but also the reasons for the voyage, that often involve considerations not only of invasion, land shortage or hunting grounds but also of totem and taboo as well as of supernatural entities. In most cases the setting for these narratives is informal in character: they are told when the need arises. But in the Lawra Bagre which was recorded in 1974, the clan history of the Kusiele plays a very important part in the recitation; it is incorporated in the Bagre itself.[18]

Apart from clan histories, there are informal types of narrative. Individuals sometimes tell stories connected with their personal lives, recollections of their earlier days, sometimes elaborated, sometimes not, as well as second-hand statements about the lives of others. What is noteworthy about the LoDagaa and the Gonja is that these narratives (indeed any narrative, in the more precise meaning of the word) play little part in their discourse. There are few contexts in which such accounts would be elicited, partly because this is a face-to-face community where such knowledge is widespread and implicit. But otherwise there is little of this kind of processing of the past. Clan histories are sometimes recited at

---

[17] According to C. de Rouville on the Lobi (personal communication). Others such as the LoBirifor have been reported as having such a recitation; indeed, the ethnographer Erbs has presented in a thesis a form that is word for word the same as my first published version, but he tells me he just translated this from my English into French.

[18] I have prepared a collection of these additional versions of the Bagre, which have been transcribed, translated and annotated but not published.

sacrifices addressed to the ancestors. Once you have heard a folk tale, however, there is no specific reason for hearing it again, although a reference to one may help to make a point. Folk tales rarely enter into adult discourse.[19] It is significant that, while clan legends contain the names of ancestors, the 'made-up' tales, the folk tales, do not normally have named characters, nor yet specific settings, though some may refer to the beginnings of the world. Many of the characters are animals, as with the Brer Rabbit of the Nancy (Anansi) tales transported to the Americas. Does this represent a distancing of fictional from real-life narrative, placing it in a special category? I certainly do not know of any concept like 'story' or 'narrative' that would cover both forms. The distance is further emphasized by the fact that all except the first and last of these genres are sung or chanted and the first also includes songs, which are performed by the LoDagaa for conveying some special types of concentrated information. Such narratives do not try to mimic reality.

Before looking in greater detail at these genres, we may remind ourselves that Malinowski distinguished three varieties of narrative in the Trobriands, on the basis of actor categories and functions. These were:

*Kukwanebu* – fireside or fairy tales;
*Libwagwe* – historical tales, legends, hearsay tales (true);
*Liliu* – myths or sacred tales.

This division parallels that of the LoDagaa, though they are not all distinguished by different terms, nor are the differences quite as clear cut as in Malinowski's case.

*Sũnsuolo* – fairy tales or folk tales;
Clan and personal histories;
*The Bagre* – a long recitation connected with a ritual.

---

[19] For an exception see Bonyiiri's story given to me, 'God wanted to kill everybody', J. Goody, fieldnotes 1949–50, p. 638.

It is relevant to note that all these three types have been referred to as myths by some author. Cardinall writes of myths of the origin of death, referring to folk tales; Fortes refers to myths of origin, meaning clan histories, while I have used the same term with regard to the Bagre. Why? Because each of them is sacred in one sense of the word. They deal with gods, animals and the origins of things, they deal with important human origins, or they are literally embedded in ritual.

Each of these forms has a different truth-status. The folk tales are often if not always told for 'amusement' and only half-believed in. I have argued that Cardinall and Paulme are wrong in taking this kind of material as an indication of how people are thinking in a general sense; for they are often part of communication with children, clearly seen as fiction. Stories of clan origins, however, are certainly believed in, as is the Bagre. They are not 'fiction', the former referring largely to mundane events, the latter to supernatural ones.

## *Folk Tales as Fiction*

Let us look in greater detail at these various genres. As far as fictional narratives are concerned, *sũnsuolo* is used for the category of folk tales, stories about God, about the Spider, a hunter and other similar characters. These are the same general types of tale that are widespread in Africa; among the Asante it is known as *anansesem*, that is, 'words about a spider', whether or not the spider actually appears in them.

It is easy to give examples of these stories but difficult to characterize them in general terms, for they partake of the nature of short story, wisdom literature and, some have remarked, 'myth'. In using the last word, it is the 'sacred' content of the tales to which attention is being called, for example, in the tales examined by Paulme on the Origin of Death.[20] She presents a story about death from Kete Krachi on the River Volta, in what used to be German

[20] Paulme 1967.

Togoland, lying just outside the kingdoms of Asante to the south-west, of Gonja to the north-west and of Nanumba to the north, with Dahomey over the mountains to the east. The tale was one collected by Cardinall, a British District Commissioner, in a volume that contains similar stories from the surrounding district. Since the destruction of Salaga in 1892, Krachi had been the centre not only of the important cult of Krachi Dente but also of a group of Muslims, including one Al Hajj Umar, the translator and composer of some sophisticated early Arabic verse and the subject of a short biography by another administrator, R. S. Rattray.[21]

The point of these remarks is to provide the context for my surprise, on reading the original tale and Paulme's comments, that this should be taken as an example of the 'thought', or the 'cosmology' of the local population. Why not as readily take something from the works of Muslim doctors? Even if we confine ourselves to the non-Muslim sphere, there seems some reason for questioning the status of this evidence about 'primitive thought'. Cardinall argues the case for belief. He points out how frequently the lore of these neighbouring peoples resemble each other and then goes on to say: 'It is not surprising therefore to find many beliefs of the grossest superstition just as one would expect to find among the country folk of remoter districts of Europe. But there is this real difference between African peasantry and European. It is that the superstitions are actually believed in and not half believed in.'[22] I do not doubt that at one level he is correct to indicate that witchcraft beliefs, for example, were more widespread, more entrenched among West African country folk of the 1920s than among Westphalian peasants of the same period. But when he goes on to say 'there is nothing out of the ordinary in them; they are the occurrences of everyday life and to the native perfectly natural. Animals speak and so do trees . . .', I part company. Certainly, any LoDagaa that went up to talk to a tree and expected it to answer back would be treated as a lunatic. When my collaborator, K. Gandah, came to the passage in the First Bagre where the Earth shrine complains

---

[21] Goody and Braimah 1967; Goody and Wilks 1968.
[22] Cardinall 1931:6.

aloud that human beings have been sacrificing and beating him on his head (or 'skin'), he burst out laughing. The reactions of a traditional LoDagaa would be the same. In other instances, individuals clearly understand narratives in a metaphorical, even allegorical sense; they do not believe in any usual meaning of that verb. Without wishing to enter a discussion about the conviction, degrees of belief, scepticism, of the actors in a particular case, is there any reason to think that, in this respect, their minds work differently from ours, that they too should not be capable of the tongue-in-cheek, the *double entendre*, the half-belief, of inconsistency between levels? The systemizations of functionalist and structuralist alike, with their emphasis on integration between institutions, on homology between layers, tend to set aside or at least undervalue the possibility. So too do many attempts to collate material from different kinds of source into a single, homogenized system of knowledge; the different truth-statuses of the variegated material is neglected, as if I were to try to interlink Snow White and the Seven Dwarfs with Christ and his disciples. To treat all 'knowledge' as of one level is like applying the same kind of interpretation to the porter scene in Shakespeare's *Macbeth* as to the scene in which Lady Macbeth eggs her husband on to murder.

The existence of a continuum between complete disbelief and full commitment requires the use of procedures by the actors for locating 'error' and for perceiving contradictions. Such procedures may involve a more generalized scepticism, which questions the very basis of belief.[23] In the Bagre the initiates are led to believe that the medicine will both kill and revive the initiates, that it will cure them from sickness and protect them from death. As the neophytes are put through the ritual, many of them believe that this is really the case. But the second phase of the ceremonies, the Black Bagre, disillusions them. The associated recitation explains that death is intrinsic to the human condition, that finally we are in the hands of God, and that nothing can prevent mortality, though we may be able to ward off the evil day and repel attacks

---

[23] J. Goody, A kernel of doubt: agnosticism in cross-cultural perspective. Huxley lecture, 1996b.

upon us. At one level, we perform Bagre even though we do not 'believe' in it. But the recitation itself acquires credibility through a frank recognition of this state of affairs and in quite a different way from folk tales.

The alternative way to regard folk tales, if they are not to be taken literally as 'primitive thought', stresses either the childishness of the beliefs or the irrelevance of their surface structure. The second is the line adopted by Lévi-Strauss (and many modern anthropologists). The other possibility, and I speak strictly of the LoDagaa and Gonja cases which are the only ones I have experienced myself, is that this category of tales is there largely 'for amusement'. It does not follow that they should not be taken seriously; the role of humour, as Freud and others have pointed out, must not be underrated. But, from the actor's point of view, the content of the story and the intention in telling it cannot be compared with narratives of a different kind with a higher seriousness.

The point is supported by the fact that African folk tales often conclude with a moral ending or proverb that seems to have little relevance to the story itself, as if to draw out a serious conclusion from a merely frivolous entertainment. We can perhaps see this feature in the same light as the 'often curiously irrelevant' moralizations appended to stories in the *Gesta Romanorum*, also found in a more sophisticated guise in much of the narrative literature of the sixteenth and seventeenth centuries.[24] The moral could serve as a kind of apology for the use of make-believe.

The context in which I have heard these stories told have nearly always been light-hearted ones: adults to children, children to one another. This seems to be the same among the neighbouring Wala to the south. According to Fikri, Wala folk tales (*silima*) are for entertainment, largely for children. In contrast to *lasire*, 'tradition or history, which is respected, serious, and mainly for elders to discuss', 'tales are considered to be lies'.[25] In other words, there is

---

[24] Nelson 1973:59–60.
[25] Fikri 1969:1, 366. The affinities with Renaissance discussions of fiction are obvious (Nelson 1973; Ife 1985).

no question of these tales in Africa (and I suggest in Europe too) being remnants of cast-off myths (though they may sometimes treat the same subject matter). They have not been downgraded by the appearance of written forms; they are of different levels of seriousness. That point relates to the difference in genre between the folk tale and a recitation like the Bagre. They work on a totally different level of belief. While they get incorporated in other standard oral forms – they appear in the Bagre just as folk tales appear in Homer, on their own they require a different reading, or rather a different listening. That may be why, in West Africa, similar tales circulate so frequently among peoples with very different socio-cultural systems, and in so doing, do not always undergo the kinds of transformation which those structural or functional theories demanding a close fit would seem to require.[26]

## The Bagre as Knowledge and as 'True' Narrative

As a source of knowledge the Bagre raises interesting questions about its relation to the culture as a whole and to how knowledge is learnt and taught. Most anthropologists assume a set body of knowledge enshrined in a cultural tradition, which various individuals get to know with varying degrees of success. As Barth suggested in discussing New Guinea, knowledge is visualized as a series of layers which individuals attain by learning processes. In certain ways this idea corresponds to one account (here I emphasize the singular) of the Bagre, which enables the neophytes to acquire a body of knowledge by a series of steps in their initiation.

Much of the Bagre, both Black and White, presents itself as such a quest, the quest of the Younger and Elder that takes them to the beings of the wild and indeed to Heaven itself, a quest that explores this world, the half-way world of the beings of the wild and the other world of God and the ancestors. It is a quest for knowledge about how to cure the ills of humankind (sickness, suicide, and the

---

[26] See J. Goody, 1992/3, 'Men, animals and gods', *Cambridge Anthropology* 16:46–60.

problems of growing plants and of rearing animals), but in the course of the quest the seekers acquire knowledge of many other things, of God, of the beings of the wild, of how humans procreate and acquire their culture. This is a curious form of knowledge in two ways. In the first place, some LoDagaa who are not members of the Bagre society do without it perfectly well; in the second, while it purports to teach about this world (the emphasis on technology is considerable), it often teaches what is already well-known (for example, how to make beer) or later discovered to be dubious (for example, about the Bagre medicine itself). Finally, the knowledge is open ended, not bounded. That openness is implied in the very notion of a quest, especially for supernatural remedies for the ills of this world which are never in the end satisfactory, never complete. It is also implicit in the nature of the recitation, which is in itself creative, generative of new forms, new knowledge. Every version of the Bagre is different, sometimes in major respects.

If we insist on myth as sacred tale, story or narrative, we are in some difficulty when it comes to analysing particular cases. Many Western observers assume myth has a primary, often exclusively, narrative form, like the epic. In some cases this may represent local reality. But it is also a question of how myths have often been recorded. Dictation can provide a complete version but it is necessarily undertaken outside the context of performance. Meanwhile, in any summary account of a film or a ritual, the narrative element is necessarily selected in an attempt to retell the listener's experience of a recitation whether or not narrative is its most significant element. This is what happened in some anthropological reporting before the advent of the tape-recorder.[27] The non-narrative elements get dropped by the wayside because they are not intrinsic to the temporal framework one has adopted (which is the most convenient, the most highly structured, from the standpoint of recall). In other words, one's judgement about the content of the myth (recitation) may be influenced by the fact that other elements

---

[27] See J. Goody, The anthropologist and the tape-recorder, *Minpaku Newsletter*, Osaka, 1995.

(for example, the more philosophical) have been omitted.

The Bagre is a case in point, though I would not deny it may not be altogether typical. The White Bagre has a temporal, but a largely non-narrative frame; the original Black Bagre I recorded has some narrative elements, but it has a great deal else, philosophy, aetiological material, commentary on itself, as well as discussion (sequential, but hardly narrative) of technological processes much of which certainly falls in the secular rather than the sacred sphere (though for the religious, all may be tinged with the work of the gods).

Outside the folk tale, animals and gods do not seem to become the objects of narrative in Africa to any great extent. It is significant that in the Bagre it is mainly people, then God (rather than gods) and the beings of the wild, that enter in. Animals and gods are very much on the periphery, though at one point the spider plays an important role which must certainly be seen in its full ethnographic context, that is to say, he is an intermediary between humans and God, whose web provides a ladder from Earth to Heaven. But the Bagre is selective in terms not only of personnel but also of topics. Even fundamental features of LoDagaa religion, such as the Earth and the ancestors, play little part and there is little personification of natural phenomena. In other words, if you took the Bagre as the sole source of even sacred knowledge, you would get a very partial view. Omitted, for example, would be many of the most important gods and shrines; it should also be added that few of these have any associated narrative structure that ties them into a pantheon (in West Africa the Yoruba and Dahomey are partial exceptions). Nor are the stars or the moon systematically integrated into a system of knowledge by this means.[28] The actors appear to treat many of these religious and natural phenomena in a more abstract way. Certainly, narrative is one of the least important things about a deity; powers, prohibitions, altar, owner, offerings, all these are more significant elements.

I have argued here that narrative is of less importance in the

---

[28] There is some reference to the stars in the opening of the Biro Bagre. I have never heard this in any other context.

Bagre than definitions of myth as 'sacred tale' suggest. That is a question which affects mythology, and to which I return in the next section. But I would also suggest that, connected with this point, myth, as distinct from mythology, also has less importance in many societies than is often assumed, since it may exclude central topics and exclude some (not only women) from hearing it. Furthermore, in many societies such long recitations simply do not exist. The relative absence of myth is not merely a negative feature, as Lévi-Strauss's approach might seem to suppose. It may also be a positive characteristic. Among the LoDagaa narrative is largely for children. I have never heard an adult tell a 'story' of the folk tale variety to anyone else except to children or to anthropologists. While I have elicited tales in a number of ways, none of the natural situations in which I heard them were basically 'adult' contexts. I do not claim this to be true throughout Africa. But it does fit with the absence, noted by many observers, of a developed mythology as distinct from a generalized cosmology. I mean that for adults, the relations God, Humans, Nature, are not held together by a series of interlinking narratives.

That is certainly the same with clan histories and legends. Each clan knows its own, but there is no common account of the history of migration into the area, no linking of the separate (rather bitty) narratives. The same holds true for local histories in the centralized state of Gonja, which are much more developed as narratives. Many of them refer to the founding hero, Jakpa. The extent of the kingdom of Gonja and its internal diversity means that myth, legend, tale, narrative, differ depending upon the interests of the groups involved, upon particular experiences and upon a number of other factors. National 'history' takes the written form of the Gonja Chronicle composed in the eighteenth century and read out in some divisional capitals at the annual festival of Damba.[29] In terms of the oral tradition there is a national drum 'history' (or set of chiefly titles) that is also recited at the annual Damba ceremony celebrated on the Prophet's birthday, but only in the capital of the

---

[29] See I. Wilks, N. Levtzion and B. M. Haight, *The Chronicles from Gonja: A Tradition of West African Muslim Historiography*, Cambridge, 1986.

kingdom.[30] That recitation is vested in specialist 'remembrancers', and its short, quite distinct verses are accompanied by particular drum rhythms. There is reason to think that, minor changes apart, the drumming is handed down in a relatively unaltered manner. What differs is the interpretation, since the verses are obscure and often in 'deep' Gonja. There is certainly no straightforward narrative structure. While the written Gonja Chronicle places greater emphasis on chronological organization, it is essentially a chronicle rather than a narrative history. There is a much more extensive corpus of oral legends, apparently historical, about the founding ancestor that are told everywhere but that differ radically from village to village, as well as over time. It is, for example, clear that some accounts reflect the claims of particular chiefs.[31] Others represent the interests of particular areas. It would be an impossible task to try to edit these various local forms into a national Gonja history; they simply would not 'add up'.

Regarding the LoDagaa, I have suggested that their cosmology too is largely non-narrative, or rather the narrative elements are in no sense intrinsic to it. Let me take the notion of the voyage across the river of death. At every LoDagaa funeral some cowries are thrown on the corpse. In my account of the ceremonies I have given an individual's version of the use of these cowries to pay for a person's journey by canoe across the river of death.[32] Now it is true that everybody knows about the river of death; there is some vague idea of crossing it, attended by a ferry man, and of the crossing as meaning the shift between the land of the living and the land of the dead. But in the normal course of events the narrative element is not more complicated than this. Individuals, such as the one whose account I took, may elaborate the content in a whole variety of ways, but there is no established form, no definite Charon sitting there to ferry the dead over to the other side. There is no set narrative to which people appeal. That absence is even more clear cut in the case of gods, and especially with the Supreme Deity. It

---

[30] See E. N. and J. R. Goody, *The Drum History of the Gonja* (forthcoming).
[31] See J. Goody 1954 for examples.
[32] See J. Goody 1962.

is consistent with the relatively abstract nature, the 'symbolic' nature if you like, of African thinking about God, about the supernatural, about the relationships between human beings and God which I have touched upon in discussing iconoclasm and which is illustrated in the works of Evans-Pritchard and Lienhardt on the Nuer and Dinka of the Southern Sudan. There is little narrative element in either of these accounts that are devoted essentially to the cosmology, to what humans know, to their knowledge of the influence of supernatural agencies on this world. In other words, it is perfectly possible to have a pantheon, to have a cosmology, without any great emphasis on narrative. Among the LoDagaa, the most important supernatural agencies are the Earth and God. There are virtually no references to the Earth in any narrative that I know, and there are very few stories about other supernatural agencies.

## *Narrative as Illusion?*

I have been trying to do several things in this chapter. First and foremost I have been concerned with the uneven distribution of 'myth', often taken to be an extended sacred narrative, and by many, confined to oral, or at least to 'other' cultures. That has entailed an attempt to sort out the different usages of the term (as well as of 'mythology') and to place it in the context of other genres, with particular reference to the LoDagaa and other West African societies. In Africa long *récits* of this kind are rare, and when we find them, as in the Bagre case, narrative is not always their most important constituent. We do, of course, find some 'true' narrative of a personal kind and as clan legends. Of fictional forms we also find the story-teller's art developed in the ubiquitous folk tale that seems only loosely linked to particular cultures.[33] But these tales are directed largely to children.

Why should narrative be less common than many assume in oral cultures? Some writers have defined 'narrative' as any 'spoken or

---

[33] J. Goody 1992/1993.

written presentation'. Clearly this definition makes any statement, such as Barthes's about the pervasiveness of narrative, quite tautological. Others see it as 'the kind of organizational scheme expressed in story form'. Once again, one can understand this in a minimalist way as the sequencing of 'the father died', 'the son cried', or we may insist upon more complex type of sequencing in the form of a plot, either fictional (often a 'story') or 'true', historical.

The psychologist Bruner sees narrative understanding as one of two basic forms of cognitive functioning, the other being the paradigmatic or logico-scientific mode. Whereas linguists, like Kinneavy, have thought of narrative as one of five basic forms of discourse, together with referential, expressive, persuasive and poetical.[34] Narrative has been described by Polkinghorne as 'the primary form by which human experience is made meaningful. Narrative meaning is a cognitive process that organizes human experience into temporally meaningful episodes'.[35] While narrative as a cognitive process is not available for observation, we can 'observe' 'personal and social histories, myths, fairy tales, novels, and the everyday stories we use to explain our own and others' actions'. Polkinghorne is a psychotherapist whose clinical activity involves creating a narrative for his clients; as social scientists we are engaged in eliciting and constructing narratives for people. Polkinghorne remarks that narrative meaning 'works to draw together human actions'; it notes 'the contribution that human actions and events make to a particular outcome and then configures these parts with a whole episode'. At a minimal level I would describe this process as 'sequencing' or 'sequential reasoning'. Narrative seems to me a more deliberate and elaborate construct which makes a more irregular appearance, partly because it raises questions of truth or falsity in a specially acute manner.

That claim runs counter to Barthes's assertion that 'there does not exist, and never has existed, a people without narratives'. Using the word in the very general manner of Polkinghorne, Bruner and

[34] Polkinghorne 1988:13–14, 17, 31.
[35] Polkinghorne 1988:1.

others, this statement becomes meaningless. If we employ the word, however, to apply to longer sequences of the kind found in folk tales, life histories and, in written form, novels, theatre or even successive pictures, the situation is quite different. In contemporary everyday life we are surrounded by narrative, in newspapers, in novels, in the theatre, cinema and more especially the television. Contrary to many discussions involving the wider usages, I see these forms (apart from folk tales) as being relatively rare in oral societies. We do not appreciate how much of narrative in this narrower sense is tied to the literate mode. Among the LoDagaa, people do not present me with narratives of their everyday life except occasionally in the settlement procedures for disputes; as observers, however, we piece together heterogeneous statements to construct a story. That is also the case with psychoanalysis, and psychotherapy generally. In oral societies, as we have seen, even art forms place relatively little stress on narrative in this sense. For that represents a standing back from life, fostering a reflexivity that is more characteristic of literate than of oral societies, especially when it takes the form of long recitations, whether narrative or not. These long recitations are necessarily presented as a monologue and are less common in oral societies than is often supposed, partly because they exclude other activities and exclude other people, quite unlike the interrupted give-and-take of ordinary discourse. I do not want for one moment to claim that narratives are unknown in oral societies, but, in the strong sense of that word, they are relatively rare, especially extended ones, and more mixed as a genre than the term might suggest. Many of the consecutive chronological narratives that appear in anthropological 'texts' are 'elicited' by the observer. It behoves us to ask, what are the situations within oral cultures where a similar perfomance would take place, and in a relatively uninterrupted and unmixed form?

Myths, in the sense of long central '*récits*', then, are rare, while mythologies are not, although in Africa it would perhaps be preferable to speak of cosmologies since the narrative backgrounds of deities and their linking in an overall pantheon receive little stress – with certain prominent exceptions in Dahomey and in

Yoruba. It is possible to see this uneven distribution as a matter of the particular development of such recitations in certain cultures where there has been the elaboration of fragmentary traditions about the Creation, for example, into a more elaborate framework. This development is especially likely to occur within the framework of a secret association such as the Bagre where the rituals may invite an accompanying myth as a commentary and elaboration and where the elders have a ready audience before whom to recite and to impart specially created knowledge (which others do not really need or in some cases already have). The question of a captive audience (informal gatherings are more restive) seems to me critical in the development of these long oral recitations.

At one level that situation could account for the uneven distribution of long recitations. But is there a further factor at work, a negative one, a doubt? Given that as art, narrative forms are largely seen as directed towards children in the shape of folk tales, and that the narrative element in cosmologies receives little emphasis, could it be that there is some resistance to the use of story telling itself for serious imaginative purposes, that there is some resistance to the development of verbal representation in its fictional form for these purposes precisely because it is not 'true'? Although we may regard story telling as revealing deeper truths, it proceeds by way of representing what is not, the absent, the fictive, the lie. It is the case that African folk tales and long '*récits*', such as the Bagre, have very different roles. The first are straightforwardly imaginative; trees talk, animals speak, yet the world we know is not like that. These stories are grounded in illusions. Whereas, accounts such as the version of the creation of culture found in the Bagre are more like *Genesis*, inviting belief rather than inciting disbelief. However, the very lack of stress on the narrative element in African cosmologies suggests that even in the case of the sacred there may be a certain mistrust of narratives that may lead to them being treated with some misgivings, avoidance, even rejection.

Myth for the LoDagaa is not simply narrative; that element has been emphasized by earlier recording practices and by literary prejudice. I suggest that one feature of the frequent absence of long mythical recitations in Africa is that narrative, imaginative tales about people and sometimes gods, has been played down by the actors in comparison with other regions. Recreational narrative in the shape of folk tales is often associated with children and with childish ways and beliefs. I doubt that among the LoDagaa they can ever be considered *yilmiona,* 'proper speech' or 'truth'. In any case, a recitation is 'talking about', it is representative rather than performative in the same sense as ordinary discourse and hence liable to arouse misgivings. It is no part of my thesis that all societies are marked by the rejection or devaluing of narrative, or, indeed, of any other artistic form. I suggest merely that there is some ambivalence about such verbal representations as with the figurative (iconic) or dramatic forms, which may lead to their uneven distribution in oral cultures. I regard the argument as less firm for narrative than it is for icons or drama, but I will try to strengthen the case in the following chapter by reviewing the protests in literate societies against the impact of fictional forms of narrative.

# 6

# Objections to the Novel

Do we find any similar situations of absence and presence of narrative, of acceptance and rejection especially of fictional narrative, in written cultures? There are problems in the very concept of fiction since the term refers to the action of fashioning or imitating, but it also means 'feigning, deceit, dissimilation, pretence, statements deriving from "mere" invention'. In other words, there is a similar ambivalence to that carried by the word 'myth'. This account seems to have been present in Greece itself where 'falsehood' (fiction) was accepted 'on low or modest levels where it could not seriously be mistaken for the truth, as in animal fables . . .'[1] Otherwise it was 'amusing and rather scurrilous anecdotes . . . and parodies of everyday life'. This account seems to parallel very closely the model I have suggested for the LoDagaa and other African societies.

In this chapter I want to deal specifically with written fiction in the form of the novel, another long, elaborate, narrative genre. I want to ask whether there are any ambivalences similar to those sometimes found with figurative icons and with theatrical performance, in fictional representations of human life? Let me begin by asking what kind of a change in sensibility novel reading represented? My evidence comes initially from Europe, not because I

---

[1] Fosdyke 1956:158.

think that was the only or even the first region to develop this genre but because it is what lies most readily at my disposal. I go on to discuss briefly the position in China and Japan. Clearly some narrative forms existed in Europe among the large section of the population who could not read. One dominant component was the religious narratives associated with the Old and New Testaments as well as the popular Lives of saints. All of these had a literate, indeed a sacred, origin. In the purely oral sphere one found the folk tales and, in a quite different genre, the ballads. Folk tales have sometimes been looked upon as the survivals of more ancient and graver myths. There seems little evidence for this. Short folk tales of this kind, the themes of which have been analysed by the folklorist Stith Thompson, the linguist Propp and many others, seem to be a genuinely universal phenomenon, found in earlier oral as well as later literate societies in rather similar forms. But in my experience both in the past and in the present, they are not narratives for adults. I do not know that this situation holds universally but it is certainly true in areas in which I have worked. Looking at the structure and content of such tales one can see that they are largely oriented to children and would hardly bear repetition in the adult world. In that world were songs, which were repeated, including narrative songs such as ballads and the kind of epic recorded by Parry and Lord in Yugoslavia in the 1930s.[2]

The development of more elaborate forms of narrative was very uneven. We find a type of novel in the late classical period in Europe as well as in Japan and in China. But in Europe it then virtually disappears, although other narrative forms appear in the late Middle Ages: Arthurian legends, the Romans de la Rose, romances, and the novellas of Boccaccio and others. The novel took on its modern form only in the period following the Renaissance and the invention of printing, with the consequent extension of the reading public.

Some have seen the novel born from the 'exhaustion of myth',

---

[2] The classicists Milman Parry and Albert Lord made some pioneering recordings of songs in Yugoslavia in an attempt to discover an oral style to compare with that of Homer.

in the words of Lévi-Strauss; Frye sees both as varieties of story telling. If, effectively, we see myth as an oral genre while the novel is essentially written, the first formulation is a hyperbolic expression of the obvious, while the second places too much emphasis on narrative. McKeon argues that the (English) novel originates at the time of the acute separation of questions of truth and virtue, which had been relatively absent in earlier ages.[3] That separation seems to run parallel to Nelson's insistence on the growing distinction at the Renaissance between fact and fiction, part of a similar dialectical process. While these distinctions were certainly emphasized at these times, at one level they seem to inhere in the production of any imaginative work of art, in any process of representation.

The Spanish Golden Age (from the 1490s to the 1650s) was one of unparalleled literary achievement. The advent of printing made possible the widespread private reading of prose fiction, a new experience for most people and heavily criticized by many authorities. The new experience involved a different attitude on the part of readers: 'In an atmosphere of silence and solitude they recreated for themselves the thoughts and fantasies of others in a language which resembled their own . . .'[4]

In fact, the extension of the reading public and its demand for works of fiction preceded the invention of printing, which it may have stimulated. In turn the mechanization of writing certainly increased accessibility, which in turn aroused opposition. Much of this was vitriolic, displaying the seriousness with which critics, not only clerics but scholars, treated the matter. The great herbalist, Montano, writes of the fashionable novels of chivalry as 'monsters, the offspring of stupidity, excrement and filth gathered for the destruction of the age'.[5] Many Spanish critics in the sixteenth century saw the reading of fiction as literally a mindless occupation, likened by de Vallés to a woman's love of dressing up; it was shallow frivolity as well as being unnatural.[6] But it also enraptured

[3] McKeon 1987:419.
[4] Ife 1985:10.
[5] Ife 1985:19.
[6] Ife 1985:56.

the reading public, which was at once its strength and its great danger. More moderately, novels were considered a waste of time to write and read; they offered bad examples, especially to women, and they distracted from serious reading. Before the thirteenth century in Spain 'the dissemination of vernacular works for recreational purposes was almost exclusively oral'; writing was for more weighty matters.[7]

Ife sees these objections as having 'their common origin in Plato', even if first-hand knowledge of his work was not widely available at the time. My own contribution is that arguments against fiction (and the arts generally) were constantly being reforged and had no need of a founding ancestor; they were present in the situation; as, in a way, Ife admits when he refers to the congruence of Plato with contemporary protesters against the television as 'a measure of the universal nature of the concern caused by the power of literacy'. As we have seen, not only reading is involved, but literacy does increase the distance of the representation and the nature of the reflexivity, especially in the case of the printed book read silently, in solitude and individualistically, outside any collective context.

Directly we find the novel, we also encounter misgivings about it. As Nelson remarks in a discussion of fact and fiction,

> it was characteristic of the Renaissance attitude . . . to depreciate the value of the narrative component of the work, to refer to that component, with a tolerance sometimes bordering on contempt, as a concession to human weakness of no real worth save as it lured the reader to partake of the solid nourishment he might otherwise reject.[8]

Criticism of the reading of novels is as old as novels themselves and is often contained within them.

Let us turn to the Renaissance and take the great novel of Miguel de Cervantes (1547–1616), *Don Quixote de la Mancha* (1604). The author's preface proclaims it 'a satire on knight-errantry', based on

---

[7] Ife 1985:8.
[8] Nelson 1973:59.

'a true history', 'this most authentic history',[9] in contrast to 'those fabulous extravagancies' which Don Quixote is determined to follow. In English the term 'romance' was used to distinguish such tales from the new realistic 'novels' that were identified with Daniel Defoe and the English bourgeoisie.[10] In French and Italian no such distinction was made and the word 'roman' covered both genres, even though they were distinguished conceptually. It was 'the authority and acceptance the books of chivalry have had in the world, and among the vulgar' that Cervantes set out to destroy. For they pertained to the 'romantic' reconstruction of a feudal way of life that had now gone. The hero, Don Quixote, was one of those 'old-fashioned gentlemen' who passed his time in reading books of knight-errantry. So affected was he that he neglected country sports, the care of his estate and sold many acres of arable land to purchase these books. The process affected his brain and changed his life, so that he was unable to distinguish truth from fiction.

> In fine, he gave himself up so wholly to the reading of romances, that a-nights he would pore on until it was day, and a-days he would read on until it was night; and thus, by sleeping little and reading much, the moisture of his brain was exhausted to that degree, that at last he lost the use of his reason. A world of disorderly notions, picked out of his books, crowded into his imagination; and now his head was full of nothing but enchantments, quarrels, battles, challenges, wounds, complaints, amours, torments, and abundance of stuff and impossibilities; insomuch, that all the fables and fantastical tales which he read seemed to him now as true as the most authentic histories.[11]

---

[9] Cervantes [1993]:11 (Wordsworth Classics, Ware).
[10] See I. P. Watt, *The Rise of the Novel* (London, 1957). The word 'romance' derives from the Old French *romanz*, originally meaning the 'roman' languages of popular speech. On the relationship of *Don Quixote* to earlier romances, which were written in the vernacular (Fr. *romanz*) rather than in Latin, and on the connection of these words to courtly love (giving another meaning of romance) and on the objections of the Church, see the elegantly concise summary in Watt 1996.
[11] Cervantes [1993]:8–9.

It is reading romances that rob him of his senses and led him to take up knight-errantry:

> Having thus lost his understanding, he unluckily stumbled upon the oddest fancy that ever entered into a madman's brain; for now he thought it convenient and necessary, as well for the increase of his own honour, as the service of the public, to turn knight-errant, and roam through the whole world, armed *cap-à-pie* and mounted on his steed, in quest of adventures; that thus imitating those knights-errant of whom he had read, and following their course of life, redressing all manner of grievances, and exposing himself to danger on all occasions, at last, after a happy conclusion of his enterprises, he might purchase everlasting honour and renown.

Consequently he polished up his grandfather's suit of armour that 'had lain time out of mind carelessly rusting in a corner', renamed both his horse and himself and found himself an imaginary mistress.

The theme of the avid reader of romances who lets fiction rule life did not disappear with the passing of knight-errantry. Cervantes, himself, had already written a pastoral romance, *La Galatea* (1582), and went on to write a further one, *Persiles y Sigismunda* (1619), a genre which derived ultimately from the Greeks in works like Heliodorus' *Aethiopica* (*c*.250 CE). While the chivalric branch disappeared, the genre continued in France with Madeleine de Scudéry's *Artamène* (1649–53) and *Clélie* (1654–60).[12] These French romances 'supported the fiction read by English young people of both sexes in the early eighteenth century'. In *The Rape of the Lock*, Alexander Pope writes of the young Baron constructing an altar to Love 'Of twelve vast French Romances, neatly gilt'.[13] That was a just comment on life, for Horace Walpole spent his time at Eton 'buried in romances and novels' to such an extent that the local landscape was completely dominated by images derived from his reading.

The reading public was both male and female and in France

---

[12] Doody 1989:xiv.
[13] Pope, Canto II, 1.161.

both sexes discussed books in the salons of the *précieuses* which were roundly satirized by Molière. Women were not only consumers but producers too. In England, after 1670, many such authors emerged, writing in a new tradition which had abandoned the earlier type of romance with its failure to meet the neo-classical standard of probability. One of these writers was Charlotte Lennox. Harriet, the heroine of her first novel *The Life of Harriet Stuart* (1750), was a great reader of romance by the time she was eleven years old and inevitably interpreted her life in terms of what she had read:

> I compared my adventure with some of those I had read in novels and romances, and found it full as surprising. In short, I was nothing less than a Clelie or a Statine. These reflections had such an effect on my looks and air next day, that it was very visible I thought myself of prodigious importance.[14]

But while it changes her behaviour the author does not see reading romances as leading her heroine astray; there was nothing better for 'retirement' in the country than such an occupation.

That situation was to be transformed with her next publication, *The Female Quixote* (1750), by which time 'the old era of romance' had gone and the new realistic novels of Defoe had taken their place. Her views of romance changed drastically as we see from the very title, where the term 'quixote' is used not as in the contemporary 'quixotic', an attacker of windmills, but as referring to someone whose life is adversely dominated by fiction; that was the situation to which she directed this satirical novel.

The story begins with the Marquis retiring from court after long years of service because of the plots of his enemies, to live in solitude in his castle. There he consoled himself with reading and brought up his motherless daughter, Arabella, to do likewise. She interested herself in the 'great Store of Romances' left by her mother, which were, 'what was still more unfortunate, not in the original *French*, but very bad Translations'.[15] The result was:

---

[14] Lennox 1751:i,8.
[15] Lennox [1989]:7.

Her Ideas, from the Manner of her Life, and the Objects around her, had taken a romantic Turn; and, supposing Romances were real Pictures of Life, from them she drew all her Notions and Expectations. By them she was taught to believe, that Love was the ruling Principle of the World; that every other Passion was subordinated to this; and that it caused all the Happiness and Miseries of Life. Her Glass, which she often consulted, always shewed her a Form so extremely lovely, that, not finding herself engaged in such Adventures as were common to the Heroines in the Romances she read, she often complained of the Insensibility of Mankind, upon whom her Charms seemed to have so little Influence.

Like the original Quixote, she even dressed in an ancient fashion – 'above two thousand years ago' states the author, but in fact following a much more recent trend.

The word 'novel' in the sense of a 'fictional prose narrative of considerable length' had come into English in the previous century. Obviously it was related to the late Latin *novella*, used by Boccaccio for his shorter tales but meaning first in translation 'a novelty', something new, perhaps slightly pejorative. In 1639, J. S., author of *Clidamis*, wrote: 'I present you with this little Novel – which though in it selfe it be nothing – may prove something.' Four years later John Milton speaks in *Divorce* (i,vi), 'this is no mere amatorious novel'. Gradually, the word 'romance' became directed to romantic novelettes aimed principally at a female readership, while 'novel' became standardized for the more 'serious' forms of more realistic fiction.

Nevertheless, it was not only the romances that were condemned. Some writers, like Rousseau in *Émile* (1762), regarded all fiction as harmful, just as he did all theatrical performance. He made but one exception of *Robinson Crusoe* because of its realism. He did not want Émile to read books (which he 'hates') because they teach one only to speak of things one does not know.[16] Barnes sees the distinction between historical accounts and fiction as distinct discourses, as going back those two centuries, although

---

[16] *Émile, ou de l'education*, quoted Watt 1996:173.

it can be seen as parallel to that of the Greeks between *mythos* and *istoria*. Fiction was specifically not true, except in the general sense of 'true to life'. In the romances that flourished before the eighteenth century there was never any question of confusion of life and art since the events were of a fantastic nature. When the question of the 'probability' of the action became a consideration, then a deliberate distinction had to be made, since, in order to establish that probability, authors of fiction often claimed to their readers that their stories were true. Defoe begins the preface to *Moll Flanders* (1722) with the words: 'The World is so taken up of late with Novels and Romances, that it will be hard for a private History to be taken for Genuine . . .' He writes of the author of the story (Moll) concealing her true name in 'the original'. His *Journal of the Plague Year* (1720) is an even more deliberate effort to pass fiction off as literal truth. And in the preface to *Robinson Crusoe* (1719), which claims to be a diary, he writes: 'The Editor believes the thing to be a just History of Fact; neither is there any Appearance of Fiction in it.' A similar equivocation marks Swift's *Gulliver's Travels* (1726) as well as Sterne's *Tristram Shandy* (1760–67). Such confusion is deliberate and even required since the reader's enjoyment of the novel depends upon his ability to enter the world of the writer and to suspend his disbelief.[17]

This is the period when Lévi-Strauss sees a shift of the literary narrative from myth to novel.[18] But novelistic forms existed earlier on in European culture, as well as in other major literate civilizations. For the Renaissance there was the work of Cervantes and other Spanish writers while shorter novelistic forms emerged in Elizabethan England. At the time of the Renaissance, Italian influence had produced the romances of Lyly, Sidney and Nashe. Fictional works resembling the longer novel made their appearance at the end of the seventeenth century with the books of Aphra Behn, then in 1719 came the great success of Daniel Defoe, *Robinson Crusoe*, followed by a series of realistic novels which set themselves apart from earlier romances. Those achievements were

---

[17] Barnes 1994:125.
[18] Lévi-Strauss 1981:652.

followed in 1740 by Richardson's *Pamela* which has been regarded as the first true modern novel, leading directly to the works of Smollett, Fielding and Sterne.

In Europe in this period the long novel represented a new genre and it flourished because of a new public interested in books even before the advent of printing.[19] Not all of this public could actually read, but books became increasingly available and the many benefited from the skills of the few. The *Spectator* of Addison and Steele reached a much larger audience than its circulation figures would suggest by being read aloud. In this way information derived from books was spread among a wider public who learnt not only from the *Spectator* but from *Pilgrim's Progress* and other works of the period. The practice spread to the new genre which had a more 'popular' appeal than much earlier reading material, especially among women. The novelist Hannah More noted that in workshops 'among milliners, mantua-makers, and other trades where numbers work together, the labour of one girl is frequently sacrificed that she may be spared to read those mischievous books to the others . . .'[20]

Later on reading clubs were formed around the novels of Dickens. For these 'mischievous books' had a wider appeal than most earlier writing. The 'serious' works of scholars, largely male, were not fictional but 'factual'. It was not until 1886, according to Taylor, that the annual output of the novel surpassed its nearest rival, theology, 'thereby gaining a lead which it trebled within the course of the next twenty years'.[21] It was not simply the content of books that changed, but the context and the public. The change in the content of communication is clear. Contextually, no longer was reading confined to the study: it now took place in the workshop, around the coffee table, in the bed chamber, none of them places for serious scholarship. This shift was related to the extension of

---

[19] Q. D. Leavis, *Fiction and the Reading Public* (London, 1932); and I. P. Watt, *The Rise of the Novel* (London, 1957).

[20] H. More, *Strictures on the Modern System of Female Education* (1818), VII, 218–19, quoted in Taylor 1943:5.

[21] Taylor 1943:6.

the reading public which increasingly comprised a larger and larger section of the population. That extension had started even before printing but later on some of this was due to the insistence of Protestants, including the growth of Sunday Schools, first established by Robert Raikes in the 1780s; according to the London bookseller, James Lackington, writing in 1795, these were 'spreading very fast in most parts of England, which will accelerate the diffusion of knowledge among the lower classes of the community, and in a very few years exceedingly increase the sale of books . . .'[22] Lackington saw that increase as directly related to the new schools and the new genre.

> It is worth remarking that the introducing histories, romances, stories, poems, etc. into schools, has been a very great means of diffusing a general taste for reading among all ranks of people . . . the children . . . have been pleased and entertained as well as instructed; and this relish for books, in many will last as long as life.[23]

Narrative, then, encouraged an increase in the reading public, an increase that began before printing and which, in turn, demanded more narrative. Moreover, those stories appealed especially to that expanding category of new reader, namely women, who were already important consumers of romances. The expansion of narrative virtually created a new genre for a new audience, an audience that was significantly more female. As Thackeray observed, 'women have always been the great novel-readers of the world'.[24] That thesis had been maintained as early as 1692 by Peter Motteux, and the position remained the same throughout the eighteenth century. Indeed, that was one of the reasons why the novel was regarded with suspicion. It was an expanding genre; it was favoured by women; and it was fictional, it was untruth. It

---

[22] J. Lackington, *Memoirs of the Forty-five First Years of the Life of James Lackington*, (London, 1795) p.427, quoted in Taylor 1943:3. The Sunday School Society was formed in 1785.
[23] Lackington quoted in Taylor 1943.
[24] W. M. Thackeray, *Roundabout Papers* in *Works*, XII, 352 (New York, 1898-9).

also became very popular, especially with the foundation of the lending libraries. For prices of books were still comparatively high, even with printing. So that already in the seventeenth century some booksellers charged a rental fee for the use of books from their shops. The first circulating libraries in London were established in the early 1740s but there had been previous ones in other cities in Britain as well as abroad. Allan Ramsey's library in Edinburgh was already functioning in 1728 when it was denounced by Robert Wodrow as a place where 'all the villainous profane and obscene books . . . are gote doun from London . . . and lent out, for an easy price, to young boyes, servnt weemen of the better sort, and gentlemen'.[25] Such libraries and their contents, especially the novels, were sometimes seen as potentially disruptive of social order, offering as they did alternative scenarios to the lower orders, since these were not simply held in the imagination, as fiction, but might be understood as possible goals and ideals. The lies might become truths, the fantasy turn to reality.

Throughout the period reading fiction was often regarded as a dangerous activity. Even allegories such as Bunyan's *Pilgrim's Progress* (1678) presented dangers for some Baptists. Only in the following century was it generally accepted that 'discourse could now transcend historical truth . . . without being stigmatized as deceitful'.[26] Nevertheless, awareness of the dangers of taking fiction for reality still persisted, especially in non-conformist circles. 'The condemnation of fiction as frivolous and vain', writes Nelson, 'was given added emphasis by post-Renaissance tendencies. Puritanism and the Counter-Reformation were at one in their intolerance of frivolity.'[27] The attitudes towards novel writing in Puritan New England are recalled by Hawthorne's vision of his ancestors commenting upon his work:

> What is he? murmurs one gray shadow of my forefathers to the other. A writer of story-books! What kind of business in life, – what mode of glorifying God, or being serviceable to mankind in his day

---

[25] Quoted in Taylor 1943:25.
[26] Barnes 1994:128.
[27] Nelson 1973:92.

and generation, – may that be? Why the degenerate fellow might as well have been a fiddler![28]

Even in the late nineteenth century, Edmond Gosse was brought up in a household of Plymouth Brethren from which 'story-books of every description' were excluded. A century earlier, in *Northanger Abbey*, Jane Austen takes her heroine to task for her addiction to the Gothic novel, somewhat the equivalent of earlier chivalric romances in which the Aristotelian canon of 'probability' was hardly recognized. Plain Catherine Morland was little interested in books of information although,

> provided they were all story and no reflection, she had never any objection to books at all. But from fifteen to seventeen she was in training for a heroine; she read all such works as heroines must read to supply their memories with those quotations which are so serviceable and so soothing in the vicissitudes of their eventful lives.

But that again was an ironic criticism of a particular tradition rather than of fiction as a whole.

The *locus classicus* for the internal criticism of fiction by an author occurs in Gustave Flaubert's novel, *Madame Bovary* (1857). Like Don Quixote and Arabella, Emma Bovary is effectively 'in retirement', living in the country, married to a boring doctor and having little to do but lead a fantasy life of the imagination in which reading plays a dominant part. But her imagination revolves about contemporary life, not the past.

She bought herself a street map of Paris, and,

> with the tip of her finger, she went shopping in the capital. . . . She took out a subscription . . . to *Le Sylphe des Salons*. She devoured every single word of all the reviews of first nights, race-meetings and dinner parties. . . . She knew the latest fashions . . . she read Balzac and Georges Sand, seeking to gratify in fantasy her secret cravings. Even at the table, she had her book with her, and she would be

---

[28] N. Hawthorne, 'The Custom-House', introduction to *The Scarlet Letter*, quoted in Nelson 1973:114.

turning the pages, while Charles was eating and talking to her. The memory of the Viscount haunted her reading. Between him and the fictional characters, she would forge connections.[29]

Emma uses novels to escape from her own present into another, imaginary present. Books dominate her life. She entertains the young clerk, Leon, with the fashion magazines she has brought along. He 'sat beside her and they looked at the engraved plates together and waited for each other at the bottom of the page. Often she would ask him to read her some poetry . . .'[30] 'And so between them there arose a kind of alliance, a continual commerce in books and ballads . . .' When a certain novel starts a fashion for cactuses, he bought some for her in Rouen. The book overshadows all and directs much of the course of events for those who immerse themselves in it. This gives rise to a dependency on fiction, to a kind of addiction, to a devaluing of the life into which one was born and a hunger for a life of luxury, of a higher stratum. These qualities were thought to be characteristic of 'women in idleness', and a novelist portraying them reveals his own ambivalence towards the feminine; in criticizing them Flaubert is consciously playing with what he called his own feminine disposition.[31]

These criticisms of the effects of fiction did not of course appear only within the pages of the novel itself, where its comments on genre seem to parallel Shakespeare's use of 'a play with a play', or more especially those references to males acting female parts – as a kind of innoculation against the possible critique of cross-dressing. Already in 1666 Pierre Nicole, in *Visionnaires*, described '*un faiseur de romans et un poète de théâtre*' as '*un empoisonneur public*'. One hundred years later Dr Pomme, in *Traité des affectives vapoureuses des deux sexes* (1767), suggests that among all the causes which have harmed the health of women, '*la principale a été la multiplication infinie des romans depuis cent ans*'. Concern about health continued. In 1900 La Baronne Staffe was still worrying about

---

[29] Flaubert [1857]:45. Trans. G. Wall (Harmondsworth, 1992).
[30] Flaubert [1857]:78.
[31] On women and the aspiring lower classes, see E. M. Forster's *Howards End*, 1910.

women in *Le Cabinet de toilette*. '*Restez assise, tard dans la nuit, à lire des romans, voilà ce qui creuse autour des yeux ces terribles petits sillons entrecroisés, qui défigurent le plus joli visage*'.

Moral health was even more at risk. In 1884 Gustave Claudin announced, '*Ce sont surtout les dames légères qui font la plus grande consommation de romans*';[32] while as late as 1938 Jacques Leynon protests that soon every novel will have to have a chapter taking place in a brothel.[33] The Holy Book and Christian literature were approved. That was the fare of Roman ladies in the first centuries of Christianity, not the light novels of today, whose reading is so dangerous.[34] Nor is their perusal confined to the towns: '*l'on rencontre dans la lande la gardeuses de brébis qui a glissé sous son capoulet le mauvais roman passé de main en main, et qu'elle a encore la pudeur de vouloir caché*'.[35]

These ideas were widespread even in this century, especially among Christian moralists who directed their attention to young girls and their novels; the covert pornographic reading of men such as Richard Burton and A.E. Housman (for pornography was predominantly a male activity) received much less attention. Nevertheless, about both there was, and still remains, a measure of ambivalence, especially about fantasy, romances and pornography (was one the counterpart of the other?). But for the same reasons as Benjamin has pointed out with regard to pictorial representation, namely saturation, these have become more, though not entirely, acceptable. Our ambivalence has now been redirected towards the television, that much more intrusive instrument of which its 'rubbish' distracts our children not so much from Christian doctrine and morality (though some groups do effectively protest at that) but from their homework, the completion of which aspiring groups see as determining their future. It is an

---

[32] Claudin, *Mes Souvenirs, 1840–1871* [1884].
[33] *L'Ordre*, 31 October 1938.
[34] Abbé Barbier 1893.
[35] Fernand Laudet, *La Libre Parole*, 25 October 1922. These quotations are taken from G. Bechtel and J-C. Carrière, *Dictionnaire de la bêtise et des erreurs de jugement*, Paris, 1984. I am indebted for this reference to Wolfgang Klein of the MPI für Psycholinguistik, Nijmegen.

ambivalence that arises not always out of the genre itself (though that may also be the case) but out of addiction, of being unable to switch off the box or put down the novel, an addiction that in psychoanalytical theory is linked to masturbation. Indulgence, perhaps luxury, lies at the basis of the objections; it is like a non-procreative sexuality both desired and deplored.

Story telling in Europe had a kind of half-life of its own in the shape of folk tales with 'pagan' implications. That in itself fed into the many religious prejudices against fictional story telling. Many religious leaders in the West, while fully accepting biblical narratives and their derivations, such as the Lives of saints, were set against secular novellas. Certainly, this art form was in bad straits during the early Middle Ages. Later on, Puritan writers were concerned to encourage their flock to read not ordinary novels, but rather sacred narratives, such as *Pilgrim's Progress*. Novel-reading was a frivolous activity, associated (though not exclusively) with women, whereas myth had been men's work; so too was religion. The rise of the (European) novel was not simply a question of the advent of urban, bourgeois society and a new reading public; it was also a matter of clearing away prejudices against fiction, especially secular, imaginative fiction.

These prejudices continued to exist not only for Puritans but even for that great eighteenth-century scholar, himself a novelist, Dr Samuel Johnson, who was well aware of the problem of fiction which he associated with fancy and imagination and contrasted with reason. He puts the following words into the mouth of Imlac, Rasselas's guide to the world outside the Happy Valley:

> To indulge the power of fiction, and send imagination out upon the wing, is often the sport of those who delight too much in silent speculation . . . the ardour of inquiry will sometimes give way to idleness or satiety. He who has nothing external that can divert him must find pleasure in his own thoughts, and *must conceive himself what he is not*; for who is pleased with what he is? He then expatiates in boundless futurity, and culls from all imaginable conditions that for which the present moment he should most desire . . . The mind dances from scene to scene . . . and feasts on the luscious falsehood whenever she is offended with the bitterness of

truth. By degrees the reign of fancy is confirmed; she grows first imperious, and in time despotick. *Then fictions begin to operate as realities* . . .[36]

Such was the distemper of the astronomer who imagined he could control the weather, and while fiction here may apply in the wider sense of falsehood, the passage bears upon the whole question of imaginative narrative, which is on one level a falsehood even though on another it may convey truth allegorically, as does *Rasselas* itself. It is interesting that the attribute so often linked to the evolution of humankind, the capacity to take another's role, is seen as the basis of this distemper of the soul, namely, that he 'must conceive himself what he is not'. All role-playing is threatened by this injunction.

What is illusionary about narrative? Imaginative narrative is, by definition, not an actual account of an experience. It represents reality, but at one remove. Obviously there is a level where it represents experience at second remove, for example, *Daphnis and Chloë* presents the experience of young lovers. But it does not usually pretend to mirror reality directly for it is fiction. It may attempt a show of truth, as Defoe did at the beginning of *Robinson Crusoe*, giving exact times and dates, giving precise circumstances, to make the reader suspend disbelief about the shipwreck. But the very process of getting the reader into this frame of mind is one of creating an illusion, of which the reader is ultimately aware. And if she or he is not, it is still a lie, an untruth.

Nor is Europe the only region in which this controversy about illusion occurred. The very early novel from eleventh-century Japan, *The Tale of Genji* by the Lady Murasaki, achieved a canonical status. Nevertheless, there were many objections to it, for Confucian scholars especially due to 'its fictional character and concentration on amorous relationships'.[37] In the Confucian tradition, the distrust of fiction is usually traced to a saying in the *Analects*: 'The subjects on which the Master did not talk, were

---

[36] Johnson 1759:xliv. In the Penguin edition (ed. D. J. Enright) 1976, pp. 133–4.
My italics. I am grateful to Juliet Mitchell for this and other references.
[37] McMullen: forthcoming.

extraordinary things, feats of strength, disorder, and spiritual beings.' Fiction was among the genres of literature scorned by Confucian literati. McMullen comments: 'In part, this distrust must derive from the rational, didactic tenor of the tradition. Events that involved fanciful or strained credulity also lacked persuasive, narrative power; they were falsehoods, the products of undisciplined, indulgent minds, that could undermine the truth'. This view was also found in Japan and is represented in the *Genji* itself. Indeed, the novel was defended by the commentator of the early Tokugawa period, Banzan, as being a true record; it is not 'a bookful of lies'. Banzan adopted another line too, however, also found in Europe, justifying a genre where 'no fact exists but where a moral truth is comprehended and a fact supplied for it'.

In the Chinese novel *The Golden Lotus (Jinping mei)*, novel-reading was considered bad for the young. That seems to have been more generally the view; the contents of novels were essentially frivolous, and indeed lewd and immoral. In Islam and in Judaism objections seem to have gone deeper. The former made a firm distinction between historical truth and religious myths on the one hand, and creative fiction on the other. That might be used, as in *The Thousand and One Nights*, to distract, but it consisted essentially of a distraction from more serious activities. In the Arab world there were, of course, objections to affabulation in historical and exegetical work, and occasional and casual expression of contempt from a learned standpoint for the Arabian Nights. But such stories were not only read before plebeian audiences; they seem to have been in favour at court, especially those containing *mirabilia*, like the voyages of Sinbad.[38] Once again objections to fiction, ambivalences to created narrative, seem to be rooted in the fact that it 're-presents' reality and is not itself the truth. Even serious narrative may be looked down upon as a way of discovering truth more appropriate for children and for those who need guidance than for the sophisticated searcher, rather like icons for early Christians and Buddhists.

Plaks remarks upon 'the outstanding coincidence that the rise of

---

[38] I am grateful to Professor Aziz al Azmeh of Oxford for his help.

prose fiction occurs nearly simultaneously, step by step, in both China and Europe', namely, in the sixteenth century.[39] He tries to explain the appearance of the Ming literati novels, 'the four masterworks', in terms of the transformation of the Ming economy, factional politics and the expanding educational system.[40]

Similar criticisms arose in China. The concept of *wen*, imitation, is discussed in the context of narrative literature, both historical and fictional. Indeed, the preferred form of fiction is often historical. As Plaks remarks, the act of fiction writing is 'the business of fabricating illusions of reality'; the opening formula of the 'Heart Sutra' that appears in *Jinping mei* reads, 'reality is emptiness, emptiness is reality'.[41] The novels themselves offer criticisms of the way of life they describe, 'the fourfold scourges of excessive indulgence in wine, women, wealth and wrath'.[42] Indeed, the novels themselves also contain some warnings about indulgence in fiction. As in the eighteenth-century English novel, 'the simulated narrator's recurrent use of the *rhetoric* of historiography in introductory sections, asides, and concluding comments . . . to emphasize the sense of judgement going hand-in-hand with the mimetic presentation of events' may encourage the 'sense that the fictional narration may convey generalized truth even where it forgoes the presumption of historical veracity.'[43] Chinese literature has an important didactic component, often with Buddhist monks or Daoist recluses coming forward 'to preach what seems to be the author's own message of worldly renunciation', showing 'the futility of it all'.[44] That moral message poses problems in the face of the manifest content often turning on 'excessive indulgence' and may lead to warnings against fiction, at least in the hands of the young. But there is a wider problem of truth and fiction which no amount of overlap (history/story) can entirely suppress and which emerges in Confucian reactions, such as the criticisms of *The*

[39] Plaks 1977:321.
[40] Plaks 1987:6ff.
[41] Plaks 1987:511–12.
[42] Plaks 1987:505.
[43] Plaks 1977:328.
[44] Plaks 1977:352.

*Tale of the Genji* in Japan. The balance that Plaks sees between the two also contains a contradiction which (under some circumstances) may lead to rejection as well as acceptance.

Particular works might be suppressed for particular reasons. *Water Margin*, a tale of outlawry and rebellion, was thought to encourage brigands. Fiction and reality were merged; the work attacked the abuse of power and misgovernment, and is reformist in tone despite 'the anarchic actions of its heroes'. However, 'many late Ming peasant rebel leaders were taking the names or nicknames of *Water Margin* heroes for themselves.'[45] The authorities perceived this as a threat and ordered the work to be suppressed in 1642. The same happened to *The Merry Adventures of Emperor Yang*, not so much because of 'its explicit descriptions of the emperor's less conventional sexual exploits' but because it raised the question of the limits of loyalty.[46] *The Prayer Mat of Flesh* was 'more effectively proscribed'.[47]

This constellation of opposition to the novel recalls immediately the similar set of societies I have discussed regarding opposition to images and to the theatre, as well as to relics (bones) and flowers. The suspicion that we are dealing with a common phenomenon is strengthened. It is strengthened still further when we look at recent events in China where again we find the suppression of flowers, of religious (and other) images and of the theatre. The novel shares in this history. In the Sichuan town of Yebin during the Cultural Revolution, Jung Chang's mother initially had a hard time in her party cell, being subject to continual criticism. But when she was moved to a new job and a new cell, things were better:

> Instead of sniping at her like Mrs Mi, Mrs Tung let my mother do all sorts of things she wanted, like reading novels; before, reading a book without a Marxist cover would bring down a rain of criticism about being a bourgeois intellectual.[48]

---

[45] Hegel 1981:77.
[46] Hegel 1981:85.
[47] Hegel 1981:227.
[48] Jung Chang, *Wild Swans*, 1991:226.

Jung Chang's father, a devoted Revolutionary, had a worse experience which extended to an attack on his library:

> One day, a group of them [the Rebels] barged into our apartment and marched into my father's study. They looked at the bookshelves, and declared him a real 'diehard' because he still had his 'reactionary books'. Earlier, in the wake of the book burning by the teenage Red Guards, many people had set fire to their collections. But not my father . . .
>
> Then they pulled out his books and threw them into huge jute sacks they had brought with them. When all the bags were full, they carried them downstairs, telling my father they were going to burn them on the grounds of the department the next day after a denunciation meeting against him. They ordered him to watch the bonfire 'to be taught a lesson'. In the meantime, they said, he must burn the rest of his collection.

When she came home that evening, her father had collapsed and was in a state of severe depression.

Some of this activity was an attack on all intellectuals and on the accumulation of knowledge in books. But the attack on reading novels was more specific – as a frivolous waste of time when more important things were happening. Novels were fiction. At one level all these acts can be grouped under the heading 'puritanism' but that is a concept embedded in the religious history of the West and the need is to look for a neutral term (moral rigour?) and a more precise explanation. This I have tried to do in elaborating the notion of cognitive contradictions about fictional narrative as representation.

The discussion has turned on the absence of fictional narrative rather than narrative itself. In earlier literate societies there was clearly some ambivalence about these creative forms, which has largely disappeared in contemporary society marked, as it is, by the mass consumption of the written word. But in the past, such ambivalence, especially when incorporated in religious ideologies, has, like iconoclasm, led to the suppression of novelistic forms at certain periods. Technically the novel became a possible genre with the advent of writing, more particularly with the ease of alphabetic writing, and yet more particularly with printing. But these techniques did not always expand the genre in ways one might expect. There were counter-pressures against such frivolity, such luxury, such deceit, against an activity so often associated with 'women in idleness'. In early New England, under the Commonwealth, in long stretches of the Middle Ages, fictional narratives came under some cognitive resistance leading if not always to complete absence, at least to the rejection from the repertoire of large sections of the community. For example, men may have preferred works of non-fiction. For the distinction between fiction and non-fiction is not simply a library classification. Non-fiction such as biography (largely a Western genre) is about 'real' people: the novel is made up, about imaginary characters.

This situation regarding the written novel seems to parallel that for narrative as a whole in some oral cultures. Once again we get an uneven distribution of a genre one might well expect to be widespread, if not universal. Why do we find the frequent absence of long myths and stories about supernatural agencies? Clearly in some cultures certain individuals are moved to develop long recitations out of the much more fragmentary mythologies that characterize most oral cultures. To do so they have to have a certain institutional context that provides them with a captive audience which will hear them out, because otherwise long recitations stand to be interrupted and their audience distracted. But why is this phenomenon not more frequent than it is? I am suggesting very tentatively that we may also find some cognitive resistance to long recitations, especially stories of this kind, a resistance that questions their 'truth', *yil miong* as the LoDagaa say. Are we being told truth or lies? My answer is speculative but seems more acceptable than the alternatives which rely on vague and circular appeals to culture and tradition. We may see such processes as being involved in handing down an existing situation, but otherwise they tell us nothing about why the LoDagaa have a recitation like the Bagre while the neighbouring Tallensi do not. That I suggest may be related to the uneven distribution of the novel and objections to its existence.

# 7

# Representations of Sex and their Denial

*'Who is at the door?' (Pārvatī asks).*
*'Digambara' (Śiva replies).*
*'Know me to be Maheśvara' [lit. great lord, sovereign].*
*'It is obvious [that you are Maheśvara] by the absence of clothes.'*

In the previous chapters I have discussed the incidence of the rejection of icons, of relics, of the theatre, of myth, and the novel. Each subject came to my attention because of their appearance in different times and in different societies, destroying any notion of universality that may have attached to these forms of representation. I do not, and could not, attempt an exhaustive account of sexual representations, only to indicate their uneven distribution, to link this, where possible, with an ambivalence about their appearance. My suggestion is that the very nature of the process of representation often gives rise to an ambivalence which can result in rejection as well as acceptance and hence is related to their different distribution over time and space. In this chapter I want to turn to the problem arising not so much out of a type of representation itself but rather the subject of these representations. This theme, differences in the representation of nudity and sexuality, grew out of a contrast that struck me many years ago between sculptural representations in India and Africa. In India these were often overtly phallic, as in shrines to Śiva; figures of fertility goddesses and attendants were nude and provocative, whereas, in actuality, Indians cover themselves in cloth and behave with restrained decorum in such matters. In Africa, the gods are portrayed with few clothes, which is how people in tribal societies appear in public, though in state systems cloth is very much part of the hierarchy of behaviour. The sexual characteristics of gods and humans receive little elaboration and the sexuality of altars is implicit rather than overtly expressed. How does this difference relate to the earlier discussion about ambivalence and cognitive contradictions?

The re-presentation of sex constitutes a special case both of verbal construction and of image making. Like the problem of the Creator God, it carries a particularly heavy emotional charge. That does not mean representation is totally banned, but, as with images more generally, it is allowed in some cultures in some contexts, and avoided or forbidden in others. Do these differences in the rejection of, or restraints on, representation relate to some ambivalence, some cognitive contradiction, about our views of the human body and its procreative acts?

I want to consider two aspects of these representations: firstly, variations in the depiction of the human body, as nude or near nude; secondly, variations in the depiction or description of human sexuality. The first will dwell largely on sculpture and painting, the second will touch upon erotica and manuals about sex. But there is another dimension, which we have not encountered before, for there may also be a tension inherent in our treatment of the body and of sexual activity itself, in our reflexive representation of and to ourselves. In other words, there is a double ambivalence: about representation in forms of art, and about the self-representation of the body. Shame, for example, may be involved in both cases. Thus, in the case of sex we are dealing partly with visual representations (with icons), partly with representation in words (as earlier with killing) and partly with an ambivalence regarding the thing itself, all of which are emotional as well as cognitive.

Part of the tension surrounding the body has to do with the use of clothing which we employ to express status, personality, and privacy (or modesty) as well as their opposites, for clothing exposes as well as conceals. Clothing is essential to our existence but it is clearly not 'natural'; it hides what might be regarded as 'the truth'. Or is the truth indeed the clothed rather than the naked self? We come into the world naked but we leave it clothed, for we dress a body for burial. Clothing *is* culture. We often take it off to wash and, usually, to have sex, which is, even more than bathing, a private rather than a public act, a personal coupling that is essential for the continuity of society.

I argue that this tension is partially resolved in art, in representation, where the human body may be portrayed nude, at least in classical and post-Renaissance art, in complete contradiction to actual behaviour. So too gods may go scantily clad when humans are clothed. No particular resolution of this tension is permanent because the underlying contradiction between the natural and the cultural remains, generating or reflecting ambivalences and raising questions about the relation between art and reality. Once again, therefore, we find changing situations over time in one and the same region and we get radically different expressions (or reactions) in different cultures.

## *India*

In this respect India appears to present a very different picture to medieval Europe, especially in the field of religion, though there is plenty of internal contradiction. Nudity does not figure in Indian paintings. Many of these are largely Mogul and influenced by Islam, but others appear earlier as wall paintings in caves and in illustrations to Jain and Buddhist texts. I do not intend to discuss representations of sex or the nude body in the Near East since all human images were rejected in Judaism and Islam, which also seem to have been notably restrained about sex in general. There was some freer expression, however, at the courts of rulers where sexual scenes might be depicted, as it were, privately, despite the general rule to the contrary. That general rule meant that Islam played a puritanical role in its expansion to countries such as India.

When women or men are depicted, as they are often in courting postures in Mogul art, they are normally clothed in the way they are in life.

Hindu gods too are clothed in paintings of the post-Muslim period, though somewhat less fully than humans. But that is not at all the case with Hindu sculpture which is remarkable for its emphasis on the rounded female form, for the busty goddesses, minimally attired, that adorn the walls of temples and of stepwells; breasts and the female body are emphasized, although female genitalia are not fully depicted (they are in the urban art of Japan). That predilection for the nude goes back to the early period of iconic representation as, for example, in figures of the Yakshas, the female nature spirits that decorated the gateways at Sanchi dating from the third century. Those structures were not Hindu but Buddhist, nevertheless, they shared this feature even with Jain temples at Ranakpur and elsewhere. One might even go 2000 years further back and trace a connection with the 'mother-goddesses' of the Harappan culture of Mohenjadaro, except that the iconographic resemblances between Sanchi and the present are much greater than with the earlier period. These resemblances characterize not only nature spirits but major female divinities, the wives and partners of the main male figures of the pantheon, for these gods rarely stand alone.

Although in Indian sculpture men, and especially women, are often scantily clad, in real life people wear great quantities of cotton cloth to cover their bodies and limbs. Nevertheless, the ambiguity towards clothing appears in the fact that nudity may be considered sacred, especially for some monks. I recently accompanied a number of Jains on a pilgrimage to the temple city of Politana, though I acquired very little merit of any kind as I found the upper reaches of the mountain too vertiginous. But on the way we encountered many nuns and a few monks of the Svetambara ('white-clad') sect (there are some 5000 of these ascetics, only a third of them men). Whenever we did so, members of my party greeted them with great respect – 'I could never do that,' remarked my senior companion, 'which is why we honour them.' Now that he has handed over a very successful family business to his son, he spends most of his time in charitable endeavours, supporting the ascetics, the temples and many other Jain activities, as his father had done before him. But the really meritorious acts are not charitable ones but those of monks and nuns who renounce everything.

Svetambara ascetics wear white clothing and carry all their belongings with them. They are required to spend no longer than three days in any one place, after which they have to be on the road again. There are monks but no monasteries in this branch of Jainism; so they seek shelter in school rooms and in any vacant space. Food they beg, or sit down unannounced at a sympathetic table; no notice is given in advance because nothing must be killed on their account (and even vegetarian food involves the slaughter of plants), though they can eat what others have gathered. For orthodox lay Jains too the restrictions placed on the consumption of food are severe; they are strictly vegetarian and my party had to stop to eat at five o'clock because any later in the evening there was a danger of consuming insects along with the meal. Jains are not farmers, since that activity entails the continual taking of animal life unintentionally. Instead they are bankers, merchants, storekeepers, jewellers, clerks, industrialists: a very prosperous community. From that point of view they can afford to reject part of the range of available foods and to get others to cultivate the rest on their behalf.

But they reject available foods in a differentiated way. Orthodox lay Jains have periods of fast when they give up yet more than normal. At times they also reject other activities, such as sex. But the ascetics, both monks and nuns, give this up on a permanent basis. Indeed the Digaṃbara (or 'sky-clad') Jains are yet stricter in their observances; the monks are completely naked; all clothing is rejected and man is stripped down to display the poor bare, forked animal he is. That is not true of the nuns, for it is realized that their naked presence would be 'socially disruptive'; in any case in this sect women were not thought able to obtain liberation.[1] A Digaṃbara woman may rise no higher than to the status of an advanced laywoman (*uttama-śrāvikā*) even though she may be

---

[1] Pal 1994:14–15, 139.

given the title 'nun' (*aryjika*) out of courtesy – the paths of female mendicants are fundamentally different to those of the males.[2] All the *jinas* (teachers) in the Digambara tradition are portrayed nude; only lesser divinities are clothed, though Svetambara *jinas* are depicted wearing a lower cloth. The only female *jina* is Malli, whom the Digambaras turn into a man.

Of course, all societies place prohibitions of this kind on the use of cultural goods and activities. Among the LoDagaa of northern Ghana food prohibitions of a totemic kind are associated with each clan. Looked at from the outside, such avoidances seem to be markers of identity; to the participants they are much more and avoidance keeps the individual out of 'mystical trouble'. Other prohibitions involve clothing. The Bagre neophytes wear no clothes when going through the most intensive part of their initiation, at the time when they are forbidden sex and observe the maximum number of food taboos. In one sense they revert to naked childhood before taking on their new identities. At the same time they are metaphorically buried (or their earlier identity is); painted in stripes of whitewash, they look like living skeletons. Certainly the procedure which they undergo is an idiom of funeral ceremonies when the widow is painted all over in whitewash, indicating her exclusion from ordinary life, indeed undergoing a kind of temporary burial away from it. Other religious activities (for example, among the neighbouring Tallensi) prohibit the wearing of cloth and only skins are to be used by the priests in the major festivals. Hunters have to be celibate before the hunt, widows until their husbands' final funerals, and so on.

There are certain family resemblances between the African and Indian prohibitions. Yet the latter are more specifically ascetic in intent, a matter of turning one's back on luxuries and in some cases even the necessities of ordinary living. Though never nude, Africans in tribal societies often have little clothing; they discard even that in certain ritual ceremonies as a way of enacting a process of rebirth and of cleansing by getting rid of all appurtenances, including body hair as well as artificial coverings. The aim is

[2] Jaini 1991:17–19.

purificatory rather than ascetic. Both elements are present in different degrees but the rejection of luxury can effectively take place only in societies that are highly stratified from the standpoint of consumption. Asceticism is a characteristic of post-Bronze Age Eurasian rather than of African societies.

While the nude body is represented two or three dimensionally in many cultures, what marks off India is its prolific representation of sexuality in major religious contexts, very different from Africa and, indeed, from earlier Europe too. For example, even in the Jain pilgrimage centre at Politana there are many representations on the temple walls of both nudity and sexuality. After the sixth century the nude Jains were often accompanied by female divinities, who were also represented on their own.

> Indeed Jainism, though stricter in its emphasis on the passionless ascetic ideal than Hinduism and Buddhism, has not found it contradictory to mix erotica (*sringara*) and tranquil (*santa*) flavours (*rasa*) in religious art. Just as there is no clear distinction between the sacred and the secular in the life of a Jain, so also the spiritual and sensual realms coexist comfortably in Jain art. The nude Jina is always an athletic, youthful, handsome and well-formed figure who remains unperturbed by the seductively elegant, half-naked female figures standing beside him.[3]

Most remarkable of all, in Hinduism, particularly in Saivite worship, Śiva is 'represented' by an erect penis, a *linga*; the god becomes a penis, the penis becomes god; each becomes the other. The 'fetish' may be interpreted as representing both penis and god in other cultures too; what is particular to India is the explicitness, the openness, of the identification to the actors themselves. Of course, the Śiva-linga is also treated symbolically – 'the all pervading space, thus symbolizes a cosmic form, serenely detached and self-sufficient'.[4] But the overt meaning of the representation, the fact that it is sexual, is in itself important since it will be recognized as such by all those unfamiliar with Tantric interpretations.

---

[3] Pal 1994:28.
[4] Mookerjee 1966.

Of the Pagoda of Konarak in Orissa, which was a major site of sexual sculpture, the archaeologist, Mortimer Wheeler, no prude by English standards, remarked that they were 'dirt and smut'. To his Brahmin companion they represented worldliness on the outside of the temple in contrast to the unworldliness and peace within.[5] But there was more to be said of this phenomenon than either allowed. Let us look at accounts of another major centre for erotic art, Khajuraho. This village in central India has more than twenty magnificent tenth-to-twelfth-century temples, each adorned with hundreds of sensuous sculptures, some of which are explicitly erotic. Since the middle of the nineteenth century when the site, apparently abandoned for 700 years, was described and documented by European scholars, many theories have been put forward to account for the incongruity they saw in religious structures decorated with frankly erotic themes. These sculptures were described as 'indecent', 'offensive' and as indicating 'the depths of decadence that Hindu society had fallen to' before the arrival of the Islamic and, later, the British rulers, thus justifying the invasions by reforming foreigners.

Others saw them as representing the practices of an esoteric Tantric cult. One related Buddhist sect of the seventh century was known as Vajrayāna, the *vajra* being the thunderbolt represented as a double-sceptre and standing for the phallus. The Vajrayāna virtually disappeared in India in the twelfth century following the Muslim conquests but lived on in Tibet, Nepal, China and in parts of southeast Asia. Hindu sexual mysticism was also practised by the Śaiva Śākta of the tenth century whose pantheon is headed by Śiva and Párvatī. Saktism continues to exist today in the form of various orgiastic practices, especially among so-called 'left-path' sects. While classical Hinduism and Hīnayāna Buddhism see salvation coming through a chain of rebirths which includes the control of carnal desire, these sects preached quite the opposite doctrine, emphasizing the widespread ambivalence about sexual beliefs and practices which is seen in attitudes towards their representation.

Yet another interpretation saw these sculptures as the equivalent of the *Kama Sutra*, providing for the sexual instruction of

---

[5] J. Hawkes, *Mortimer Wheeler* (London, 1982), p. 238.

newly-weds. Such volumes were essentially aimed at defining aristocratic (luxury) behaviour, like Castiglione's *The Courtier*. That is true partly because the books were expensive (luxury) products which could be kept as bedside companions only by the rich. Consequently the information they contain is not a general description of behaviour but a set of instructions, developing, for example, new or restricted knowledge concerning sexual positions, and thus contributing to the degree of differentiation of subcultures in Indian society. To a lesser extent the same is true of some Mogul miniature painting, the miniaturization being a partial avoidance of mimesis, of reality.

The sensuality of the temple sculptures looks back to paintings in the Ajanta caves such as the sixth-century paintings of lovers.[6] On the walls of these caves, made for Buddhist *bikhsu* (wandering monks) to form a *sangha* (or community), appear rows of dancers which are mentioned in the fourth-century works of the Sanskrit playwright, Kalidasa. Both have a combination of 'modesty and sensuous pleasure, of offering and withdrawal... As Rabindranath Tagore once put it: he has here "fully painted all the blandishments, playfulness and fluttering of the intoxicating sense of youth, the struggle between deep bashfulness and strong self-expression"'.[7] The counterpart to the sensuality of court life was the ascetic hermitage of the monks associated with the forest.

In this perspective India has been seen by some in the modern West as giving sex, love and physical pleasure their rightful place in human existence, and the temple, as a seat of learning, was held to provide free 'sex education' for all devotees.[8] Shobita Punja, on the other hand, understands these sculptures in Khajuraho as associated with the temple ritual, with the divine marriage of Śiva and Párvatī. One of the central features of temples dedicated to Śiva is his *linga* or mark in the form of a phallus, this example of which one early explorer described as the largest in India. Some

---

[6] C. Sivaramamurti, *South Indian Painting* (National Museum, Delhi, 1968), figure 7.
[7] Gray 1981:18.
[8] Punja 1992:x.

of these lingas are natural formations, immovable; this is what the Byzantines called *acheiropoetai*, 'images born of themselves without the hand of man'.[9] Others are man-made, set up on a *yoni* (female) platform, and considered less sacred, a difference that displays the ambivalence often felt about manufacturing one's own gods; hence the many myths about discovering the 'natural' representations of deities or the holy books descended from heaven. Lingas can be made of any material, including temporary ones out of cooked rice, cow dung, riverside clay and sandal paste. Constructing lingas, according to the *Shiv Purana*, was a way of getting wealth or defeating the enemy. One version of the associated myth tells how Śiva seduced the wives of the sages, his devotees, when they were at prayer. Another relates how it was the devotees who seduced the god. In both cases, when the sages returned they cursed him saying his penis would fall off, which in due course it did. Śiva commanded that from then on people should worship his linga.[10]

In fact, the site of Khajuraho had not been altogether abandoned and the place is still frequented by pilgrims at a particular date in February–March. The congregation is large and the tax revenues that such occasions produced were one of the main reasons for the royal patronage of this and other religious centres. The pilgrims celebrate the marriage of Śiva and Párvatī in which the congregation believes itself to be actually participating, especially in dressing the bridegroom; dressing the god is a recurrent theme in Indian religion. That divine marriage was not altogether a straightforward one because after contracting a union that failed, Śiva attempted to conquer all desire and his later marriage came about as the result of penance.

There is another level of explanation of religious erotica that may be connected with the Tantric vision but has much wider ramifications – the metaphor is quasi-universal. The sexual union of man and woman is seen as representing the union of the male and female forces that lie at the basis of creation, the unity arising out of duality. 'When represented or pictured in anthropomorphic

---

[9] Clément 1995:23.
[10] For an account of Śiva and sexuality, see O'Flaherty 1973.

forms, "they embrace each other, touching at all points of contact". This shows a total resolution of opposite forces as the two become essentially one.'[11] Such notions are obviously close to the Chinese concepts of the yin and the yang and, in a less generalized, more concrete form are expressed in the Bagre myth of the LoDagaa where the rain represents the male element fertilizing the female earth.

A more performative version of this idea is used by Desai in her account of Khajuraho, especially of the earliest erotic art (*c*.950 CE) in that centre, the first examples elsewhere dating from the fifth century CE. The architect, she explains, was quite familiar with the use of the erotic motif in temple art as an *alamkāra* or ornament 'auspicious and protective in function'.[12] Sexual motifs such as *mithuna*, the couple in coitus, were 'believed to be endowed with magical powers for prosperity, luck, auspiciousness', and to protect from and ward off evil spirits and calamities. The exposure of nudity, for example, is described as a fertility ritual. Such themes were apparent by that date in many temples of the Western Deccan; the erotic motifs at Khajuraho had their roots in a much wider tradition in Indian art, in the temples of various sects and religions so that the explanation has to be somewhat more general than the rather specific one of re-enacting a marriage.

Desai argues that any interpretation must take into account several levels, since what is involved was 'intentional language' endowed with double or triple meanings to disguise certain doctrines. What we find is the philosophical level, the magical one and the 'delight to people', the sexual one. Some representations may represent only one of these levels and some require a literal interpretation, others a symbolic one. Both are potentially possible.

While the male–female relationship receives its extreme expression in the explicit portrayal of the sexual act in the temple sculptures, sexual relationships are also central to earlier books of instruction such as the *Kama Sutra* of the first century CE which may appear in vivid graphic forms as well. Under Islamic influence

---

[11] Mookerjee 1966:29.
[12] Desai 1984:144.

Mogul miniatures are somewhat more restrained; nevertheless, a constant theme of such art is courtship and lovemaking among the aristocracy.

It is the contrast that strikes one between ordinary life and religious representation. In India, women are heavily clothed. While their dress occasionally reveals bare flesh at the waist, skirts are long, the breasts firmly bound (though that is more recent), and the whole enveloped in a loose cloth or *sari* that conceals the curves of the body. This is true of upper-caste women in general, but less so of working women, such as Maharashtran fisher folk who will pull up their skirts around their thighs and are less careful about their bodily covering. The deities, on the other hand, are usually portrayed with a minimum of clothing. Bosomy goddesses lean against bare-waisted gods in a total iconic reversal of everyday life.

There is a similar reversal in the representation of sexual behaviour. In ordinary life there is little obvious sexuality displayed between men and women. Of course, there are exceptions; the aristocracy indulge in courting behaviour; as in other complex societies, prostitution is well developed and in ordinary life assignations between the sexes clearly take place outside as well as inside the marriage bond. Once again there is a class element; Freeman's account of *harijan* life provides evidence of frank talk of sex that is also true of some recent *filmi* novels. But in life there is little explicit reference to sexuality in act or in talk. While figures of gods may be 'naturally naked', in iconic displays such as the temple of Konarak, everything goes; the figures are aggressively sexual. Once again we find iconic (or representational) reversal. What is shown openly in textbook and temple is in life enacted in complete privacy. Such a discrepancy is likely to raise cognitive contradictions in the minds of some of the actors at least; or, alternatively, this discrepancy may be a result of their prior existence.

## *Africa*

In Africa we find abundant representations of nudity but few of sexuality. Indeed, the nudity is largely asexual as one would expect in cultures where there was often limited access to cloth. In West African sculpture there is little explicit emphasis on sexuality as distinct from gender. The abundant wooden figures of women of the Senufo are bare breasted and there is little iconographic reversal since the people themselves, at least the 'pagans', do not wear much cloth. Or rather, cloth is a variable. The Asante of the forest area of West Africa went well clothed on most occasions, beating cloth from the bark of trees in earlier days, and later weaving materials from cotton and silk into their splendidly colourful *kente* cloths. These people, living in a relatively complex state, looked down upon many of the inhabitants of northern Ghana such as the 'naked Lobi' as human booty. But from their standpoint the latter, while scantily clad, were never totally nude, for men wore penis sheaths and women perineal bands and bunches of leaves.

In wooden sculpture, genitalia, especially of males, are portrayed but rarely in the exaggerated form found in Hindu worship; those of women are only sketchily outlined. Sexuality does play some part in the sculpture associated with the female initiation rites of the Bemba of present-day Zambia, and has been described in Richards's account of *Chisungu* (1956). Other examples are found among neighbouring Congo peoples who are also distinguished by their matrilineal institutions, though the association may well be fortuitous.

While visual representations of sexuality are few, and textual ones necessarily absent in non-literate societies (folk tales and legends give the topic little attention), references are made in the rare secular theatre that has been reported for the Ibibio in southeast Nigeria and the Bamana of Mali. Sexual themes enter into the plots of the stories themselves, and among the Bamana one finds 'the man with a long penis' and 'the woman who loses her vagina in the river'.[13] Performances include erotic dancing and the invention of new, often bawdy, tales.[14] That is also true of the Ibibio where many of the plays have sexual themes. In one skit a man's

---

[13] Brink 1977:36.
[14] Brink 1977:62.

penis is cut off. At those performances witnessed by the Messengers, the anthropologist's wife was confronted by an actor who prodded her with his wooden penis.[15] In the 1930s, Jeffrey commented on the 'crude bawdyism of the peasant', which was possibly encouraged by the fact that men played women's parts. For the actors circulate among the audience flirting with the men. Whether homosexuality is connected with the theatre for this reason is not stated but that may well be the case. Although women actors appeared early on in Chinese opera, sometimes in male roles, young male actors nevertheless became sexual substitutes for women, especially when legal constraints led to the decline in numbers of 'flowers' (women) in the nineteenth century.[16] In the present century, the film *Farewell, My Concubine* portrays a theatre troupe consisting entirely of males, orphans brutally trained for their parts from childhood, some of whom eventually find it difficult to separate life and art.[17] But equally I have seen opera in Hong Kong where women played the leading parts, both male and female. Cross-dressing and transvestite behaviour is characteristic of much early theatre, giving rise to accusations of perversity and to anti-theatrical prejudice but also acting, I have suggested, as a brake on illusion.

Ibibio songs celebrate women as more strongly sexed, a belief said to be related to the practice of clitoridectomy by women's fertility associations during the fattening period prior to marriage. It is believed that

> wives are the repositories of sexual knowledge, are usually the initiators of coitus and often assume the female-superior position, are capable of multiple orgasms nightly, are far more adulterous than men and threaten the physical and spiritual strength of their husbands (as do female witches who come in the night to copulate).[18]

---

[15] Messenger 1971:24.
[16] Mackerras 1983:105.
[17] The film of Chen Kaiga.
[18] Messenger 1971:219.

That idea is obviously part of a set of male fantasies that has its counterpart in many other societies, for example, in the Plain Girl of the Chinese handbooks of sexual instruction.

Theatrical expressions of sexuality clearly differ radically between societies, as the presence and form of the theatre do. I have no evidence from Africa that cultures also differ over time. In general, pictorial representations of sexual acts seem to have been rare for as long as we know; although these appear in the few examples of theatre (entertainment) we have, they are uncommon in ritual. Verbal expressions, however, were more common and did vary in this respect in adjacent cultures. The anthropologist, Meyer Fortes, observed a difference in Ghana between the Asante (who were relatively free) and the Tallensi (who were relatively tight). A similar contrast obtained even between the Tallensi and their close neighbours, the Gorensi. I do not have much to add for the LoDagaa and Gonja since I heard few expressions or stories about sexual activity. That corresponds to my general view of most African societies, in which nudity is sexually neutral and sexuality little represented. But there is enough evidence to suggest some ambivalence about its open expression (or suppression) leading to differing outcomes in different areas and different contexts.

In previous chapters I have seen cognitive contradictions as appearing in the more advanced, literate, societies as well as in the simpler oral ones, but these have taken different forms in Eurasia, on the one hand, and Africa on the other. In the present instance the overt sexuality of Indian sculptural representations has little counterpart in Eurasia either westward in earlier Europe or eastwards in China. Let us look briefly at these two situations.

## *Europe*

As before, I turn first to the question of nudity in early representations. Greek statues, especially of gods, were often of unclothed figures. These statues were usually of males but sometimes of females, not always entirely nude. Nudity represented purity. In Plato's *Giorgias*, Socrates recounts the story of Zeus' establishment of a system of law in the afterlife. Pluto and others had complained of miscarriages of justice because many wicked souls were dressed in the trappings of physical beauty, that is in their clothes of which their splendour, symbolism, and inversely their poverty influenced the decision of the court. So he ordered 'they must all be tried naked, that is, when they are dead, and to ensure complete justice the judge too must be naked and dead himself, viewing with bare soul the bare soul of every man as soon as he is dead, when he has no kinsmen to aid him and has left behind on earth all his former glory'.[19] Justice required nudity. In life people were normally well clothed although, for males, great importance was attached to nakedness in competing for the Olympic Games and exercising in the gymnasium. Standards were not always the same throughout the ancient world. The Spartans shocked the Athenian Greeks by allowing women to compete in their games lightly clothed, while some later Romans saw all such behaviour as a sign of real decadence.[20]

These variable attitudes to nudity were paralleled by major gender differences in art. Despite the existence of prehistoric Venus figures and the exquisite Cycladic dolls of the Mediterranean world, the Greeks developed the nude female form later than the male. We have only two sculptural records of nude women from the fifth century and there is evidence of some active antipathy well into the fourth. The people of Cos rejected the nude Venus of Praxiteles in favour of one that was draped; since the statue had to find a home, it was erected at Cnidos instead in about 350 BCE.[21] In fact, this nude figure of Venus may represent oriental influences among the Greeks who sometimes draped the goddess in a moist shift to cover her body.

The nude ceased to be produced before the end of classical antiquity; no new statues were made after the second century CE. Its absence became part of the aniconic, puritanical trend that dominated early Christianity and objections to statues, especially

---

[19] Plato, *Giorgias* 523, translated W. Hamilton (Harmondsworth, 1960).
[20] Clark 1956:21.
[21] Clark 1956:71.

secular ones, continued throughout the Middle Ages, though occasionally they made an appearance. When they did return, whether in the Middle Ages or the early Renaissance, all gods were clothed and, in Sir Kenneth Clark's words, nudes 'have lost their meaning'. The notion of the unclothed body in art, whether in painting or sculpture, was rejected except for some near-nude figures of Adam and Eve, who were in a state of pre-lapsarian purity. After their fall, nudity became a sign of the inferiority, even bestiality, of wild men or savages. As a result, nudity could signify both inferiority and innocence. The Expulsion from Eden, when 'our ancestors' first knew shame, was one of the five areas in Christian art where nude figures were appropriate. The others were the Flagellation, the Crucifixion, the Entombment and the Pietà, all events dominated by the pathos surrounding the dying Christ. However, in the representation of these events Christ was rarely completely nude; a loin cloth covered his genitals. Images of the crucifixion appear no earlier than the fifth century and are of two types, the undraped Antioch figures and the Jerusalem type in a long tunic. Both continued to be made but there was some ambivalence attached to the first, to the nude Christ. Towards the end of the sixth century, Gregory of Tours tells how in the Cathedral of Narbonne there was a painting of a naked Christ on the Cross, but the Lord appeared to the Bishop in a dream and commanded that His body be covered with drapery.[22]

Under Charlemagne antique forms were consciously imitated. With the later ninth century we find some nude figures with drooping heads, especially of the suffering Christ echoing perhaps the drooping penis. The nude, however, had largely disappeared between late Rome and the golden doors of the Baptistry of the cathedral of Florence carved by the sculptor Ghiberti (*c*.1378–1455) with his creation of Eve. Then, during the first hundred years of the classical Renaissance, the nude flourished exuberantly in secular as well as in religious contexts; at one extreme was Michelangelo's *Last Judgement*, at the other, nude females on door-knockers and on the carved handles of knives and

[22] Clark 1956:223.

forks. It was still objected by some that nakedness was unbecoming in the representation of Christ and His saints but others, such as Veronese, protested that in such images there was nothing that was not spiritual.[23] Disagreement continued. In 1564, Pope Pius IV declared that some of the figures in Michelangelo's *Last Judgement* were indecent and ordered the artist, Daniele da Volterra, to paint in some loin cloths. Even during the recent restoration of the Sistine Chapel these additions were left as 'facts of history'.[24]

Three-dimensional statuary in the round was especially at risk to such objections. In the fourteenth century, according to Ghiberti, even before the Italian Renaissance, an ancient statue was dug up in Siena and erected in the town centre. In 1357 a citizen made a speech pointing out all the disasters that had befallen the city from the time it was set up: 'since idolatry is not permitted by our faith there can be no doubt whence these disasters arise'. The prohibitions of the Old Testament were still present in people's minds as were contemporary ambivalences about such representations. So the statue was taken down by public decree and buried in Florentine territory in order to bring bad luck to the enemy.[25] The ambivalence towards statuary, especially of the nude, is brought out by the fact that, fifty years earlier, Pisano had given it positive value by placing a replica of the Venus Pudica as one of the Virtues on the pulpit of the cathedral of Pisa, one of the first examples of the classical revival in the 'false Renaissance'. But problems continued, as we see from Siena as well as from the fact that in northern Europe the drawing of the nude presented considerable difficulties even for some great artists such as Dürer, although that was not the case for his contemporary, Cranach, whose Eve is naked except for a hat.[26]

That retreat from the nude largely disappeared at the Renaissance, after which Nead sees the female nude as particularly

---

[23] Clark 1956:23.
[24] *The Times*, 19 June 1995, p. 5.
[25] Clark 1956:89.
[26] Compare Donatello's David (for example, in B. A. Bennett and D. G. Wilkins, *Donatello*, Oxford, 1984, p. 216).

significant within Western art and aesthetics, 'a metaphor for the value and significance of art in general', symbolizing 'the transformation of the base matter of nature into the elevated forms of culture and the spirit'. It must be understood as 'a means of containing femininity and female sexuality' in a 'patriarchal' culture.[27] The theme of her study, she writes, is 'frames and framing'. Art of course frames all experience, all sense impressions, whether of a flower or a body; that is what it is about. Greek art frames male nudes more insistently than female ones. The problem still remains of why one society or one period frames female as distinct from male nudes, or why there are no nudes at all, no representation of explicit sexual acts or no representations.

If nudity was rare in European representations after the Roman period, sexuality was more so. This had been frequently represented in classical times, not only on Attic vases (especially homosexual acts) but also in wall paintings such as those at Pompeii, where they appeared in brothels, possibly to stimulate the appetite of clients. However, except in representations of Adam and Eve, in the Christian period there was little reference to the sexual characteristics of male and female, and none to sexuality itself. That is not to say there was no overt phallic element in 'popular art'; about that we know little, except that on the borders of the Bayeux tapestry, and on the margins of Gothic manuscripts we find drawings of sexual acts.[28] But in high art, sexuality, like the nude, effectively returned only with the secular art of the Italian Renaissance.

Accounts of sexuality in literature were more frequent. *The Miller's Tale* of Geoffrey Chaucer develops a long line of medieval *fabliaux* that are much more explicit than the oblique tradition of courtly love associated with the troubadours and the *Minnesänger*. Boccaccio was in the same tradition as Chaucer, as were monkish productions such as the Carmina Burana. There were fictional accounts of sexual experiences (quite distinct from the romance of the *Roman de la Rose* tradition), but these certainly did not meet

---

[27] Nead 1992.
[28] Camille 1992.

with universal approval. Such manifestations divided society, members of which held radically differing views about propriety depending on their social position and their individual tastes.

More practical advice about sexual behaviour was earlier offered by sex manuals with which the ancient world seems to have been supplied. With one exception no examples have survived but the names of their authors are found in the writings of Christian Fathers such as Clement of Alexandria and Justin Martyr 'who condemn these pagan works as licentious, immoderate and excessive'.[29] Known as 'writers of shameless things', these authors apparently gave lists of recommended positions for heterosexual intercourse and much more besides; their work seems to have been parodied in sections of Ovid's *Art of Love*.

How complete was the disappearance of these manuscript books as a result of Christian Fathers clamping down on openness in bodily and sexual matters? Of course, there are many references to sexual matters in the Bible, though there seems to be a significant change in attitude between the Jewish and Christian sections. The Old Testament (as well as the Mormon Bible which followed it closely in the nineteenth century) has many references to sex, though these were often re-interpreted by later commentators. The extreme case of this process, displaying changing attitudes over time and an ongoing ambivalence, is the attempt of the Christian Church to turn the highly erotic *Song of Songs* into an allegory of Christ's relationship with his church. Allegorical interpretation is an obvious technique for dealing with a text that no longer reflects current attitudes; at the same time allegory, as an original creation, exists in its own right as a mode that continues to maintain an ambiguous relation between the literal and layered meaning.

Whatever the religious pressures in favour of suppression, there is obviously no question in matters of sex (and even of the body, since we all have, at times, to derobe) of a complete elimination of interest in such matters as well as in their visual and verbal representations. The marginalia in manuscripts of the Middle Ages demonstrate this continuing concern. Visually, in painting and

[29] King 1994:3.

sculpture, we continue to have images of Adam and Eve. There is even some evidence of the existence of books on sexual description, for example, in references to the library of a certain dean of Cadiz,[30] as well as from literature. Just as Ovid appears to be making an allusion to the Roman manuals that have largely disappeared, the incident in *Sir Gawain and the Green Knight* where the lady attempts to seduce the hero appears to suggest formalized procedures for seduction which may have achieved written expression. Certainly that happened less overtly in the tradition of courtly love.

The representation of sexuality cannot be separated from the practice, especially from the question of constraints or freedoms, since at one level we are dealing with the problem of whether the image or the word does indeed represent the actuality of human action and belief. We have noted profound differences between many representations of the human figure in the Renaissance and the care that in everyday life people took to clothe themselves abundantly, to hide their nudity, sometimes even in bed. Art deviates radically from actuality and one of the attractions of the nude or of the pornographic is precisely that this is *not* how life is usually lived (though their presence in representation may change the nature of that life as happens today perhaps with video tapes).

How was the representation of sex related to its practice? The practice has always been accompanied, throughout human societies, by a measure of denial. The latter may take the form of taboos on persons, taboos on place or taboos on time (not to speak of taboos on methods). Take the LoDagaa of northern Ghana. With regard to persons, they prohibit intercourse with any 'sister' or 'mother' (or 'brothers' and 'fathers'). Regarding place, sex is forbidden out of doors. Regarding time, it is taboo with menstruating, pregnant and parturient women, with widows until released by the final funeral, and in a certain sense with all married women other than one's wives. In other words, restraint is a transcultural aspect of sexual behaviour, but on the other hand, chastity, total

---

[30] See Linehan, forthcoming, concerning the 'most pornographic specimen of Alfonso's poetry'.

abstinence, is virtually non-existent for men or for women, either as a practice or as an ideal. Asceticism in matters of sex does not figure significantly. Among the LoDagaa all girls get married soon after puberty and the sleeping arrangements are such in polygynous households that a man sleeps in the room of every spouse in turn, even if he does not have sex with them all.

The contrast with Christianity, especially early Christianity, is clear. In his book, *The Body and Society*, Peter Brown offers a study of:

> the practice of permanent sexual renunciation – continence, celibacy, life-long virginity as opposed to the observance of temporary periods of sexual abstinence – that developed among men and women in Christian circles in the period from shortly before the missionary journeys of Saint Paul, in the 40s and 50s CE, to a little after the death of Saint Augustine, in 450 CE.[31]

Only at the end of that period does the cult of the Virgin Mary emerge.

> Clerical celibacy, though finally advocated by some, was practised in a manner totally unlike that now current in the Catholic Church. The ascetic movement, though a constant presence in much of this period, lacked the clear and orderly profile later associated with the Benedictine monasticism of the Latin West.[32]

Brown is concerned with the specificity of Christian beliefs and practice, so he does not deal with the Roman, Greek and Jewish worlds. Indeed, he thinks that 'the sharp and dangerous flavor of many Christian notions of sexual renunciation, both in their personal and their social consequences, have been rendered tame and insipid, through being explained away as no more than inert borrowings from a supposed pagan or Jewish "background"'. He does accept, however, that 'an effort to do justice to the particularity of certain strains of Christian thought and practice should

---

[31] Brown 1988:xii.
[32] Brown 1988:xv.

not be held to justify the systematic dismissal of the complex and resilient ecology of moral notions that characterized the Mediterranean cultures of the age . . .'.[33] At the same time he concentrates on the particularities of Christianity and of the age, reinforcing Foucault's warning about 'the cozy, even arch, familiarity with which a modern person often feels entitled to approach the sexual concerns of men and women in a distant age'. However, apart from the differences, there are certain similarities which are not necessarily to be explained by 'inert borrowing' but rather with reference to parallel solutions to common problems.

The problem of differences and similarities raises the obvious but continuing dilemma of the enquirer into human action. Obviously, one must allow for cultural and individual differences. But, especially in the field of heterosexual behaviour, closely linked as it is to biological continuity, there are also some quasi-universal aspects, one of which I would argue is a certain ambivalence about the sexual act, and more generally nakedness. That ambivalence characterizes 'savage' as well as 'civilized' society, but in different ways. However, there are some broad differences (as well as other individual ones). I would suggest that asceticism of the Christian type, including sexual renunciation, can be found in other world religions. It is especially well developed in Christianity, but there is an obvious comparison with Buddhism. Monasticism of the Tibetan variety institutionalizes celibacy, both for males and females; celibacy, in turn, is linked (either as consequence or as cause) to the desire to exclude a plurality of sons from inheriting or even reproducing (hence the preference for polyandry), as well as to a high percentage of unmarried women.[34] Among the Jains too, while they have no monasteries, monks and nuns give up not only sex, a wide variety of foods and a settled dwelling place, but in some cases, even clothing. Hinduism has few permanent monks, let alone monasteries; the priests are married Brahmins. But the notion of renunciation is nevertheless deeply embedded in Hindu thought and action. One has only to recall the personal history of

---

[33] Brown 1988:xvi.
[34] See J. Goody 1990, ch. 5; Carrasco 1959.

Mahatma Gandhi in which the renunciation of the eating of meat, of violent action to humans and of sexual intercourse was interwoven in complex ways. Even the idealized practice of sex, mainly of *coitus reservatus*, that was also adopted in China, implied an ambivalence about the act, which constituted a loss as well as a gain. There is danger as well as delight both about the act and about the other actor (women, for men; men, for women).

Whatever the medieval situation, that changed dramatically after the Renaissance with the reassertion of bourgeois merchant culture against an ambience that had been dominated by the Church. That we see, for example, in the new demands merchants made upon the educational system.[35] A critical factor here was the development of the printing press which permitted a wider and more rapid distribution of written knowledge, including sexual knowledge, especially among the middle classes. Visually they had only some limited access to the reproductions of representations of nudity and of sexual play in post-Renaissance art such as that of Titian, for the clientele for the originals was largely aristocratic and the upper echelons of Church and bourgeoisie. However, even the largely illiterate majority was affected by the increased circulation of written matter, since part of what circulated consisted of graphic material, calendars as well as the illustrations to popular ballads. Moreover, the transfer of other forms of knowledge, even when generated in the written channel, can be carried out by word of mouth.

Apart from the question of transmission, however, in these matters of sexual behaviour there was undoubtedly some resistance to adopting the practice of other classes, although in different contexts (the design of material objects for instance) there was much emulatory adoption. In their social behaviour lower groups might desire to differentiate themselves as 'respectable' not only against the licentious activities of higher ones but even against that of the non-respectable poor.

Attitudes to sexual behaviour were certainly class based. In the country and in towns, upper seems to have been distinguished

---

[35] See Pirenne 1929.

from lower by its greater freedom or licence, depending upon the point of view of the observer. The local French historian Beteille has documented the reluctance of peasant women in nineteenth-century France to expose themselves to their husbands in households where there was multiple occupancy of rooms for sleeping. In the towns similar attitudes are recorded. In working-class families it was common for people to sleep more than one in a bed. The lack of privacy among the poor led to the development of particular habits. 'Typically, everyone slept in their underclothes and avoided undressing in front of other family members.'[36] In the Viennese working class, 'parents took great care to avoid appearing naked before their children'.[37] Despite the close physical proximity, they grew up without ever being aware of their parents making love. Even today in middle-class Europe, similar reticences are common. But the very close presence of children may have earlier inhibited the activities of the couple, although other internal restraints were clearly felt. 'Non-coital forms of sex play were clearly beyond the pale for the vast majority of working-class couples, a testament to the rigidity of their sexual socialization.'[38]

So in Europe the situation varied over time, both with regard to practice and to representations. Greece and Rome represented the human body as nude. Christianity changed all that (except for the Crucifixion and the Fall), until the Renaissance when nudes again became popular. There was little by way of representation of sexuality in the high artistic culture but some in marginalia. After the Renaissance, however, sexuality became a sub-theme in the artistic, and to some extent the literary, world, except during periods of dominance by puritanical Protestants and their Catholic equivalents. In England, the Cromwellian situation was reversed by the advent of aristocratic Restoration drama and with the early realistic novel such as Defoe's *Moll Flanders*. All this was 'dressed' sexuality but it represented a substantial shift of focus. In the visual arts that change was illustrated in the works of satirists such as

---

[36] Seccombe 1993:144.
[37] Seccombe 1993:145.
[38] Seccombe 1993:161.

Hogarth and of cartoonists such as Rowlandson, expanding dramatically the repertoire of sexual and bodily representations.

The nineteenth century was marked by a greater puritanism in bourgeois quarters but nevertheless an erotic undercurrent came to the fore in the life and work of figures such as Richard Burton (who translated not only *The Thousand and One Nights* but also the *Kama Sutra*) and his colleagues. Sexuality is now very much about clothing, not so much about nakedness but about the very act of undressing; the excitement lies in the de-robing, not in the nakedness itself, potential or otherwise – a very different interest from Greek art. Gradually, the sexual undercurrent became increasingly acceptable and sexual knowledge more public, so that sexual representation is now a dominant theme, especially in the cinema.[39]

Tensions continued to exist, however. Puritanism objected to that which the Renaissance encouraged. Two different trends were present: knowledge expanded through the nineteenth and twentieth centuries and, at the same time, the Reformation led to a withdrawal of the interest in sexuality and nudity which had developed since the fifteenth century. Nudes were hardly a prominent feature of the early New England living space; indeed aniconic trends were dominant both there and among the Puritans of the Old World. Their objections gradually weakened with the growth of knowledge and the rise of secularization, though they are still found among some fundamentalist sects and almost universally regarding representations suitable for children. Nevertheless, as Benjamin argues for images generally, representations of sex are now so common a feature of the many colour magazines decorating newsstands that the element of rejection has been largely over-ridden by sheer numerical dominance.

## *China*

Moving westwards to Europe from India, we have found a much greater restriction on the expression of nudity and sexuality, at least

---

[39] On sexual knowledge, see Porter and Teich (eds) 1994.

until the revival of classical forms in the Renaissance. There is an obvious tension between private behaviour and public expression which leads at times to greater openness and then to periods of repression.

That situation appears to repeat itself when we make the eastwards passage to China where visual expression is singularly restrained, though this is not altogether the case with written works either of fiction or of instruction. I start, as before, with the nude. According to Clark, 'The offering of the naked body for its own sake as a serious subject of contemplation, simply did not seem to occur to the Chinese or Japanese mind . . .'[40] although in later Japanese prints such representations appear as part of *Ukiyoe*, 'the passing show of life'. That seems to have been true of Chinese painting and of sculpture. The Buddha may be half clothed but other figures like Guanyin are fully dressed, while Confucian painting is very restrained, with the immortals dressed in human clothing. But another element altogether enters with the written word, whether we look at novels or at instructional material.

Classic Chinese novels, such as *The Dream of the Red Chamber*, contain a great deal of bawdy material, and more so in the *Golden Lotus* and the *Prayer Mat of Flesh*. An even greater openness is found in instructional handbooks about sex and in the prints that accompanied them. These handbooks are recorded from the beginning of the Common Era but no doubt existed well before. As in India they were largely directed to the upper classes, although the same constraints on production were not present since a mechanized form of reproduction existed from an early period. In these works women are often the guardians of the arcana of sex and the repository of all sexual knowledge.[41] At an earlier period Confucians approved of the principles embodied in these handbooks, provided that practice was confined to the bed chamber and was for procreative purposes only. All physical contact with women had to be limited to the marriage couch.[42] During the Han period

[40] Clark 1956:7.
[41] van Gulick 1974:8.
[42] van Gulick 1974:59.

(202 BCE to 220 CE), handbooks were illustrated with drawings of sexual positions and the text was written in the form of dialogues between the Yellow Emperor and one of his female teachers, usually the Plain Girl. These books were well known among better-off families and might form part of a bride's trousseau. It was the custom of rich parents in Japan until well into the nineteenth century to give their newly-married daughter a set of these pictures. They were placed by the bedside to stimulate the responses of a bashful companion. One poem refers to their use for just this purpose:

> And you feast and sport with her,
> Pointing at the pictures you observe their sequence,
> While she keeps being bashful and ashamed
> And coyly protests –

Despite what is on one level an openness towards the representation and associated practice of sex, the system of beliefs on this topic shows much ambivalence. In China a sexual mysticism was developed, closely resembling that of the Indian Buddhist and Hindu practices known as Tantrism, of which one central tenet was 'making the semen return' in *coitus reservatus*. The semen withheld is then supposed to be transformed into the Elixir of Life.[43] Such beliefs were linked to particular sects and in accounts of sexual intercourse influenced by those cults the man is instructed on how to retain his semen, stressing the female component of his body, at the same time as bringing the woman to orgasm. In so doing he is thought to overcome the inherent dualism of the human body.

Van Gulick sees the tradition of these handbooks on sex as passing from India to China with the attachment to Buddhism, but sexual mysticism based on *coitus reservatus* seems already to have flourished under Daoism in the early years of our era and so may

---

[43] For the continuation of such beliefs into the present, see the references to Dr Xia in Jung Chang's autobiography, *Wild Swans* (1991). Or, in my own field-notes, the beliefs of a young shopkeeper in Degham, Gujarat.

have travelled in the opposite direction, possibly through the mediation of the seventh-century King of Assam who claimed Chinese origin and had regular relations with the Tang court.[44]

Attitudes to sex were rarely homogeneous at any one period, however, and the situation changed radically over time. As we have seen there were always some Confucian reservations about such texts. Early translators of Indian works up to the Tang period (618–907) tried as far as possible to spare Confucian sensibilities; for instance, they glossed over Sanskrit passages about lovemaking and prostitution. Later on, during the Tang dynasty, when Chinese Buddhism was flourishing and the erotic Tantric works had been introduced from India, such reticence was no longer necessary. But when Neo-Confucianism triumphed during the Southern Sung, a drastic expurgation of Buddhist texts was undertaken. There were similar swings in Europe.

In the fourteenth century an authoritarian Chinese state, based on Neo-Confucian principles, was established by the Ming dynasty. Engaging in 'immoral cults' became a capital offence, so the Buddhists and Daoists themselves practised self-censorship and expurgated their canon, although in Japan Tantric practices continued among the members of the Tachikawa sect. In China during this period the handbooks no longer circulated as freely as before; while this genre of literature was still seen by some as useful, it 'did not lend itself to public discussion'.[45] On the other hand, a considerable production of erotic and pornographic novels, and even of paintings, took place during the Ming, especially among the literati of the Nanking circle.

With the crumbling of the Ming Empire and the conquest by the Manchu, Confucian principles were applied even more strictly. Everything belonging to the women's quarters became strictly taboo. Chinese officials exorted their Manchu masters to ban the erotica of the Ming. 'In this manner developed the Chinese phobia regarding the divulging of sexual matters, a phobia that has characterized the Chinese attitude to sex throughout the last four

[44] van Gulick 1974:351.
[45] van Gulick 1974:268.

centuries.'[46] So China has seen very sharp changes in its attitudes towards representations of sex, in writing, in speech, in some figurative art, as well as in practice. This alternation can be interpreted in terms of the conflict between Confucian 'puritanism' and Buddhist or Daoist 'freedom', but the very existence of those divergent views represents an ambivalence on the part of individuals and contradictions at a societal level, giving rise to a temporary balance between the secrecy and display in sexual matters that marks many cultures and relates to basic tensions surrounding sexuality and the cognitive processes associated with it.

Let me try to draw the threads of this discussion together. My initial observation derived from the contrast between open representations of sex, including instructional handbooks, and a more restrained, highly-clothed practice in India on the one hand, with the prevalence of nudity in Africa, in practice and in images, but the relative absence of representations of sexuality. In both these cases, there was some suggestion of tension between restraint and freedom but the evidence was drawn from static situations. Looking at Europe and China, where fuller historical records exist, we find not only the tensions between attitudes but note that the dominant view changes over time in a manner that suggests the existence of cognitive contradictions of the kind we have come across before.

I am interested in situations where people are ambivalent about representations of nudity and sex (as well as about the activity itself). In different societies and at different times in the same society, we find attitudes varying between encouragement and rejection. Why should this be? Regarding nudity, we usually strip both to wash and to have sex, although Europe and the East have produced some bizarre clothed forms of both.[47] Nudity and sex form a central part of our experience, yet there have been frequent objections to their representation in words or in pictures. That contradiction is related to a distinction between the private and the

---

[46] van Gulick 1974:355.
[47] See Beteille 1987.

public. Publically, we are (usually) clothed, keeping sex and nudity private. Hence, representations (which are potentially public and may be demanded both for instructional and for entertainment purposes) run up against these notions of privacy. There are other contextual contrasts. Statues may be nude but humans are not. Gods may be naked, humans clothed.

A further question arises because to be nude is also to be in the state in which we come into the world – it is pure as well as shameful and even 'beastly'. Clothes comfort and decorate but they also conceal the truth. That presents us with a cognitive problem that finds expression in the Adam and Eve myth, and relates to our understanding of the world, including our own bodies. Nudity is both good and bad. The same is true of sexuality. The act is essential for procreation and at the same time highly enjoyable, but it is almost always a private act. Why? Modesty is an insufficient answer. It is, I suggest, related to the very personal coupling which may give rise to envy and hostility on the part of others, certainly as a public act; in its very nature it excludes those outside the couple and yet involves putting oneself in the hands of another person (usually a member of the opposite sex) and so threatening one's innermost identity which is part of the private self.[48]

Privacy is not an attitude to sex taken up equally strongly in all parts of the world. Bougainville's eighteenth-century account of his voyage to Tahiti told of the lack of inhibition young men and women had about their first sexual encounters which were the subject of public display. Or that is how Diderot, the editor of the *Encyclopédie*, understood the matter, although his interpretation has been challenged.[49] Similar accounts have been given of Hawaii, but in most of the world sexuality is a distinctly private affair. So too is complete nudity. Some outside observers may see 'savages' as unclothed and naked, but from the actor's standpoint

---

[48] This situation is also a strong factor in relations between ex-partners who have exposed themselves to each other in ways they now regret and wish to conceal.

[49] Diderot, *Supplement to the voyage of Bougainville, or dialogue between A and B on the inappropriateness of attaching moral ideas to certain physical actions that do not accord with them*. See *Political Writings*, ed. J. H. Mason and R. Wokler (Cambridge, 1992).

there is a lot of difference between wearing a penis sheath and wearing nothing at all.

There is a further contradiction lying at the heart of sexuality, which relates to the union of dirt and desire, epitomized in the double function of the genitalia. In the East this paradox is represented by the lotus, the beauty that emerges from the mud, but it was also well understood by Jonathan Swift.

So why we find 'puritanism' (as we may call this denial by a blanket term) in different societies at different times, and greater freedom at others, is because sex and nudity pose cognitive contradictions in our understanding of ourselves. Hence their representation gets elaborated at one time and forbidden at another. Forms of representation often occur in particular contexts, in the sense that statues (especially of gods) may be nude while people are clothed. Or the temple may have a phallus as its central focus, whereas the rest of the society is prudish about the reality. As with totemism, expression in one context, absence in another, may partly resolve the tension between the two for the society as a whole.

There is also the wider problem raised by any representation. Why some societies reject nude forms, as in the early European Middle Ages, may be because they reject all three-dimensional representations, or indeed all representations. That rejection takes place partly on theological grounds – you do not repeat the Creator's unique act of creation. This theological position raises the question of the relationship between the original creative act of God and the subsequent ones of man and woman. In the 1972 Bagre, God directly shows humanity the act of creation itself. The beings of the wild reveal most other things about culture. While he created and shows how to create, he did not show humanity the way to create continuously, to procreate. That is revealed to woman by the snakes, and she passes on this natural knowledge to her partner. In many societies a special problem lies in representing (or even thinking about) sexual procreation in relation to the first non-sexual creative act. One partial resolution is to provide a supernatural dimension to sexuality: Śiva's phallus (*linga*) is divine because one aspect of Śiva is the creator. But there is a further problem on the secular side arising from the fact that representation is never the original presentation itself, never the real thing.

Sexuality, then, is largely absent from public representations for reasons having to do with privacy, intimacy and identity. Of course, representations may circulate 'privately' in the form of sex manuals or erotica, above all among upper groups with the readership extending more widely with changes in the mode of communication. Among adolescents knowledge undoubtedly passes by word of mouth in a less formal manner. However, not only the information but the sexual act itself is generally of private concern. Among the LoDagaa, to copulate outside a house (even though not in public) was a major sin against the Earth. That taboo relates to the Confucian injunction, that sex was approved only if it took place on the marital couch. Privacy was favoured and restrictions on openness were widespread, both regarding the act and its representation.

I am suggesting that though they are different, the kind of puritanism or moral rigour we find in Europe (in certain contexts, at certain times and in certain places) occurs in other societies. People have taken different attitudes to the representation of sex because of cognitive contradictions intrinsic to its conceptualization and its practice. In that perspective openness may be seen as a characteristic of beasts (or savages), concealment as marking civilization. Those sentiments are concisely summarized in Ovid's *Art of Love*:

> Beasts everywhere and openly unite:
> Maids oft avert their faces at the sight.
> Locked bedrooms suit the joys we humans steal
> And coverlets the parts of shame conceal.
> And if not darkness, still a twilight blurred
> And something less than open day's preferred.
>
> *(Book II, 1990:616)*

Even 'simple tribesmen' set store by shame, distinguishing themselves from the beasts, a feature of the human situation that lies behind the myth of Adam and Eve.

The tension between the shame and the enjoyment of sex, between the desire for knowledge and the wish for privacy, is a quasi-universal phenomenon that takes different forms in different societies and in different clusters of societies. Those differences may also take a hierarchical form within the same society; what is forbidden down below being practised up above. Mediterranean regimes of the classical period display this feature in common with the other major civilizations of Eurasia; a highly differentiated society is marked by 'luxury' as well as by literacy. In such a situation there is the cultivation of plenty, even excess, at the top and the presence of poverty, even penury, at the bottom. Epicureanism is accompanied by asceticism, excess by restraint. Both are encouraged by the development of writing, which brings out more explicitly the tensions and contradictions in the situation, often establishing an alternative tradition in the works of intellectuals, especially philosophers.

Sexuality and its denial rest partly upon such general factors but there are also the more specific ones that I have discussed. It is not only that luxury societies accumulate sexual services at the top, though that they do, creating envy (and possibly actual shortages) below and encouraging restraint in the eyes of commentators. It is also that aristocratic behaviour involves greater freedom as well as restraint more generally. The act of baring oneself to another involves stripping away the clothing (actual and symbolic) that incorporates one's ego and declares one's identity. The private act revives the vulnerability of the newborn, while its public face (including its representations) may give rise to shame as well as to prurience. That dual orientation leads to shifts between the two poles of openness and concealment with regard to the human body and to human sexuality.

# 8

# Culture and Cognition

Cognitive contradictions exist at a societal or institutional level, at least potentially. I have treated the contradictions involved in the process of representation, especially in the form of images, theatre, relics and of oral and written narrative. The contradictions, which make possible absence as well as presence, are cognitive in that they are embedded in the use, indeed the existence, of language. What are contradictions at the level of the observer are activated when embodied as ambivalence for the actor; in the minds of individual agents they become the instruments of change. This cognitive aspect has been played down in the social sciences in past decades in their search for hidden functions and structures which has tended to neglect the dynamic explanation of difference and change. In this concluding chapter I want to place my discussion in a wider context of theoretical concerns.

In the nineteenth century, major anthropologists such as E. B. Tylor and James Frazer took a stance on the customary practices and ways of thinking of non-European society which the French sociological school of Émile Durkheim dubbed 'intellectualist'. For the former attempted to set out the reasons why individuals held the beliefs they did about the world, whereas Durkheim considered the central question to be what particular beliefs contributed to a specific social institution (or to society as a whole) and how they functioned in relation to other aspects of customary social interaction (or culture). There was no clear-cut contrast, however. One can describe the second approach (in Weberian terms) as focusing on meaning to the observer rather than meaning to the actor. But the term 'intellectualist' could also be interpreted as implying an imposition of external ideas about how those minds worked, for those writers were always concerned with the general rather than with the particular; they were not field-workers making observations of specific groups but wrote about the 'primitive' world as a whole. On the other hand the functionalists who followed Durkheim did work in the field, were concerned with particular societies and, therefore, it could be argued, got closer to the actors' frame of reference. We see here two axes of differentiation. One has to do with whether the focus of attention is on the actor or the observer. The second, related, axis concerns whether we are dealing with surface (meaning to the actor) or with deep structure, the latter referring to underlying (functional) meanings inevitably hidden from him. Of course, what is hidden may none the less be acceptable to the actor once it is made explicit. This is one of the major outcomes of written communication, which enables us to see as well as to hear what we are thinking, to see in a concrete, manipulable form; it makes possible the extraction of grammar, as an object, as a deep structure, from the ongoing flow of speech; it makes explicit what is otherwise implicit in oral discourse.

In Britain and elsewhere, social anthropology of the inter-war and post-World War II period took over many Durkheimian notions. The approach produced many results, but for certain problems it was less than adequate. The French sociologists did not collect their own data; like the earlier 'English intellectualists' they relied upon the observations of others. But for the generations of research workers from the 1920s onwards, meaning to the actor was inevitably what their field data were about. One learnt the language not only so one could ask about the number of children an individual had, but to elucidate notions about childhood and procreation, for individuals as well as for collectivities, to appreciate what was particular and what was general, most importantly the latter. Thus, Evans-Pritchard enquired about Zande notions of the logic behind their witchcraft beliefs, that is, about the nature of their sequential reasoning. Yet the weight of the interpretation offered by most anthropologists fell elsewhere, not so much on the witchcraft beliefs themselves but on who was accusing whom and how these accusations served to indicate underlying tensions in the society. The results were significant, and it seems a pity that this line of enquiry has not been followed up more systematically. When anthropologists begin to make a contribution, they become only too prone to turn away from what has been achieved and to seek out novelties for their own sake. Whatever its advantage, however, such a focus did lead away from two other important aspects of witchcraft beliefs, namely the cognitive ones, that is, not only their meaning to the actor but the more general question of why, and indeed how, people hold such beliefs intellectually. Included in this neglect was the distributional aspect, the presence and absence of these beliefs (and their variants) on a broad comparative level.

Let me turn to the distributional aspect first. Tylor and Frazer, among others, did discuss world-wide examples of ancestor-worship, beliefs in the soul, witchcraft and similar practices, pointing to sets of beliefs and customs that make up what Tylor called 'primitive culture' and what Levy-Bruhl saw as manifestations of the 'primitive mentality'. The field-working generation tended to scoff at such broad-ranging attempts, and contemptuously dismissed out of hand 'the comparative method'. They claimed that had their predecessors actually gone to the field, they would have found that every culture or society had different ideas about the soul. That claim immediately raised the problem of translation, since to provide a word in English or French may imply a set of associated beliefs, irrelevant to the non-European case; for 'the soul' is not a neutral analytic term like 'oxygen', but one embedded in Christian theology. At one level, that claim was true enough. Yet at another the complaint was profoundly unsatisfactory. Clearly soul-type concepts (or ones of witchcraft or the ancestors) exist in a wide range of human societies displaying significant similarities, and for these one needs to find a term. However, field-work inevitably threw the focus on particular cultures and how they were differentiated, rather than on human beings in general or even as neighbours, and the similarities in their institutional arrangements and in their cognitive processes. In those cultures that they studied, the observers tended to interpret social action as meaning something more than that which the actors themselves maintained. But there was some acknowledgement that, if the beliefs varied, their functions (for example, whether witchcraft, expressed, encouraged or diminished social tensions) were widespread.

Field-workers began to expand from their particular cultural nests when they looked at neighbouring societies (perhaps through the eyes of colleagues or students they had encouraged to work there). They found similar, but not identical, concepts (as well as functions), which served to illuminate each other, as in the case of the work on religion carried out by Evans-Pritchard on the Nuer and by Lienhardt on the neighbouring Dinka. So they returned tentatively to a regional form of comparison under the tutelage of approved field-working anthropologists like Radcliffe Brown for the Australian aborigines, Eggan for the Pueblo Indians, Schapera for the south-west Bantu, Richards for the central Bantu, and others. This opening raised the problem of how a practice or belief in one society related to that in another, how they could be seen as transformations, in for example the work of Lévi-Strauss on myth or of Dumont on marriage. The notion of transformation was a morphological one; it saw forms of marriage, for example, as represented by different geometrical models and tended to set on one side a consideration of the historical process by which one form changed to another, partly because the historical material was often thin, but partly too for theoretical reasons, since history was often rejected as a mode of explanation.

Of course, wider comparative and historical questions did engage the attention of a few anthropologists but they remained minority interests. For most there was an unbridgeable gap between the study of particular cultures and the study of human culture in general although, in practice, the wider issues still gnawed away at people's understandings. What field-working anthropologists tended to do in the absence of acceptable alternatives, was to let the Nuer or the Trobriands stand for the whole of the non-European or pre-industrial world, without providing any systematic proof that they were representative. The result tended to be a world of binary distinctions, 'we' versus 'they'.

I have referred to one important attempt to deal with the wider comparative question, namely the ambitious enterprise of Lévi-Strauss. His enquiries into Australian systems of (cross-cousin) marriage led him to isolate a category of elementary forms which he contrasted with those complex ones where the choice of partner was not specified in kinship terms. But it was his work on myth and on *la pensée sauvage*, 'primitive thinking' ('the savage mind'), that comes closest to the subject of cognition and culture, since there he was avowedly dealing with some general aspects of 'l'esprit humain', the human mind. He did this by dwelling upon the binary distinction between the scientific procedures of the modern human and what he called the alternative approach of the *bricoleur*, of the neolithic handyman who pieces bits of things together and cobbles his beliefs out of this and that.

His analysis of 'mythical thought' led away from the work of his predecessors, either intellectualist or functionalist, towards a search for the building blocks of cognitive operations, an analysis not of explicit meaning but of underlying structure. In the work of various of his followers the search took the form of examining the conceptual apparatus of human (or, at least, pre-industrial) thought in terms of basic binary distinctions. The model was that of the Prague school of linguistics, especially the work of Roman Jakobson, which distinguished, for example, between the basic sounds of speech in terms of oppositions:

| voiced | unvoiced |
|--------|----------|
| p      | b        |
| d      | t        |

They attempted to apply this method to concepts arranged as polarities (opposites) and analogies (similarities):

| | |
|---|---|
| right | left |
| light | dark |
| white | black |
| man | woman etc. |

Tables of this kind were supposed to provide keys to unlock the mythical (or symbolic) thought of particular peoples. Yet the result was a set of rather similar tables emerging from a wide range of societies.

Whether viewed as particular or general phenomena, these lists raised a number of questions including what can be called 'The black is beautiful' problem. This problem can be illustrated by referring to a central notion in Conrad's tale, *Heart of Darkness* (1902). One editor, Cedric Watts, explains that the title and the tale are richly ambiguous:

> 'Darkness' suggests variously the obscure, mysterious, unknown, sinister, or evil. The phrase 'heart of darkness' suggests the interior of Africa, the 'Dark Continent', but London is described as the centre of 'a brooding gloom'. The phrase can also refer to an individual (Kurtz, for instance) whose heart is dark (mysterious, sinister, evil). The tale associates light with civilization but also with the brightness and destructiveness of fire, and it associates whiteness with hypocrisy ('a whited sepulchre'), ivory, bones and death. In Virgil's Aeneid, Book VI, the ivory gates of the Underworld are the gates by which 'false dreams' are sent to the world above. Kurtz's career may occasionally evoke that of Lucifer (whose name means 'light-bringer'), the brightest of the angels, who fell through pride and reigned in Hell.[1]

Paris is a whited sepulchre; ivory is the object of the search in the Congo and also used for dominoes with which the adventurers occupy their time. No binary formulation can tabulate this array of ambiguous usages, except possibly in a processional way, over time. In single lists and in similar highly decontextualized attempts to represent cognitive structures graphically, the flexibility which

---

[1] Watts 1990:262–3 (Introduction to Conrad's *Heart of Darkness*).

metaphor and the use of language encourage are automatically excluded because we are presented with a stationary, frozen system (black = evil). Yet ambiguity and contradiction lie close to the heart of the communicative and cognitive processes and are essential in accounting for the generative aspects of socio-cultural phenomena.

With structural analysis we appear to have returned to the cognitive level. But Lévi-Strauss and others saw these tables as statements not about the surface level of meaning (meaning to the actor) but about the deep structure, which was hidden to the participants in the same way as the grammar of his language. In fact Lévi-Strauss was somewhat dismissive of the surface level of mythological meaning (as he had been with marriage), which one of his students described as 'absurd'.[2]

There are, I believe, some technical reasons for this attitude. Briefly, before the advent of the tape-recorder, the myths that appeared in ethnographic reports were often truncated narratives, which omitted the more speculative, thoughtful passages of a recitation, partly because of the communicative situation that existed between the actor and the observer in the hegemonic context of an interview that was out of place in local society, except possibly in an inquisitorial setting. The observer asked for a narrative; that was the part the actor remembered, and that was right for the situation. Like children, outsiders could grasp the narrative elements without difficulty, so that was what they were offered.

Be that as it may, an important aspect of cognition, how the actor understands the world at an explicit level, gets put on one side in the search for the static oppositions of a deeper structure (sometimes seen as the rules that guide, sometimes as the model that interprets). Whereas, if we look at the Bagre myth of the LoDagaa it is a more overt level of intellectual concern that first engages our attention. Among its central aspects is the problem of why God created a world that included disease and misery, and the more abstract concern of how to represent the immaterial spirit by material objects.

[2] Sebag 1964.

These intellectual elements, these potential components of the actor's world, of meanings, have obvious links to our own understanding, for example, of the problem of evil and of the concern of iconoclasts (one of which was how to represent the immaterial by the material). Hence, those particular elements are in no way limited to mythical thinking, to the 'savage mind'. This is important because while the human mind is not everywhere the same, since mental processes are necessarily interactive – they are different, for example, when writing intervenes, because that medium is potentially more self-reflexive so that the implicit becomes explicit – nevertheless, the basic apparatus is similar. So that there is no room for a notion of the 'mythopoeic mind' as such, that is, of mental processes that are constitutionally distinct rather than situationally different.[3] That is what I have been trying to say in suggesting that doubts about representation are certainly found in oral societies but in less explicit forms than in the critical traditions of literate ones.

To return to Lévi-Strauss, he was posing problems to do with the nature of the mind. He saw this as 'cultural' in the sense that its basic notions were internalized as learned behaviour, not as statements but as the structure of statements, in the form of deep structure rather than of surface meaning. Questions arising out of this approach (especially regarding the similarities of the elicited structures that emerged and suggested universality rather than difference) led some of his successors to concentrate on those universal aspects of *l'esprit humain*, to reject explanations in terms of culture and learning theory, which would lead towards differences, and to look more seriously at what elements could be considered to be built in to our mental make-up and what could not. Sperber makes his position clear regarding the analysis of Lévi-Strauss when he sees his structuralism (in relation to totemism) as related to the specific kind of organization the human mind is able, and liable, to impose on its representation of the

---

[3] The same point is made about mentalities by Lloyd (1990). Nevertheless, such a notion in more subtle forms is intrinsic to the ideas of Weber as of Habermas (see J. Goody 1990).

world. He would push further in this rationalist direction, and argue that 'cultures have developed not simply in response to external demands but, more fundamentally, in accordance with the human mind's internal constraints'.[4] That view is undoubtedly correct; the empirical question remains as to what specific affect these constraints have and in what sense they can be considered more fundamental than external ones. Sperber draws Lévi-Strauss closer to his view and argues that the title of *La Pensée Sauvage* 'gives a false idea of Lévi-Strauss' general purpose . . . for him *la pensée sauvage* is the way human beings – all human beings – think when they are not following explicit restrictive rules, or using aids and techniques such as writing'. In other words, we are talking about a certain type of basic intellectual process. I accept this as one interpretation which has something to be said in its favour. But it is not clear to me how unambiguous Lévi-Strauss was on the question of mentalities; there are certainly other implications contained in notions such as 'neolithic' thought and in the binary way he tabulates its characteristics which point to a more exclusive distinction.[5] In any case, the resort to a notion of universal basic intellectual processes and the treatment of writing and rules as extraneous additions involves an essentialist approach to mental activity that seems to allow too little room for the transforming effects of modes of communication and their products.

In this project, of working out the constraints of the human mind, one dominant model was the Chomskian view of language, that the ability to learn languages must be inherited in humans, who are pre-programmed because infants learn the grammar of a language so quickly without being sufficiently taught. But the more specific debt was to cognitive science, to cognitive philosophy and psychology. Some French cognitive anthropologists have tried to apply such an approach to clusters of categories (that is, to domains, to cognitive systems of classification) and to beliefs. Category systems in natural history have been analysed by Atran in his book, *Cognitive Foundations of Natural History: Towards an*

---

[4] Sperber 1985:64.
[5] Lévi-Strauss 1962. See J. Goody 1977, ch. 4.

*Anthropology of Science* (1990). Following research in cognitive science, he maintains that there are two broad types of domain in natural history, one dealing with living things, the other with artefacts, each having its own rules.[6] The classification of the latter is defined by function, while that of the former is in-built like grammar. And he employs a similar argument to that of Chomsky, namely, that children take an extraordinarily short time to acquire the ability to distinguish a category of living things. This line of thinking owes much to the work of the psychologist Keil who, in his account of *Semantics and the Conceptual Development* (1979), announced that he 'became convinced by the work of Chomsky and Osherson, among others, that the acquisition of knowledge in virtually any conceptual domain was guided and facilitated by a set of *a priori* constraints, many of which were specifically tailored for that domain'.[7] As a result, he tried to examine 'how ontological knowledge develops within the guidelines set down by certain constraints' in order to illuminate semantic and conceptual development. Ontological knowledge refers to conceptions of the basic categories of existence and is seen as constituting a highly structured domain so that a child rapidly builds up knowledge because of the pre-existing constraints.

There are certainly in-built elements in human action. Some are more obviously physical. Psychologists have written of them in connection with a neonate's built-in reaction to the serpentine movement of snakes or to the loud cry of birds. Davey (1992, 1994) claims that just as disease and germs drove a lot of evolution, so people are particularly likely to fear agents of disease, such as rats and insects.[8] This fear represents a more specific case of Seligman's notion of 'evolutionary preparedness' (1971) to

---

[6] See Keil 1986.
[7] Keil 1979:vii.
[8] An important trend in recent research on neonates, for example, in the work of Trevarthen (1988, 1979a and b) and Stern (1977), is away from the *tabula rasa* view of infancy, emphasizing not only the reactions but the actions of the child towards the mother, even in the intra-uterine state. Such action develops before speech, before birth, but in an interactive context.

acquire certain phobias with only a limited exposure or a few social cues.[9] While we may be ready to accept the preparedness to categorize living things distinct from artefacts, there is a big jump from making such a quite specific claim to including as built-in entire systems of classification.

The other point these authors make is a comparative one. While there are many differences in category systems in natural history, raising at the simplest level the Saussurian problem of the arbitrariness of whether you call an animal (living or dead) 'sheep' or 'mouton', there are also similarities in the ways these terms are structured into families and grouped together at different levels.

Similar ideas have been applied by Boyer to religious symbolism in his discussion of 'cognitive constraints on cultural representations'. While not ignoring their variability, Boyer is struck by the recurrent features betrayed by religious ideas. In other words, he returns to certain Tylorian preoccupations (as he himself recognizes) that were largely suppressed during what I may call the period of field-worker hegemony. He, too, suggests these common features may not have been acquired through socialization but are related to the fact that the processes of acquisition and memorization place strong constraints on the contents and organization of cultural representations. Varieties of mental representations may emerge in a particular population and the most likely to be retained will persist because their structural properties more closely mirror the cognitive constraints.[10] The theory does not require cultural universals, it is claimed, only that cognitive constraints on acquisition and representation account for widespread recurrence.

For Boyer, it is the 'unnaturalness' of religious ideas that is critical. 'Religious representations typically centre on claims that violate commonsense expectations concerning ordinary things, beings, and processes. For instance, religious entities are described as invisible beings, yet located in space . . .'[11] One task of a cognitive approach, he proposes, is to find why and how human minds

---

[9] I am indebted to M. Cole for these references.
[10] Boyer 1994a:391–2.
[11] Boyer 1994a:393.

are led to entertain such notions and to find them plausible, to probe the contrast that lies between ordinary cognition and the extraordinary claims of religious ontologies which violate even the actors' notions of biological and physical phenomena. Religious representations are real events but not ordinary ones, and since they are recognized as such intuitively, no distinct concept of the supernatural is necessary. They demand attention because of what he calls their counter-intuitive claims.

Recurrent religious ideas are, according to Boyer, the consequence of a configuration of optimal combinations of violation and confirmation of intuitive knowledge. That is, they violate everyday understandings but at the same time are capable of being learned because their extraordinary claims are constrained by domain-specific assumptions that are part of a universal intuitive understanding of basic ontological categories.

The argument depends on making a radical distinction between religious and other categories, effectively between natural and supernatural, between what is intuitive and counter-intuitive. The notion of domain-specific assumptions in the field of religion may be more appropriate to Western societies where religious action (belief and acts) is frequently set apart from secular action. Most observers of non-literate societies have not recognized such a sharp division. This is partly because it is only with the increased reflexivity that literacy encourages that some of these domains emerge as clearly differentiated. Like grammar, they are literally 'discovered' by written procedures. Even if we grant the quasi-universality and early acquisition of concepts and classification, this feature is not necessarily dependent on built-in wiring. For example, in relation to botanical classification it is not easy to see that the investigators have eliminated the possibility of parallel functional evolution. Rather than see items allocated by evolutionary preparedness to different domains, we may want to look at constraints in the situation of interaction whereby language-using humans face the outside world. That is to say, quasi-universals may arise not from internal constraints alone but from the interface between mind and externalities, which is the crux of higher mental processes.

The intensely interactive nature of human life, largely but not entirely related to the use of language, means that little is totally unquestioned. That idea runs against many notions of earlier society, where beliefs were thought to be fixed, and held by everybody. Hence there is the idea of the static nature of earlier societies. It is certainly true that the tempo of questioning and change has increased in the last few centuries, but changes, changes of considerable magnitude, have taken place in the earlier past; we can only account for the differences between neighbouring groups by assuming that these are due to changes from a common original, some internally, others externally generated. Secondly, it runs against the anthropological notion of long-term continuity, of culture. Whereas I suggest doubt already exists because of the cognitive contradictions that are present in certain spheres of human action.

The situation I have examined in earlier chapters involves representations, and the process of creating and using them is likely to give rise to doubts about this very nature, which in turn may affect the system of domains. Not only doubts, but contradictions may cross-cut the categories, making them more flexible, at least in certain contexts, in just the way we know language to work in practice. Take the example of spatial location. A human being cannot be in two places at once and that clearly differentiates him from deities or ancestors. Yet we all have the experience in dreams of being where our bodies are not. The same notion is intrinsic to many explanations of the activities of witches, who meet in covens when their bodies remain on the mat, who attack other people's 'souls' rather than their flesh. Body and soul are not simply to be allocated to separate domains; the human persona consists of both, one of which can be located in one place, the other in another. Indeed, it is far from clear to me that, in most contexts, the LoDagaa place these two elements in separate domains; for some purposes, perhaps, but not for all. Moreover, even the living body sometimes has the ability to move rapidly from place to place in mysterious ways. One early District Commissioner, Duncan-Johnstone, was known as *muriye*, the burrower, because he would suddenly appear in unexpected places. *O tera tĩĩ*, 'he had medicine', the LoDagaa would say, employing a concept that certainly crossed our own usual boundaries between natural and supernatural, for he was a human possessed of 'superhuman' powers.[12] There is a cognitive problem here, as Boyer points out; such ideas, he declares, are 'unnatural', they 'violate commonsense'. I would also add that there is no built-in resolution; they remain potential contradictions for the actors and can, therefore, give rise to scepticism.[13]

There is a related theoretical problem raised in these studies. According to Maurice Bloch, this particular approach dispenses with the 'anthropological theory of cognition', associated with the 'theory of exhaustive cultural transmission' which sees representation as 'being entirely determined by what was given to them by adult members of the group'. Such a theory hardly needs defending, since few would, in practice, deny either the contribution of biology or the capacity of people to change their representations over time (including by the invention of tradition or by creativity).[14] It is based upon what is largely a false opposition. Most scholars, even cultural anthropologists, are quite happy with the notion that transmission involves biological elements, though these may not be the ones in which they are interested. Others are concerned with learning in the wider sense of 'learning to learn'. That is, cultural transmission involves the programming of individuals to generate new forms of behaviour just as they do new sentences; indeed, new forms of widely accepted sentences are precisely what 'culture' is about. While some elements may be relatively static, we are constantly faced with the invention not only of tradition but of the individual sentences out of which it is constructed, as well as those novelties that are forced upon us by political dominance or other external pressures. In any case 'social learning' is established as a feature of not only human but of animal behaviour, where imitation (copying behaviour) is present in some

---

[12] For alternative explanations of this name, see S. W. D. K. Gandah's manuscript, *Gandah-yiri, the House of the Brave*.
[13] J. Goody 1996b.
[14] Boyer 1994a:396.

higher species as well as other forms of learning, such as stimulus enhancement (individual trial and error as a result of focusing on an object or action), exposure and goal emulation.[15] Apes can apparently imitate but not monkeys; the former can take roles (that is, store representations in delayed imitation), the latter cannot. Imitation, Bruner has long argued, requires that the mimic is able to put itself into the mental position of the model: 'in contemporary terms, to represent mentally the knowledge and plans of another individual'.[16] In other words, imitation is not a simple activity but part of the complexity of primate behaviour, involving a rapid method of learning compared to other possibilities.

The alternative to the assumption that all behaviour is learned is not necessarily that all programmes are in-built. That latter suggestion seems to allow too little room for change unless the proposed programmes are seen as highly flexible, that is, highly undetermined and therefore open to learning. Given the rapid rate of change in contemporary societies (as well as in some earlier ones), there can be little doubt about the need for programmes of 'learning to learn', though that leaves open the question of whether those programmes are in-built, culturally prescribed or resulting from the creativity that language use and social intelligence encourage. There is probably no one answer for all activities; certainly the verbatim learning of which Bloch writes is only one aspect.

Let me give an example from my own field-work among African adults. When I first wrote down the recitation ('myth') of the Bagre in 1950, I was convinced by my local friends that this long recital was learnt verbatim by the initiates (not by all but by some) and that there was a process of deliberate teaching. That conviction was reinforced by anthropological notions of the centrality of myth based upon the single (often truncated) version which was more or less all that many investigators could collect in the lived-in cultural context before the advent of electronic recordings. When I recorded further versions and reflected on the problems that

---

[15] Whiten and Ham 1992.
[16] Byrne 1995:45; Bruner 1972.

Bartlett found in the exact transmission of even short messages or tales, I realized that my understanding of this process was fundamentally flawed.[17] Even the invocation of the first dozen or so lines, which may well have been learned in the orthodox way, varied in each recital. How much more did the full myth vary! Speakers recited, remembering some things, forgetting others and recreating yet others in innovative ways. Some of these innovations were encouraged by the particular social situation of the actors; others were more unrestrainedly creative, making use of human experience in a wider sense, while yet others exploited cognitive ambiguities in an earlier version to produce variations, sometimes of an important thematic kind.

This discussion raises certain questions about the nature of 'culture'. From one point of view we see LoDagaa (or, for that matter, French) culture at one moment in time as regular and fixed as if it was the product of a purely authoritative mode of transmission having a strong continuity with the past. Looked at over time we find considerable variation emerging from endogenous as well as exogenous sources. To account for the sum of cognitive activity, we need to consider creativity (invention) as well as the contribution of learning and the presence of in-built structures or tendencies.

If we find the recurrence of certain themes in different societies, that convergence may be related to situational similarities that produce similar cognitive responses, or a limited set of responses. These responses are not wired-in but arise from the nature of the human condition, the situation of language-using individuals faced with the world at large, including other culture-bearing agents who are also reflective in the way that language promotes (and literacy increasingly encourages). Now what is intrinsic to many of these encounters is that individuals and groups may be offered a limited set of alternative courses of thinking or action, which includes the queries and the doubts about any one particular course. As a consequence a long-term dynamic is thrust upon humanity by the cognitive contradictions (or by less marked

---

[17] Bartlett 1926.

ambiguities) involved in holding particular sets of beliefs, or in adapting some more overt behaviours, which is the process I have set out to analyse. In so doing I have tried to take into account both unity and diversity. While cultural approaches dwell on diversity between cultures, the associated theories of learning and transmission make little provision for producing that diversity, for generating differences. This would also seem to be the case with those theories that look to in-built mechanisms; inevitably their focus is on unity.

The cognitive constraints and contradictions of which I speak are not built in genetically nor necessarily even held in the memory and transmitted. Learning and inheritance have important roles to play but a third force needs to be taken into account, a more overtly cognitive process of acquisition than is assumed by either process.

Cognitive contradictions exist in those situations where an understanding of the world could go in two or more directions because of the very nature of that cognition. Those situations are necessarily unstable in the long run. That is to say, if a group chooses one line of thinking, the other remains a potential alternative, either at the societal or at the individual level. At the societal level we have a potential contradiction (an actual one at the analytic level) and at the individual level we have ambivalence. When such contradictions become explicit (as they are more likely to do when the formulations take a written form), but sometimes even when they remain implicit, they may lead to a shift from one alternative to another.

Relative stability may occur when one cognition protects itself from another by recognizing its existence, either in a ritual act or by some individuals or groups adopting the alternative mode of understanding. Alternative choices may be built into the social system, perhaps resolving individual ambivalence. It is not that there is always ambiguity about these norms since they may often be separated off from one another. Nor are they indeed paradoxes, that is, 'statements or tenets contrary to the received opinion or belief' though they may give rise to such, especially in the form of antinomies which, in Quine's words, 'produces a self-contradiction by accepted ways of reasoning' and may 'bring on the crisis of thought' leading to the taking up of an alternative position.[18]

The rejection of images and other artistic forms falls into this category of cognitive contradictions. I argue that the process of re-presentation is essential for human society (for example, in language use) but has a negative side in that what is re-presented is never what is presented in the first place. And the very absence of the object may give rise to other problems and queries. A 'horse' (the word) is not a horse (the animal) but its absence. That situation may give rise to cognitive contradictions regarding images, which are reinforced when we are dealing with images of divinity, especially of the Creator. Relics again seem to fall in the same category since they both are and are not the original whole person. Theatre, also, follows images as a matter of re-presentation. Fiction, too, can be said to display similar characteristics, truthful perhaps at one level (and certainly entertaining) but a fabrication at another. Myth too, like other religious accounts, may raise questions for common sense. Regarding sex, we are in an adjacent domain since the problem concerns self-representation primarily, and why we shy away from it.

The relation between the notion of cognitive contradiction appears to approach the psychologist Festinger's concept of 'cognitive dissonance'. Dissonance is produced when a cognition is contradicted by events, for example, at the failure of a prediction in which one has invested a great deal of affect. Cognitive contradictions have to do with contradictions involved in the cognition itself. The two may overlap. In the case of the failure of a prophecy that the world will end on a specific day (and that one will be saved), the conflict may be between the notion of a catastrophic end of the universe (the inverse of the Creation by the Big Bang) and that of the gradual dissolution of an ongoing state (the inverse of evolution), or again between common sense and religious conviction, or between prediction and failure.

Let me elaborate this example of the Creation. Human beings

---

[18] W. V. Quine, *Ways of Paradox*, 1966, i, 7. The term 'paradox' is often given a wider significance.

inevitably speculate about the origin of their world and one recurrent result is the idea of a Creation and of a Creator that is often embodied in accounts of the origin of things. Another, as Frazer pointed out, is gradual evolution rather than the Big Bang. I argue that both the 'pre-scientific' versions of these doctrines, contradictory as they are, reflect aspects of man's experience of his world; yet both are incomplete, containing internal ambiguities or contradictions. The paradox about the Creation is that it is a unique act carried out by an agency that is necessarily superior to humankind, superior in its powers and in its essence. While it is believed to exist, it cannot be seen and does not take a material form except in its creation. Moreover, having created the world (or humankind), it then withdraws; the all-powerful renounces power.

At least two specific cognitive problems are raised in these speculations which we have already identified in talking of the intellectual components of the Bagre, namely the problems of evil and of the (material) representation of the immaterial. Each one carries concomitant (built-in) contradictions. Any one set of assumptions involves not only statements about this world but raises a kernel of doubt about our understanding of it, which can lead to scepticism about, and even to rejection of, that set of beliefs and hence to the adoption of alternatives. In the case of the LoDagaa and the problem of evil, one solution is to set the Creator God above the fray he created and in which he now no longer intervenes. Even an altar is lacking, since the *deus otiosus* does not require one; active intervention would, of course, need some such material focus, shifting the nature of conceptualization. With the withdrawal of the Creator God intermediaries, such as medicine shrines, bear the brunt of the scepticism. As a result of their inevitable failures they become obsolete both for individuals and for societies, and new ones are invented, or adopted, that promise better results, while the old ones languish or are rejected. That turn-over, I have suggested, may leave the door open to a more active concept of God.

There is a problem, however, not only about addressing, but about representing God. Unlike other entities the High God is not figuratively imaged because of doubts about the representation of the Creator by the created, of the immaterial by the material. How can you re-create the Creator, especially in visual form, and especially in a three-dimensional one where the effort at reality is more obvious? The problem is sometimes seen to apply, though in a less severe way, to other divine creatures, and, in Islam and Judaism, to all that the Creator has created. For a human to create an image is to repeat His unique act of Creation. That notion of the uniqueness of Creation is also central to many African cosmologies, and can be seen as challenged by some human actions.

My approach in no way discounts the possibility of in-built mechanisms or constraints in transmission, although it would limit their application to well-established cases. Rather, it draws attention to another level of cognitive process that refers to recurrent features of the human situation. These features are subject not so much to constraints (of transmission, and so on) as to inherent dilemmas or contradictions. So that, in making certain assumptions about the world or in taking certain actions, the solution may frequently give rise to a kernel of doubt (about the effectiveness of supernatural agencies, for example, the situation of 'doubting Thomas') which will lead to adopting an alternative course, even to a possible change in the structure of ideas. This process arises from the presence of cognitive contradictions, potential ambiguities in the human situation which derive from the interactive context and which are themselves part of transmitted culture. In other words, culture does not simply consist of in-built tendencies or customary (traditional) procedures of a socialized kind, but includes a kernel of doubt, its own critique of itself that may lead to the adoption of opposed forms of behaviour. This is what happens in many instances of re-presentation.

Let me look at this question again in connection with the use of flowers. In my study of this subject I dealt mainly with the presence and absence of natural flowers and mentioned the artificial variety only in passing. Artificial flowers are representations of flowers, as are icons, paintings. One reason why some peoples tend to reject artificial flowers for religious and secular purposes is that there is a contradiction inherent in their use. They do not accomplish what fresh ones do because they are permanent representations rather than the effervescent realities which serve as temporary tributes needing constant renewal and therefore the embodiment of perpetual care. To some they also represent a lie, an untruth.

In relation to figurative representations, as with my discussion of flowers, I have pursued this theme over time as well as over space, historically as well as comparatively, and have found similarities as well as differences between Eurasia and Africa. The use of such icons raised problems not only in the monotheistic religions deriving from the Near East but in others too. In Asia there were sects of Jains who rejected all icons just as there were also sects of Buddhists. In other words, the iconoclasm we find in Europe cannot be looked upon as a facet of its own history alone but must be seen in terms of wider ambivalences about icons.

What about Black Africa? Was there any evidence of iconoclasm? Obviously there was in Islam and in some branches of Christianity that came from Eurasia. But even in oral cultures not affected by, indeed resistant to, those literate world religions, representation was not always a straightforward matter. Cognitive contradictions were involved. We need to distinguish the problems attached to religious and secular icons respectively, especially figurative ones. There is a special problem about imaging the immaterial (as Aquinas among others has pointed out), particularly about imaging the High God, the Creator God, which raises the problems of creation in a very direct fashion. That problem also existed in Africa as we see from the intermittent absence of images.

In addition there is always the wider secular problem that representations are never the thing itself. They have their own real existence but they may also be seen as lies, untruth, and hence rejected as such in the Platonic tradition, since they present what they are not. While these notions regarding either the religious or the secular are not explicit in Africa in the same way that they are in the written traditions of Eurasia, there is some evidence of such tendencies which would account for the uneven *spatial* distribution of all figurative images in Africa just as it does the uneven *temporal* distribution in Eurasia (that is, the bursts of iconoclasm).

I applied aspects of this argument to dramatic representations. First, I touched upon the wider problem of performance. There are dangers in including ritual and theatre (or even drama) in a single category of performance (though there are obvious overlaps and similarities) because the nature of participation, the views of the actors, are different. In ritual you *are* the archbishop. In *Murder in the Cathedral* you *mimic* his nature; you take on a role. And that process is again different from unstructured mimicry outside the theatre.

I argue that this difference is related to the greater likelihood that a kernel of doubt will arise regarding drama, which is pretence, making it more likely that it will be deliberately rejected just because it is mimetic. It is re-presenting something we may wish to call 'reality', though in another sense the original is not any more 'real'. There are layers of reality which any system of representations constructs and which has a hierarchical dimension. While we normally regard these layers as equally real, there are moments of perception when one queries the relation between word, icon or gesture and the object or experience to which they refer. Ritual does not give rise to the same queries since it is believed to be performative. But secular drama does, which makes it a more likely candidate to be set aside or rejected, not only in the simpler (oral) cultures (where other socio-economic factors limit the scope of theatre) but from time to time in the complex ones of Eurasia as well.

Of course, there are intermediary cases between the secular and the religious, including mixed modes, carnivals as well as certain phases of LoDagaa funerals. In social life forms of mimetic activity are continuously emerging but, there too, lies a potential kernel of doubt, about, for example, the charivari. Those doubts may take a formal shape in the ban and indeed rejection of such activities that took place in England in the mid-sixteenth century. Such a rejection was not simply an instance of the imposition of Church authority; that assumption would not account for its recurrence or its persistence. The objection rang a bell among the populace, and that response needs to be taken firmly into account.

Ritual is not altogether immune from similar objections, but the word itself refers to too general and unspecific activities (or aspects thereof) for these ever to be completely banned. However, specific rituals may certainly be criticized for their extravagance, for their formality, for their elaboration as well as for their inability to produce the expected results. In some cases, extreme reformers, such as Quakers and Puritans, rejected virtually all forms of ritual activity, although elaboration always had a tendency to creep back in. That situation again reflects a kernel of doubt, which may express itself in the total rejection of supernatural agencies, as by some individuals and groups in China or India, or even in the scepticism one encounters in Africa but which, without writing, does not get formalized into a specific doctrine or a continuing tradition. Scepticism is a precipitate of the human situation in which gods and rituals promise but often fail. Failure of efficacy does not go unnoticed by the actors who are not always to be comforted by the sociological doctrine that such rites none-the-less encourage felicity or solidarity.

Let me give a further example of cognitive contradiction from my own field-work, but from another domain, concerning the killing of humans and animals. Doing my first spell of field-work in northern Ghana, I was struck by the ambivalence, at both an individual and a collective level, that was displayed about killing. I was with the LoDagaa in the post-World War II period when some men had been soldiers, were thought to have killed and had to go through a homicide ritual involving what was regarded locally as a series of highly unpleasant tasks, including a modified form of eating human flesh (nowadays a dog). Indeed, as an ex-soldier, I had to undergo this ritual, for even those who had killed honourably had to go through the same acts as a murderer. Blood was on their hands and it had to be removed; killing humans was dangerous in itself, regardless of motive or context.

The human situation always involves intraspecific killing that inevitably sets up a dichotomy between those legitimate killings made for the sake of the group (once a declaration of combat has been announced and the shift of conduct made) and the illegitimate slaughter of fellow members, the difference between homicide and murder. Both involve the shedding of human blood, however, so that even a meritorious killing is dangerous for the perpetrator.

The same ambivalence was often true in the case of animals. One evening when I was writing under a pressure lamp, I stopped from time to time to swat the insects that were bothering me. My friend, Timbume, who was certainly no vegetarian and whom I had seen killing a lizard which had colours that made people think of leprosy, came into the room and reprimanded me for killing 'God's creatures'. There was a similar duality about the killing of wild animals as there was of men. In the hunt one aimed to kill, for the collectivity as well as for oneself. Yet in some cases serious rituals had afterwards to be performed and the successful hunter might also be forced to erect a shrine either to the beings of the wild or to the dead animal (which belonged to the flocks of the beings of the wild). A similar duality applied to domestic animals. They were raised to be killed for food (in the end) but if you did not also preserve them, you would have no flesh to eat. Once again their killing involved the shedding of blood from the consequences of which the group can be seen as protecting itself by each constituent clan tabooing a certain wild creature and, in the case of most domestic animals, by consuming the flesh only as the result of sacrifice to some supernatural agency so that the slaughter is sacralized.

Those homicide rites were not simply formal acts handed down from the ancestors. They related to a wider *cognitive* problem, to an ambivalence that was partly explicit. In the case of the belief expressed by Timbume, no doubt a fairly widespread one, the wanton destruction of animal life, the unnecessary shedding of blood, was seen as 'unnatural', 'against nature', 'against the law'. To describe this as a taboo, a non-rational prohibition, seems inadequate. In any case, it did not have the diacritical significance assigned to many taboos, nor the status of an anomaly, nor did it fit neatly into any wider categorical system that I knew of. Rather, in a society that was always taking part in killing (there were no specialist butchers or soldiers on whom one could devolve responsibility), the rite seemed to be more of an apology.

These divergent attitudes to killing, that you killed some part of the time and cherished some at others, were associated with cognitive contradictions, even ambivalences, for the members of those societies which were handled (I will not say resolved) by the ritual and by other acts and beliefs. These are cognitive because they have to do with human understanding of the world; if you point it out to them, make explicit the notion 'kill some, spare others', they are likely to recognize the problem. But the cultural handling of it is implicit rather than explicit. It does not matter whether any individual recognizes this as a contradiction at any moment in time; my point is not that this awareness is present in the psyche of every member of that society. I see this contradiction as arising from the human situation itself, in what philosophers see as critical to the process of cognition, that is, the interaction between the knowing mind and the external reality, recognizing that external reality includes other knowing minds. And these interactions, the use of the book, for example, must be seen as no mere addition but as part of the internal as well as the external cognitive process. Human mental operations are almost intrinsically interactive. The outside is also within, as in the case of reading and writing.

Writing has a particular effect on these understandings. The partial rejection of killing people and animals in oral cultures is supplemented in literate ones by the emergence of explicit doctrines that partially resolve the question in a different way, by the rejection of all taking of life by certain categories and groups, such as Benedictine monks, Buddhists and Jains. The extensive distribution of these attitudes and practices suggests that the problem was very widespread, but in literate societies there evolved a complex division of religious labour, one group taking on the burdens of all.

An alternative view of the rejection of the killing of animals has seen 'the widespread disgust expressed at the prospect of consuming animal foods' as related to the issue of taking on animal characteristics.[19] In most societies, however, rejection is partial, that is, of some animals or by some people; the feelings towards such consumption are always divergent, since great pleasure and nourishment are derived by many from eating flesh. Moreover, the particular thesis is weakened by the fact that greatest disgust is,

---

[19] Rozin et al. 1993.

almost universally, reserved for the eating of human flesh, the flesh of those to whom we are closest and whose characteristics we could acquire unproblematically.

Looking at the consumption of food more widely, a further question that arose in connection with the rejection of flowers, and to some extent of icons and drama, had to do with the appearance of luxury in differentiated societies. Distinct stratification by wealth almost inevitably gives rise to some criticism about its distribution. I have previously argued that this is the case with food; the differentiation of cooking into high and low gives rise to an internal critique, which is not present in every individual but is potentially there in the social situation. Not, in this case, the pan-human situation, but in a type of hierarchically differentiated society; largely not in Africa, but it is expressed in the writings that philosophers such as Mencius directed against inequality and in the programmes of revolutionary parties, for example, of Cromwell and of Ho Chi Minh, both of whom placed restrictions on lavish consumption.[20]

Many of the same people who objected to an *haute cuisine* and to the stratification of food also turned down the use of flowers; it was a question of the embarrassment of riches turning into a rejection on the part of some as a result of the critique embedded in the social situation itself. The uneven distribution of wealth itself invited criticism, partly from the weak ('When Adam delved and Eve span, Who was then the gentleman?'), but also in the minds of some of the strong who were forced to think about the support of others. Charity, gift giving, aid for the poor, the rejection of riches by St Francis was a feature not only of Christian Europe but in different degrees of all the major Eurasian societies. It appeared in Islam, in Indian religions, in China and Japan, not only in deeds but in scholarly writings. In his commentary on *The Tale of Genji*, the seventeenth-century Japanese author, Banzan, sees that world as far healthier than his own. The observance of 'ritual and ceremony' rendered unnecessary the expenditure of social and material resources and wealth on physical or coercive forms of restraint; it limited consumption and this preserved the

[20] J. Goody 1982.

harmony of society and a healthy ecology. The avoidance of expenditure on magnificent tombs, on spectacles, the consumption of frugal meals, keeps taxation low, avoids the depletion of natural resources as well as civil disturbance.[21]

The inevitable differentiation that arises from complex market activities (and, of course, from conquest) tends to give rise to some countervailing notions of redistributive justice.[22] The existence of differentiation based on highly unequal access to goods and services in the market is counteracted by socialistic (welfare) trends aimed at mitigating the worst effects of those very activities. Conservatism and socialism are inevitable counterparts of one another, the contradictions of each promoting its opposite. The idea of 'from each according to his ability, to each according to his needs' is both impractically utopian and a necessary sentiment to make society work, to make concrete the idea of 'One Nation'.

In relation to the theme of this book, luxury in the arts, the near monopoly of certain art forms, such as painting or theatre, by the upper class, may create resentment which leads to rejection, especially at times of revolutionary change. Luxury and its concomitant critique is certainly a relevant factor here, above and beyond the wider problems of representation, and has to do with the presence of class societies.

In talking of luxury cultures I am selecting one aspect of class societies as they have emerged since the Bronze Age. That transformation is important not because it introduced stratified societies. African societies had states differentiated by social estates. But there was little to differentiate one cultivator from another since their tools limited the amount of land they could farm and hence the surplus they could produce; so there was usually enough land for each and few opportunities for exploiting the labour of others (except slaves). Hence limited differentiation occurred. What happened with the Bronze Age in Eurasia was that individuals and groups became differentiated in relationship above

---

[21] McCullen, ms:30–32.
[22] See Radcliffe-Brown 1968, and for the anarchist background, J. Goody, 'Anarchy Brown', forthcoming.

all to access to the means of production. There were landless labourers in the country as well as peasants and other farmers and, as in the towns, they were distinguished in significant ways by their 'styles of life', by their subcultures.[23] That differentiation extended to artistic activities ('culture' in the restricted hierarchical rather than the inclusive sense) as well as to other aspects of consumption, all of which produced protest against the distribution of goods and services, especially luxury ones, sometimes taking the form of class conflict but also as the expression of an ambivalence not only about unequal distribution but about the very forms of representation.[24] Nowhere is the cognitive contradiction about distributive justice better expressed than by the radical aristocrat, Percy Bysshe Shelley, in his tirade against one human's exploitation of another, the poor by the rich.

> The seed ye sow, another reaps;
> The wealth you find, another keeps;
> The robes ye weave, another wears;
> The arms ye forge, another bears.

Such a highly stratified distribution of cultural goods, including art, only begins to disappear for the majority (and not then for the minority) with the mass production of the Second Industrial Revolution which sets the stage for consumer, as distinct from luxury, cultures.

The notion of cognitive contradictions may therefore be linked to the idea of contradiction lying within a particular mode of

---

[23] It is a failure to see the full cultural implications of the differences in material means of production as between, say, Eurasia and Africa, including in their artistic activities, that renders ineffective efforts of scholars to identify feudal, Asiatic or even tributary modes of production in the hoe-cultures of Africa. In this work I have hinted at some of the relationships between modes of production and more specifically modes of communication on the one hand, and modes of artistic activity on the other, but I have not traced out any systematic links, except the obvious ones.

[24] On culture as 'the total way of life' or a restricted literacy phenomenon, see the account of the debate between Thompson and Williams in Swindells and Jardine 1990.

production, as perceived by Marx and other scholars. In discussing nineteenth-century capitalism in England, Raymond Williams isolated an alternative tradition in literature to what he saw as the dominant conservative Great Tradition mapped out by the critic, F. R. Leavis. That was to include the oppositional element in English thought. But while that oppositional element could be said to constitute a tradition of discourse, it arose out of a contradiction of capitalism, the division into the rich and poor and the failure to achieve what could be considered a reasonable distribution of worldly goods. It is an explicit cognitive, as well as an underlying social, contradiction because not only do some of the producers (and potential producers) experience deprivation but some of the better-off recognize this problem. So the protest is not confined to a single class, as we see from the case of Shelley; to that extent the oppositional tradition is not a distinct alternative but a facet of the social and intellectual system itself. Industrial production generates attacks upon itself, which lead both to modification in its organization (for example, the support of those it fails to employ) as well as to proposals for, and attempts at, revolutionary change, which may turn out to be utopian: 'Weave robes – let not the idle wear.'

The consideration of a wider range of societies adds another dimension to the comparison which I see as essential to the creation of an adequate theory and which is lacking in so much writing based on the classical or Judaeo-Christian tradition. Much of this book has centred on topics that are familiar to us from the history of Western Europe. That continent was not my only focus. On each occasion I started with an African problem and asked how much light could be shed on it if we assumed that cognitive processes that characterize the history of Western thought might also operate elsewhere, in Asia and in Africa, in other forms. In the case of Asia I was trying (for example, with flowers) to overcome what I saw as an exaggerated developmental and typological differentiation between West and East. In the case of Africa, I was arguing that such differences, for example, in modes of communication and in modes of production, had to be taken into account, especially when looking at the expression of contradictions and ambivalence, as well as in notions of luxury. But in the former case we had also to recognize the presence of less explicit forms of cognitive activity which were based on similarities embedded in the wider human situation.

While I did not, at first, direct attention to Europe, much less to differences within Europe, what I was saying clearly touched very directly upon aspects of the great transformation that occurred in many places at the time of the Renaissance and the Reformation and that still occupies so much of our historical and sociological attention. The frugality and puritanism of the Reformation, as in the case of Bazan, has been linked to prosperity and the growth of capitalism. The rejection of luxury, an embarrassment about riches, is associated, among Calvinists, with the rejection of icons, theatre, relics and fiction, as well as with scepticism about elaborate rituals and about imposed hierarchies. I have discussed these features in connection with widespread dilemmas; they are in no sense confined to Europe and aspects of Protestantism can be seen as an example of the cognitive contradictions that are embedded in such activities. Even in Europe, there were areas in the south that were considered by some as being impermeable to such movements. But the notions expressed in the Reformation were not confined to lands where Protestantism came to dominate. Even in the extreme south these trends were rapidly taken up, for example, by a number of Maltese intellectuals not long after the beginning of the movement in Germany in 1518.[25]

The rapidity of their adoption suggests that the seeds of doubt in existing practice were already sown; this resembles the arguments of Chomsky and Sperber, but I see the preparedness as having different roots. The dissemination of contrary ideas was obviously aided by the advent of printing and the circulation of the book. But the files of the Inquisition seem to indicate that while these doctrines were spread through schools and through printed books (often coming from France and Sicily, and printed in those languages), some of the ideas struck chords in the minds of the inhabitants because they corresponded to existing doubts which

---

[25] First mentioned in Italy in 1529 (Cassar 1988).

had been embodied in earlier heresies. That kernel of doubt led to the emergence of a tradition of scepticism, although I do not see that tradition as necessarily continuous in a specific culture, but as grounded in widespread contradictions, ready to emerge at an appropriate time.

A school in the ecclesiastical capital of Mdina in Malta became a centre for discussion among the inhabitants. There the participants addressed one another as 'brother', kissed each other on the face and broke bread together. One day, picking up a small book, the leader, Don Adrea Axac, openly declared 'that there was no Purgatory, that it was illicit to pray to saints as God needed no lawyers, and that there was no need to pray for the dead'.[26] Those ideas meant abandoning hierarchy, eliminating Purgatory (an introduction of the late twelfth century and one closely associated with indulgences and masses for the dead) as well as doing away with much of the cult of the saints and that of the dead themselves, intermediaries between human and God. The proposed transformation of everyday life went yet further since the food this group ate on a Friday included meat, which was forbidden to Catholics (though not in biblical sources). One enquirer was told that it mattered not what entered the mouth, only what came out, reverting to earlier Christian claims that all God's creatures were good to eat.[27]

Axac was the curate of a parish, and the reports of the Inquisition claimed he 'used to scandalize the flock by preaching publicly that no one should revere the saints and their images'. It was not simply the saints as such; iconoclasm entered in, as did anti-theatricality (or rather, an opposition to elaborate ritual). On one occasion Axac was accused of making fun of a procession and referred to those taking part as 'animals who adore images'.[28] On the surface much activity in contemporary Malta seems to centre on images, on saints and on public enactment, so that these notions of Axac were profoundly 'counter-cultural'. But were the objections simply a

---

[26] Cassar 1988:58.
[27] Porphyry [1965].
[28] Cassar 1988:62.

matter of imported ideas adopted by the educated? It was obviously the educated who made up the thirty-five inhabitants accused of perusing or owning forbidden books between 1546 and 1580.[29] But the rapidity of the diffusion, the fact that it emphasized widespread themes occurring not only in earlier heresies but outside Christianity altogether, suggests that we are in the presence of doubts of a deeper kind, including those that regard the longstanding impulse to represent as flawed. The inhabitants of Malta, no less than those of Sicily, were aware of the iconoclastic tendencies of Muslims, who smashed the noses of Roman statues just as they defaced Christian icons.[30] Did this too strike a chord? Some historians have seen the failure of Protestantism to take hold in the south as an intrinsic aspect of those cultures and their 'mentalities' which may have been 'emotionally ill-disposed to take to heart the rationalising and rigid mentality' of transalpine Europe.[31] Such a contention seems highly doubtful since the Islamic Mediterranean was as 'rigid' as the north with regard to images, dramatic representations and the stress on the word and on direct communication with God. In any case, the reform did make some headway in Spain and Italy and, as in Malta, was eliminated only by censorship, torture and propaganda – that is, by total domination; the Church of the Counter Reformation 'involved itself in everything'.[32] On the surface Maltese culture appears unambiguously in favour of pasqual processions and other holy feasts, just as British society does on royal occasions. But the turn-out may be as much for the nougat as for spiritual nourishment; or perhaps for the company, or to see how Paolo acts his part. Even those who take off their shoes and tell their beads at the passage of the *Mater dolorosa* on the Day of the Annunciation may reflect at times that what they see is 'only a statue'. Or in the Easter procession, that the bloodied face of Christ is only Paolo with greasepaint.

---

[29] Cassar 1988:67–8. The list was only published in 1559; the reformed Inquisition in Italy was set up in 1552.
[30] On the former, see the Roman heads in the Cathedral Museum, Mdina.
[31] Braudel 1973:766; Cassar 1988:65.
[32] Febvre 1982:349, quoted in Cassar 1988:65.

In conclusion, we need a plurality of approaches to cognitive processes. I do not wish to deny the possibility of in-built elements or constraints, only to insist that in each case these have to be demonstrated, not assumed. I do not reject the validity of a deep-structural account, suggesting only that adequate allowance be made for disconfirmation and that the surface level of meaning to the actor (which I take to be the primary level that cognitive enquiry should recognize and attend to) cannot be neglected. I do not discount the importance of cultural transmission; only suggest that sufficient account by taken of changes, including radical changes, in the system of acts and beliefs. Any adequate theory of cultural transmission must include an account of the mechanisms of change, not simply those of continuity which occupy the attention of most theories, especially of oral cultures. Hence, the very static assumptions made about myths and, to my mind, the inadequate statements about the fixity of memory storage and the verbatim reproduction of long recitations.

There is a number of ways in which cultures acquire new knowledge and change endogenously, quite apart from exogenous inputs. There is the recognition that some forms of communication (writing, though its advent is usually exogenous) or technology are superior to others, that one has a comparative advantage. There is also a kind of cultural drift comparable to genetic or linguistic drift. There are the generative aspects of linguistic communication, which is a cultural creation, the invention of tradition, and difficult to restrain. Finally, there is the mechanism to which I have drawn attention, the canker in the rose, the grit in the oyster: that inherent contradictions of a cognitive kind may give rise to ambivalence in the actor's mind, especially in relation to certain kinds of representation. As a consequence, forms such as those we have been examining, and of which images can stand as the case in point, are differentially distributed in human societies over time and over space.

# Bibliography

Adedji, J. 1969 Traditional Yoruba theater. *African Arts* 3:60–3.
Arhin, K. 1994 The economic implications of transformations in Akan funeral rites. *Africa* 64:307–22.
Anon. 1986 *La Voie des Ancêtres*. Paris.
Arnoldi, M. J. 1986 Puppet theater: form and ideology in Bamana performances. *Empirical Studies of the Arts* 4:131–50.
———. 1988 Performance, style, and assertion of identity in Malian puppet drama. *Journal of Folklore Research* 25:87–99.
———. 1989 Reconstructing the history and development of puppetry in the Segu region, Mali. In *Man Does Not Go Naked*. Basel: Ethnologisches Seminar der Universität und Museum der Volkerkunde:221–34.
———. 1995 *Playing with Time: art and performance in Central Mali*. Indiana.
Artaud, A. 1964 *Le Théatre et son double*. Paris.
Atran, S. 1990 *Cognitive Foundations of Natural History: towards an anthropology of science*. Cambridge.
Augé, M. 1982 *The Anthropological Circle: symbol, function, history*. Cambridge.
Axton, R. 1974 *European Drama of the Early Middle Ages*. London.
Bahrani, Z. 1995 Assault and abduction: the fate of the royal image in the ancient Near East. *Art and History* 18:363–82.
Barth, F. 1987 *Cosmologies in the Making: a generative approach to cultural variation in inner New Guinea*. Cambridge.
Barthes, R. 1966 *An Introduction to Structural Analysis of the Narrative*. Occasional Paper, Centre for Contemporary Cultural Studies, University of Birmingham.

Barish, J. 1981 *The Anti-Theatrical Prejudice*. Berkeley.
Barnes, J. A. 1994 *A Pack of Lies: towards a sociology of lying*. Cambridge.
Barns, M. 1990 Pots as people: Yungur ancestral portraits. *African Arts* 23:50–60
Bartlett, F. 1926 *Remembering*. Cambridge.
Beadle, R. (ed.) 1994 *Cambridge Companion to Medieval English Theatre*. Cambridge.
Beare, W. 1950 *The Roman Stage: a short history of Latin drama in the time of the Republic*. London.
Beattie, J. 1968 Aspects of Nyoro symbolism. *Africa* 38:413–42.
——. 1976 Right, left and the Banyoro. *Africa* 46:217–35.
Bechtel, G. and Carrière, J-C. 1984 *Dictionnaire de la bêtise et des erreurs de jugement*. Paris: R. Laffont.
Bemille, S. 1983 *Dagaara Stories: the wisdom that surpasses that of the king*. Brazzaville.
Benjamin, W. 1968 (1st edn 1936) The work of art in the age of mechanical reproduction. In W. Benjamin, *Illuminations: essays and reflections* (ed. H. Arendt). New York.
Besançon, A. 1994 *L'Image interdite: une histoire intellectuelle de l'iconoclasme*. Paris.
Beteille, R. 1987 *La Chemise fondue: vie oubliée des femmes de Rouerge*. Rodez.
Bloch, M. 1991 Language, anthropology and cognitive science. *Man* (n.s.) 26:183–98.
Bosman, W. 1967 *A New and Accurate Description of the Coast of Guinea, divided into the Gold, the Slave, and the Ivory Coasts* (first published 1705). London.
Bourdieu, P. 1976 Le sens practique. *Actes de Recherche en Sciences Sociales* 1:43–86.
Boyer, P. 1994a Cognitive constraints on cultural representations: natural ontologies and religious ideas. In L. A. Hirschfeld, and S. A. Gelman (eds), *Mapping the Mind: domain and specificity in cognition and culture*. New York.
——. 1994b *The Naturalness of Religious Ideas: a cognitive theory of religion*. Berkeley.
Brain, R. and Pollock, A. 1971 *Bangwa Funerary Rituals*. London.
Braudel, F. 1973 *The Mediterranean and the Mediterranean World in the Age of Philip II*. Glasgow (Fr. edn 1949).
Bravmann, R. A. 1974 *Islam and Tribal Art in West Africa*. Cambridge.
——. 1981 *Islam in Africa*. Washington, D.C.
Bremond, C. 1973 *Logique du Récit*. Paris.

Brink, J. T. 1977 Bamana Kote-tlon theater. *African Arts* 10:36–65.
——. 1980 Organizing satirical comedy in Kote-tlon: drama as a communication strategy among the Bamana of Mali. Ph.D. thesis, Indiana University.
——. 1980 Speech, play and blasphemy: managing power and shame in Bamana theater. *Anthropological Linguistics* 24:423–31.
Brown, P. 1971 *The World of Late Antiquity, AD 150–750*. London.
——. 1981 *The Cult of the Saints: its rise and function in Latin Christianity*. Chicago.
——. 1988 *The Body and Society: men, women and sexual renunciation in early Christianity*. New York.
Bruner, J. S. 1972 Nature and uses of immaturity. *American Psychologist* 27:687–708.
Burwick, F. 1991 *Illusion and the Drama: critical theory of the Enlightenment and the Romantic era*. University of Pennsylvania.
Byrne, R. W. 1995 The ape legacy: evolution of Machiavellian intelligence and anticipatory planning. In E. Goody (ed.) *Social Intelligence and Interaction*. Cambridge.
Camille, M. 1992 *Image on the Edge: the margins of medieval art*. London.
Cardinall, A. W. 1931 *Tales told in Togoland*. London.
Carrasco, P. 1959 *Land and Polity in Tibet*. American Ethnological Society, Seattle.
Cassar, C. 1988 The Reformation and sixteenth-century Malta. *Melita Historica* 10(1):51–68.
Cervantes. 1993 [1604]. *Don Quixote de la Mancha*. Wordsworth Classics: Ware.
Chan, S. Y. 1991 *Improvisation in a Ritual Context: the music of Cantonese opera*. Hong Kong.
Chang, Jung. 1991 *Wild Swans*. London.
Chattopadhyaya, D. 1959 *Lokāyata: a study in ancient Indian materialism*. New Delhi.
Cheetham, M. A. 1991 *The Rhetoric of Purity: essentialist theory and the advent of abstract painting*. Cambridge.
Clark, K. 1956 *The Nude: a study of ideal art*. London.
Clément, J.-F. 1995 L'image dans le monde arabe: interdit et possibilités. In G. Beaugé and J.-F. Clément (eds), *L'image dans le monde arabe*. Paris.
Cole, H. M. 1989 *Icons, Ideals and Power in African Art*. Washington, D.C.
Collin de Plancy, J. A. S. 1821–22 *Dictionnaire critique des reliques et des images miraculeuses*, 3 vols. Paris.
Collins, J. 1985 *Musicmakers of West Africa*. Washington, D.C.

Conrad, J. 1990 [1899] *Heart of Darkness and Other Tales* (ed. C. Watts). Oxford.
Constable, G. 1976 Opposition to pilgrimage in the Middle Ages. *Studia Gratiana* 19:123–46.
Cox, M. 1893 *Cinderella*. Folklore Society Monograph Series, no. 31. London.
Cressey, D. 1989 *Bonfires and Bells: national memory and the Protestant calendar in Elizabethan and Stuart England*. Berkeley.
Culler, J. 1975 *Structuralist Poetics*. London.
Davey, G. C. L. 1992 Characteristics of individuals with fear of spiders. *Anxiety Research* 4:299–314.
——. 1994 Self-reported fear to common indigenous animals in an adult UK population: the role of disgust sensitivity. *British Journal of Psychology* 85:541–54.
Desai, D. 1975 *Erotic Sculptures of India: a socio-economic study*. New Delhi.
——. 1984 Placement and significance of erotic sculptures at Khajaruho. In M. Meister (ed.), *Discourses on Śiva*. Philadelphia.
De Groot, J. J. M. 1910 *The Religious Systems of China*. New York.
Detienne, M. *Les Jardins d'Adonis*. Paris.
Dolby, W. 1983 Early Chinese plays and theater. In C. Mackerras (ed.), *Chinese Theater: from its origins to the present day*. Honolulu.
Doody, M. A. 1989 Introduction to C. Lennox, *The Female Quixote*. London.
Dowd, D. L. 1953 'Jacobinism' and the Fine Arts: the revolutionary careers of Bouquier, Sergent and David. *Art Quarterly* 16:195–214.
Dunbabin, T. 1957 *The Greeks and their Eastern Neighbours: studies in the relations between Greece and the countries of the Near East in the eighth and seventh centuries BC*. London.
Dundas, P. 1992 *The Jains*. London.
Eliot, T. S. 1948 *Notes Towards a Definition of Culture*. London.
Elmslie, W. A. L. (ed.) 1911 *The Mishna on Idolatry 'Aboda Zara*. Cambridge.
Engelbrecht, B. and Gardi, B. 1989 *Man Does Not Go Naked: Textilien und Handwerk aus afrikanischen und anderen Landern*. Basel.
Erian, J. B. 1914 *Pourquoi les Prêtres de l'église ont condamné le théatre de leur temps*. Paris.
Evans-Pritchard, E. E. 1937 *Witchcraft, Oracles and Magic Among the Azande*. Oxford.
——. 1940 *The Nuer*. Oxford.
——. 1956 *Nuer Religion*. Oxford.

Febvre, L. 1982 *The Problem of Unbelief in the Sixteenth Century: the religion of Rabelais*. Cambridge, Mass. (Fr. edn 1947).
Fernandez, J. 1982 *Bwiti: an ethnology of the religious imagination in Africa*. Princeton.
Figueras, P. 1983 *Decorated Jewish Ossuaries*. London.
Fikri, M. 1969 Wa: a case study of social values and social tensions as reflected in the oral traditions of the Wala of northern Ghana. Ph.D. thesis, Indiana.
Finnegan, R. 1970 *Oral Literature in Africa*. Oxford.
Firth, R. 1940 *The Work of the Gods in Tikopia*. London.
Fodor, J. 1984 *Representations: philosophical essays on the foundations of cognitive science*. Brighton.
Fontaine, J. (ed.) 1967 *Sulpice Sévère, Vie de Saint Martin*, vol. 1, vol. 2 (1968). Sources Chrétiennes no. 133. Paris.
Fortes, M. 1945 *The Dynamics of Clanship among the Tallensi*. London.
———. 1949 *The Web of Kinship among the Tallensi*. London.
———. 1983 *Oedipus and Job* (ed. R. Horton). Cambridge.
Fosdyke, J. 1956 *Greece Before Homer: ancient chronology and mythology*. London.
Freedberg, D. 1985 *Iconoclasts and their Motives*. Maarsen, Netherlands.
———. 1989 *The Power of Images: studies in the history and theory of response*. Chicago.
Geary, P. J. 1978 *Furta Sacra: thefts of relics in the Central Middle Ages*. Princeton.
Geertz, C. 1976 *The Religion of Java*. Chicago.
———. 1980 *Negara: the theatre state in nineteenth-century Bali*. Princeton.
Ginzburg, C. 1991 Représentation: le mot, l'idée, la chose. *Annales ESC* 46:1219–34.
Gluckman, M. 1974 The philosophical roots of masked dances in Barotseland (Western Province), Zambia. *In Memoriam António Jorge Dias*, vol. 1. Lisbon.
Goldhill, S. 1986 *Reading Greek Tragedy*. Cambridge.
Goldmann, L. 1960 Sur le peinture de Chagall. *Annales ESC* 15:667–83.
Good, D. 1995 Where does foresight end and hindsight begin? In E. Goody (ed.), *Social Intelligence and Interaction: expressions and implications of the social bias in human intelligence*. Cambridge.
Goody, E. 1973 *Contexts of Kinship: an essay in the family sociology of the Gonja of northern Ghana*. Cambridge.
———. 1982 *Parenthood and Social Reproduction: fostering and occupational roles in West Africa*. Cambridge.
———. 1995 (ed.) *Social Intelligence and Interaction: expressions and*

*implications of the social bias in human intelligence.* Cambridge.

Goody, E. and Goody, J. (forthcoming) *The Drum History of the Gonja.*

Goody, J. 1954 *The Ethnography of the Northern Territories of the Gold Coast, West of the White Volta.* London: Colonial Office mimeo.

——. 1956 *The Social Organisation of the LoWiili.* London.

——. 1961 Religion and ritual: the definitional problem. *British Journal of Sociology* 12:142–63.

——. 1962 *Death, Property and the Ancestors.* Stanford.

——. 1970a Marriage policy and incorporation in northern Ghana. In R. Cohen and J. Middleton (eds), *From Tribe to Nation in Africa.* San Francisco.

——. 1970b Reform, renewal and resistance: a Mahdi in northern Ghana. In C. Allen and R. W. Johnson (eds), *African Perspectives.* Cambridge.

——. 1971 Class and marriage in Africa and Eurasia. *American Journal of Sociology* 76:585–603.

——. 1972 *The Myth of the Bagre.* Oxford.

——. 1975 Religion, social change and the sociology of conversion. In J. Goody (ed.), *Changing Social Structure in Ghana: essays in the comparative sociology of a new state and an old tradition.* London.

——. 1977 *The Domestication of the Savage Mind.* Cambridge.

——. 1981 Sacrifice among the LoDagaa and elsewhere: a comparative comment on implicit questions and explicit rejections. *Systèmes de Pensée en Afrique Noire.* EPHE, V$^e$ Section, Cahier V:9–22.

——. 1982 *Cooking, Cuisine and Class: a study in comparative sociology.* Cambridge.

——. 1983 *The Development of the Family and Marriage in Europe.* Cambridge.

——. 1986 *The Logic of Writing and the Organisation of Society.* Cambridge.

——. 1987 *The Interface Between the Written and the Oral.* Cambridge.

——. 1990 *The Oriental, the Ancient and the Primitive: systems of marriage and the family in the pre-industrial societies of Eurasia.* Cambridge.

——. 1991 Icones et iconoclasme en Afrique. *Annales ESC*:1235–51.

——. 1992/93 Men, animals and gods in northern Ghana. *Cambridge Anthropology* 16(3):46–55.

——. 1993a *The Culture of Flowers.* Cambridge.

——. 1993b East and West: rationality in review. *Ethos* 58:6–36.

——. 1996a *The East in the West.* Cambridge.

——. 1996b A kernel of doubt: agnosticism in cross-cultural perspective. The Huxley Lecture. *Journal of the Royal Anthropological Institute* 2:667–81.

Goody, J. and Braimah, J. A. 1967 *Salaga: the struggle for power*. London.
Goody, J. and Gandah, S. W. D. K. 1981 *Une Récitation du Bagre*. Paris.
——. (forthcoming) *Variants of the Bagre*.
Goody, J. and Poppi, C. 1994 Bones and flowers: approaches to the dead in Italian and Anglo-American cemeteries. *Comparative Studies in Society and History* 36:146–75.
Goody, J. and Watt, I. P. 1963 The consequences of literacy. *Comparative Studies in Society and History* 6:304–45. Reprinted in J. Goody (ed.), 1968, *Literacy in Traditional Societies*. Cambridge.
Goody J. and Wilks, I. 1968 Writing in Gonja. In J. Goody (ed.) *Literacy in Traditional Societies*. Cambridge.
Grabar, A. 1946 *Martyrium: recherches sur le culte des reliques et l'art chrétien antique*. Paris.
——. 1968 *Christian Iconography: a study of its origins*. Princeton.
Graham, A. C. 1964 The place of reason in the Chinese philosophical tradition. In R. Dawson (ed.), *The Legacy of China*. Oxford.
Graves, R. 1955 *Greek Myths*, 2 vols. Harmondsworth.
Greimas, A. J. 1966 *Sémantique structurale*. Paris.
Greimas, A. J. and Rastier, F. 1968 The interaction of semiotic constraints. *Yale French Studies* 41:86–105.
Gray, B. 1930 *Persian Painting*. London.
——. (ed.) 1981 *The Arts of India*. Oxford.
Habermas, J. 1984 *Theory of Communicative Action*. Boston.
Habib, I. 1963 *The Agrarian System of Mughol India*. Bombay.
Hacking, I. 1983 *Representing and Intervening: introductory topics in the philosophy of natural science*. Cambridge.
Halbertal, M. and Margalit, A. 1992 *Idolatry*. Cambridge, Mass.
Hawkes, D. 1989 [1964] *Classical, Modern and Humane: essays in Chinese literature*. Hong Kong.
Hawkes, J. 1982 *Mortimer Wheeler*. London.
Hegel, R. E. 1981 *The Novel in Seventeenth-century China*. New York.
Heim, F. 1985 *Virtus: idéologie politique et croyances religieuses au IV$^e$ siècle*. Berne.
——. 1985b L'éxperience des pèlerins occidentaux en Terre Sainte aux alentours de 400. *Ktema* 10:193–208.
Herkovits, M. J. 1944 Dramatic expression among primitive peoples. *Yale Review* 23:683–98.
Hodges, R. and Whitehouse, D. 1983 *Mohammed, Charlemagne and the Origins of Europe*. London.
Holas, B. 1960 *Cultures matérielles de la Côte d'Ivoire* (preface de F. Houphouet-Boigny). République de la Côte d'Ivoire, Ministère de

l'Education Nationale, Centre des Sciences Humaines, Paris.
Hufton, O. 1995 *The Prospect Before Her: a history of women in Western Europe*, vol. 1, *1500–1800*. London.
Hunt, E. D. 1982 *Holy Land Pilgrimages in the later Roman Empire, AD 312–460*. Oxford.
Huntingdon, J. C. 1985 Origins of the Buddha image: early image traditions and the concept of Buddhadarsanapunya. In A. K. Narain (ed.), *Studies in the Buddhist Art of South Asia*. New Delhi.
Huntingdon, S. 1985 *The Art of Ancient India*. New York.
Hyers, C. 1989 The paradox of early Buddhist art. *Asian Art* 11:2–6.
Ife, B. W. 1985 *Reading and Fiction in Golden-Age Spain: a Platonist critique and some picaresque replies*. Cambridge.
Imperato, P. J. 1980 Bambara and Malinke Ton masquerades. *African Arts* 13:47–55, 82–5.
——. 1981 The Yayoroba puppet tradition of Mali. *The Puppetry Journal* 32:20–6.
Innis, H. A. 1950 *Empire and Communication*. Oxford.
Izerda, S. J. 1954 Iconoclasm during the French Revolution. *American Historical Review* 60:13–26.
Jaini, P. S. 1979 *The Jaina Path of Purification*. New Delhi.
——. 1991 *Gender and Salvation: Jaina debates on the spiritual liberation of women*. New Delhi.
Jeanmaire, H. 1951 *Dionysos: histoire du culte de Bacchus*. Paris.
Jeffreys, M. D. W. 1951 The Ekoŋ players. *Eastern Anthropologist* 5:41–7.
Johnson, S. 1759 *Rasselas*. London.
Johnston, A. F. 1991 'All the world a stage': records of Early English Drama. In E. Simon (ed.), *The Theatre of Medieval Europe: new research in early drama*. Cambridge.
Kaplan, T. 1977 *Anarchists in Andalusia 1868–1903*. Princeton.
Kandert, J. 1990 Tradition of metal-casting in Eastern and Western Cameroons between 1840 and 1940. *Annals of the Náprstek Museum Praha* 17:7–110.
Keil, F. C. 1979 *Semantic and Conceptual Development: an ontological perspective*. Cambridge, Mass.
——. 1986 The acquisition of natural kind and artefact terms. In A. Masrar and W. Demopoulos (eds), *Conceptual Change*. Norwood, N.J.
——. 1989 *Concepts, Kind and Cognitive Development*. Cambridge, Mass.
Kenyon, K. M. 1935 The Roman theatre at Verulamium, St Albans. *Archaeology* 84:213–61.
Kenyon, K. M. and Frere, S. S. *ca* 1963 *The Roman Theatre of Verulamium (St Albans) Official Guide*.

Kibbey, A. 1986 *The Interpretation of Material Shapes in Puritanism: a study of rhetoric, prejudice, and violence.* Cambridge.
King, H. 1994 Sowing the field: Greek and Latin sexology. In R. Porter, and M. Teich (eds), *Sexual Knowledge, Sexual Science.* Cambridge.
Kirby, E. 1975 *Ur-drama: the origins of the theatre.* New York.
Kirk, G. S. 1970 *Myth: its meaning and functions in ancient and other cultures.* Cambridge.
Kirshenblatt-Gimblett, B. 1990 Performance of precepts/precepts of performance: Hasidic celebrations of Purim in Brooklyn. In R. Schechner and W. Appel (eds), *By Means of Performance: intercultural studies of theatre and ritual.* Cambridge.
Knight, G. W. 1938 *The Wheel of Fire: essays in the interpretation of Shakespeare's sombre tragedies.* London.
Knights, L. C. 1933 *How Many Children Had Lady Macbeth?* Cambridge.
Kötting, B. 1950 *Peregrinatio religiosa, Wallfahrten in der Antike und das Pilgerwesen in der altern Kirche.* Münster.
Labouret, H. 1932 *Les Tribus du rameau Lobi.* Paris.
Labouret, H. and Travélé, M. 1928 Le théâtre mandingue (Soudan français). *Africa* 1:73–97.
Laburthe-Tolra, P. 1985 *Initiations des sociétés secrètes au Cameroons.* Paris.
Lackington, J. 1795 *Memoirs of the Forty-Five First Years in the Life of James Lackington.* London.
Lancashire, I. 1984 *Dramatic Texts and Records of Britain.* Cambridge.
Leavis, Q. D. 1932 *Fiction and the Reading Public.* London.
Legner, A. (ed.) 1989 *Reliquien: Verherung und Verklärung.* Koln.
Le Goff, J. 1967 Culture cléricale et traditions folkloriques dans la civilisation mérovingienne. *Annales ESC* 22:780–9.
Lennox. C. 1989 [1751]. *The Female Quixote.* London.
Levine, I. 1994 *Men in Women's Clothing: antitheatricality and effeminization 1579–1642.* Cambridge.
Lévi-Strauss, C. 1962 *La Pensée sauvage.* Paris.
——. 1970 *Le Cru et le cuit.* Paris.
——. 1971 *L'Homme nu.* Paris (London, 1981, *The Naked Man*).
Levy-Bruhl, L. 1978 *Primitive Mentality.* London.
Linehan, P. 1997 The king's touch and the dean's ministrations: aspects of sacral monarchy. In Miri Rubin (ed.) *The Works of Jacques Le Goff and the Challenges of Medieval History.* Woodbridge.
Lloyd, G. E. R. 1990 *Demystifying Mentalities.* Cambridge.
Lord, A. B. 1960 *The Singer of Tales.* Cambridge, Mass.
Ludwig, A. I. 1966 *Graven Images: New England stonecarving and its symbols, 1650–1815.* Middletown, Conn.

MacCulloch, J. A. 1918 Relics (Primitive and Western). *Encyclopaedia of Religion and Ethics* (ed. J. Hastings), vol. 10, Edinburgh.
Mackerras, C. 1983 The drama of the Qing dynasty. In C. Mackerras (ed.), *Chinese Theater: from its origins to the present day*. Honolulu.
Mackreth, D. F. 1987 Roman public buildings. In J. Schofield and R. Leech (eds), *Urban Archaeology in Britain*, Research Report 61, The Council for British Archaeology.
Mair, V. H. 1988 *Painting and Performance: Chinese picture recitation and its Indian genesis*. Honolulu.
Maraval, P. 1985 *Lieux saints et pèlerinages d'Orient*. Paris.
Marçais, G. 1957 *La Question des images dans l'art musulman. Mélanges d'histoire et d'archéologie de l'Occident musulman*. Algiers.
Marcus, L. S. 1986 *The Politics of Mirth: Jonson, Herrick, Milton, Marvell and the defense of the old holiday pastimes*. Chicago.
Marshall, G. 1987 *In a Distant Isle: the Orkney background of Edwin Muir*. Edinburgh.
Massip, J. F. 1984 *Teatre Religós Medieval als Països Catalans*. Barcelona.
McKeon, M. 1987 *The Origins of the English Novel, 1600–1740*. Baltimore.
McMullen, I. J. (forthcoming) *Confucianism and Protest in Seventeenth Century Japan: Banzan and the Tale of Genji*.
Meillassoux, C. 1964 The 'koteba' of Bamako. *Présence Africaine* 24:28–62.
Meredith, P. and Tailby, J. E. 1983 *The Staging of Religious Drama in Europe in the Later Middle Ages: texts and documents in English translation*. Kalamazoo, Michigan.
Messenger, J. C. 1962 Anang art, drama, and social control. *African Studies Bulletin* 5:29–35.
——. 1971 Ibibio drama. *Africa* 41:208–22.
Meyer, P. 1981 *Kunst und Religion der Lobi*. Zurich.
Minard, P. (ed.) 1991 *Gregoire le Grand. Registre des Lettres*, vol. 1 (*Sources Chrétiennes* no. 370). Paris.
Mookerjee, A. 1966 *Tantric Art: its philosophy and its physics*. New Delhi.
More, H. 1818 *Strictures on the Modern System of Female Education*. London.
Müller, M. 1868–75 *Chips from a German Workshop*, 4 vols (vol. 1: *Essays on the Science of Religion*) 2nd edn, London.
Murray, A. 1978 *Reason and Society in the Middle Ages*. Oxford.
Nakamura, H. 1967 *A History of the Development of Japanese Thought* AD *592–1868*, 2 vols. Tokyo.
Nead, L. 1992 *The Female Nude: art, obscenity and sexuality*. London.

Needham, R. 1967 Right and left in Nyoro symbolic classification. *Africa* 37:425-52.
——. 1976 Nyoro symbolism: the ethnographic record. *Africa* 46:236-46.
Nelson, B. 1969 *The Idea of Usury: from tribal brotherhood to universal otherhood* (2nd edn). Chicago.
Nelson, W. 1973 *Fact and Fiction: the dilemma of the Renaissance storyteller.* Cambridge, Mass.
Nunley, J. W. 1976 Sisala Sculpture of Northern Ghana. Ph.D. dissertation, University of Washington, Seattle.
O'Flaherty, W. D. 1973 *Asceticism and Eroticism in the Mythology of Śiva.* London.
Olson, D. 1994 *The World on Paper: the conceptual and cognitive implications of writing and reading.* Cambridge.
Orgel, S. 1996 *Impersonations: the performance of gender in Shakespeare's England.* Cambridge.
Ovid [1990] *The Love Poems* (transl. A. D. Melville). Oxford.
Ozouf, M. 1988 *Festivals and the French Revolution.* Cambridge, Mass.
Pal, P. 1989 Art and ritual of Buddhism. *Asian Art* 11:33-55.
——. (ed.) 1994 Introduction to *The Peaceful Liberators: Jain art from India.* Los Angeles.
Panofsky, E. 1946 *Abbot Suger on the Abbey Church of St Denis and its Art Treasures.* Princeton.
Parry, M. 1971 *The Making of Homeric Verse* (ed. A. Parry). Oxford.
Parsons, T. 1937 *The Structure of Social Action.* Glencoe: Ill.
Paulme, D. 1967 Two themes on the origin of death in West Africa. *Man* n.s. 2:48-61.
Peacock, J. 1987 *Rites of Modernisation: symbolic and social aspects of Indonesian proletarian drama.* Cambridge.
——. 1990 Ethnographic notes on sacred and profane performance. In R. Schechner and W. Appel (eds), *By Means of Performance: intercultural studies of theatre and ritual.* Cambridge.
Pegeard, R. 1962 Travestis et marionettes de la région de Segou. *Notes Africaines* 31:17-20.
Pelikan, J. 1990 *Imago Dei: the Byzantine apologia for icons.* Princeton.
Père, M. 1988 *Lobi: tradition et changement, Burkina Faso,* 2 vols. Paris.
Perrois, L. 1992 *Byeri Fang* (Exhibition Catalogue). Marseilles.
Peters, E. L. 1956 A Muslim passion play: key to a Lebanese village. *Perspective of the Arab World* (supplement to *Atlantic Monthly*) 58-62.
Phillips, H. 1980 *The Theatre and its Critics in Seventeenth-century France.* Oxford.

Phillips, J. 1973 *The Reformation of Images: destruction of art in England, 1535–1660*. Berkeley.
Phillips, T. (ed.) 1995 *Africa: the art of a continent*. London.
Pierce, C. S. 1931–38 The icon, index and symbol. In *Collected Papers*, vol. 8. Cambridge, Mass.
Pirenne, H. 1929 L'instruction des marchands au moyen âge. *Annales d'Histoire Économique et Sociale* 1:13–28.
——. 1955 *Medieval Cities: their origins and the revival of trade*. New York (1st Fr. edn 1927).
Pitkin, H. F. 1967 *The Concept of Representation*. Berkeley.
Plaks, A. H. (ed.) 1977 *Chinese Narrative: critical and theoretical essays*. Princeton.
——. 1987 *The Four Masterworks of the Ming Novel: ssu ta ch'i-shu*. Princeton.
Polkinghorne, D. 1988 *Narrative Knowing and the Human Sciences*. New York.
Porphyry. 1965 *On Abstinence from Animal Food* (trans. T. Taylor). London.
Porter, R. and Teich, M. (eds) 1994 *Sexual Knowledge, Sexual Science*. Cambridge.
Pound, E. 1931 *How to Read*. London.
Prendergast, C. 1986 *The Order of Mimesis: Balzac, Stendhal, Nerval, Flaubert*. Cambridge.
Pronko, L. 1969 *Theater, East and West*. Berkeley.
Prouteau, M. 1929 Premiers essais de théâtre chez les indigènes de la Haute Côte d'Ivoire. *Bulletin du Comité d'études historiques et scientifiques de l'AOF* 12:409–75.
Punja, S. 1992 *Divine Ecstasy: the story of Khajuraho*. New Delhi.
Quine, W. V. 1966 *The Ways of Paradox and Other Essays*. New York.
Radcliffe Brown, A. R. 1968 *Method in Social Anthropology: selected essays*, ed. M. N. Srinivas. Chicago.
Radin, P. (ed.) 1926 *Crashing Thunder: the autobiography of an American Indian*. New York.
Rao, T. A. G. 1914–16 *Elements of Hindu Iconography*, 2 vols. Madras.
Rattray, R. S. 1927 *Religion and Art in Ashanti*. Oxford.
Ricard, A. 1986 *L'invention du théâtre: le théâtre et les comédiens en Afrique noire*. Lausanne.
Richards, I. A. 1929 *Practical Criticism: a study of literary judgement*. London.
Rozin, P., Haidt, J. and McCauley C. 1993 Disgust. In M. Lewis and J. M. Haviland (eds), *Handbook of Emotions*. New York.

Sahas, D. J. 1986 *Icon and Logos: sources in eighth-century iconoclasm*. Toronto.
Sangave, V. A. 1959 *The Jaina Community: a social survey*. Bombay.
Schechner, R. 1969 *Public Domain*. New York.
——. 1985 *Between Theater and Anthropology*. University of Pennsylvania.
——. 1988 *Performance Theory* (rev. edn). New York.
——. 1993 *The Future of Ritual: writings on culture and performance*. New York.
Schechner, R. and Appel, W. (eds) 1990 *By Means of Performance: intercultural studies of theatre and ritual*. Cambridge.
Schildkrout, E. 1990 Reflections on Mangbetu art. In E. Schildkrout and C. A. Keim (eds), *African Reflections: art from Northeastern Zaire*. Seattle.
Schimmel, A. 1976 The celestial garden in Islam. In H. Ettinghausen (ed.), *The Islamic Garden*. Washington, D.C.
Schmidt, J.-C. 1987 L'occident, Nicée II et les images du VIII$^e$ au XIII$^e$ siècle. In F. Boscplug et al. (eds), *Nicée II 787–1987: douze siècles d'images religieuses*. Paris.
Schwartz, G. 1988 (1972) *Iconoclasm and Painting in the Revolt of the Netherlands 1566–1609*. New York.
Scott, A. C. 1983 The performance of classical theater. In C. Mackerras (ed.), *Chinese Theater: from its origins to the present day*. Honolulu.
Scribner, S. and Cole, M. 1981 *The Psychology of Literacy*. Cambridge, Mass.
Sebag, L. 1964 *Marxisme et Structuralisme*. Paris.
——. 1971 *L'Invention du monde chez les Indiens Pueblos*. Paris.
Seligman, M. E. P. 1971 Phobias and preparedness. *Behavior Therapy* 2:307–20.
Shanks, D. 1993 Breaking Chomsky's rules. *New Scientist*, 30th January, 26–30.
Shyrock, J. R. 1932 *The Origin and Development of the State Cult of Confucius*. New York.
Smith, P. 1975 *Le Récit populaire au Ruanda*. Paris.
Smith, V. A. 1918 art. Relics (Eastern). *Encyclopaedia of Religion and Ethics* (ed. J. Hastings), vol. 10. Edinburgh.
Snellgrove, D. L. (ed.) 1978 *The Image of the Buddha*, Unesco, Paris.
Sommer, D. A. 1994 Images into words; Ming Confucian iconoclasm. *National Palace Museum Bulletin* (Taiwan) 29:1–24.
Soyinka, W. 1990 *Literature and the African World*. Cambridge.
Sperber, D. 1985 *On Anthropological Knowledge*. Cambridge.
Spieser, J.-M. 1985 La christianisation de la ville dans l'Antiquité tardive.

*Ktema: civilisations de l'Orient, de la Grèce et Rome antiques* 10:49–55.
Spurgeon, C. F. E. 1935 *Shakespeare's Imagery and What it Tells Us.* London.
Stannard, D. E. 1977 *The Puritan Way of Death: a study in religion, culture, and social change.* Oxford.
Stanner, W. E. 1959–63 *On Aboriginal Religion.* Oceania Monographs no. 11. Sydney.
Stern, D. N. 1977 *The First Relationship: infant and mother.* London.
Stevenson, A. M. (Mrs Sinclair) 1915 *Heart of Jainism.* London.
Stranks, C. J. 1973 *This Sumptuous Church: the story of Durham Cathedral.* London (rev. edn 1993).
Strong, J. S. 1983 *The Legend of King Asoka.* Princeton.
——. 1987 art. Relics. *Encyclopaedia of Religion* (ed. M. Eliade), vol. 12. New York.
Sumption, J. 1975 *Pilgrimage: an image of medieval religion.* London.
Swindells, J. and Jardine, L. 1990 *What's Left? Women in culture and the Labour movement.* London.
Taralon, J. 1978 La majésté d'or de Sainte-Foy du trésor de Conques. *Revue de l'Art* 40–1:9–22.
Taylor, J. T. 1943 *Early Opposition to the English Novel: the popular reaction from 1760 to 1830.* New York.
Tessmann, G. 1913 *Die Pangwe.* Berlin.
Thackeray, W. 1898–99 *Roundabout Papers* in *Works.* New York.
Thapar, R. 1966 *A History of India.* Harmondsworth, Middlesex.
Thompson, S. 1977 (orig. 1946) *The Folktale.* Berkeley, California.
Thrower, J. 1980 *The Alternative Tradition: religion and the rejection of religion in the ancient world.* The Hague.
Trevarthen, C. B. 1979a Communication and cooperation in early infancy: a description of primary intersubjectivity. In M. Bullowa (ed.), *Before Speech: the beginning of interpersonal communication.* Cambridge.
——. 1979b Instincts for human understanding and for cultural cooperation: their development in infancy. In M. von Cranach, K. Foppa, W. Lepenies and D. Ploog (eds), *Human Ethology: claims and limits of a new discipline.* Cambridge.
——. 1988 Universal co-operative motives: how infants begin to know the language and culture of their parents. In G. Jahoda and I. M. Lewis (eds), *Acquiring Culture: cross cultural studies in child development.* London.
Turner, V. 1979 *Process, Performance and Pilgrimage: a study in comparative symbology.* New Delhi.
Turner, V. and E. 1978 *Image and Pilgrimage in Christian Culture: anthro-*

*pological perspectives.* Oxford.
Tylor, E. B. 1871 *Primitive Culture: researches in the development of mythology, philosophy, religion, language, art and custom.* London.
van Gulick, R.H. 1974 *Sexual Life in Ancient China.* Leiden.
Vassal-Phillips, O. R. 1917 *The Work of St Optatus Bishop of Milevis against the Donatists.* London.
Vogel, S. M. 1977 Baule art as the expression of a world view. Ph.D. dissertation, University of Michigan.
Waddell, L. A. 1905 *Lhasa and its Mysteries, with a record of the expedition of 1903–1904.* London.
Wang Ch'ung 1911 *Lien-Hêng* (trans. A. Forke). Berlin.
Watt, I. P. 1957 *The Rise of the Novel.* London.
——. 1996 *Myths of Modern Individualism.* Cambridge.
Whiten, A. and Ham, R. 1992 On the nature and evolution of imitation in the animal kingdom; reappraisals of a century of research. *Advances in the Study of Behavior* 21:239–83.
Willet, F. 1971 *African Art.* London.
Wirth, J. 1988 La représentation de l'image dans l'art du Haut Moyen Age. *Revue de l'Art,* 9–21.
Worsley, P. 1957 *The Trumpet Shall Sound.* London.
Wright, A. F. 1959 *Buddhism in Chinese History.* Stanford.
Wright, T. 1861 *Essays on Archaeological Subjects,* 2 vols. London.

# Index

abstract painters   68ff, 124
actors, status of   114, 137
    China   127
    Judaism   123
    Rome   103–4
Adorno, T.   22
Africa
    and images   55
alienation   22, 118, 151
allegory   122, 223
altars   59ff, 64, 90
    and relics   88
ambiguity   18
ambivalence   1, 13, 16, 17, 18, 22ff, 28, 51, 52, 65, 66, 92, 100, 104, 112, 116, 146, 150, 151ff, 181, 182ff, 196, 199, 202, 204, 206, 211, 213, 218, 220, 221, 226, 227, 231, 233, 238, 254, 258, 261, 265ff, 270
ancestors   240, 250
ancestors and figuration   62ff
aniconism   38, 40ff, 44, 47, 51, 55, 56, 58, 68, 73, 94, 219, 229
    Hindu   49
animate–inanimate   75
animism   56
antinomies   254
art, absence of   2ff
art and life   150, 187, 188, 190ff, 206ff, 217
asceticism   225, 237

Bagre   153ff, 164ff
Barthes, R.   6
belief   172, 180, 240, 250
    of children   181
Benjamin, Walter   21, 68, 151, 196, 229
binary concepts   73, 242, 246
    left and right   38
'black is beautiful'   243
bones   75ff, 84ff, 95, 97
    bone-gathering   86, 96
    clean   89
    disposal of   86
    dried   89

## Index

Brahmā, image of  51
breasts  207, 215, 216
Brecht, Bertold  22, 118, 151
Bronze Age society  3, 14, 24, 136, 264
    and asceticism  210
Buddhism  12, 13, 230, 232, 258, 262
    and images  48, 51, 93, 149, 206, 212
    Vajrayāna  211
    Zen  53, 60, 94, 134
Byzantine influence  46

Calvinism  19, 44ff, 67
cannibalism  81, 84, 97, 263
carnivals  259
Chagall, Marc  38ff
change  238, 241, 253, 264, 270
change in representation  9ff
    Africa  66
charity  106–7, 113, 263
    Judaism  208
charivari  259
Chomskian model  246
chronicles  176
church accumulation  11, 104ff
class  227, 236ff, 264ff
cloth, use of
    dressing the god  213
    India and Africa  205, 209ff, 215ff, 218, 219
clothing  224, 226ff, 233
cognitive contradictions  13, 16ff, 28, 51, 57, 64, 65, 73, 84ff, 91, 94, 98, 103, 116, 135, 146, 150, 152, 202, 218, 233, 235, 236, 238, 250, 251, 253ff, 255, 258, 260, 261, 265ff, 270

cognitive dissonance  255
cognitive science  28, 51, 246
concert parties  147–8
Confucians  230, 236
conservatism–socialism  264
consumer cultures  18, 135, 265
conversion  54, 73
cooking  263, 268
cosmology  158, 169, 176ff, 179ff
courtly love  224 ff
creation  150, 151, 154
Creation, the  11, 39, 58, 73, 134, 180
Creator  38, 235, 255ff, 258
cross-dressing  110, 114, 117–18, 135, 137, 139, 146, 149, 195, 217
    China  127
cuisine, cooking  23, 208
culture  253, 257, 268
Cultural Revolution  23, 72, 129, 151, 201

defacing  40
    Durham  44
differences  226
disbelief, suspension of  25, 118, 190, 198
disguise  55, 109, 113, 145
distributional unevenness  2, 16, 18, 35, 55, 65, 73, 100, 125, 135, 150, 160, 165, 177, 181, 203, 204, 258, 265
    myth  159
    narrative  180
    theatre  112
divinity, the dilemma of  54
domain-specificity  51, 247

doubt, 16, 21, 27, 38, 51ff, 118, 132, 143, 153, 245, 250, 253, 256, 259ff, 267ff, 269
   Hindu 49
   kernel of 91, 25, 28, 134
   about narrative 180
   theatre 116

Durkheim, Émile 17, 238

East and West 266
education,
   education and images 234
   exemption from ban on images 46, 68, 199

Eliot, T. S. 22, 162
English intellectualism 17
entertainer 145
entertainments 140, 142, 168, 171, 181, 185ff, 192, 214, 218
erotica 205, 210ff, 216, 229, 232, 236
   religious 213
essentialism 69, 246
Europe, decline of 11
evil, problem of 57, 244ff, 256
explicit–implicit 16, 17, 28, 48, 55, 58, 64, 65, 73, 85, 98, 136, 146, 150ff, 158, 205, 210, 239, 245, 254, 258, 262
eyes, and images 51

fabliaux 222
fetish 27, 35, 55, 56, 59, 64, 66–7, 210
fiction (*see also* narrative) 12, 128, 153, 168ff, 172, 177, 182ff, 197ff, 203ff

fiction and fact 21, 155, 184ff, 193, 200, 201
figurative images 40, 47, 56, 59, 65, 66, 98, 124
   Africa 63
   and Confucianism 61
   general 51
figurative sculpture 35, 39, 75ff, 134
   fear of 63
   Mangbetu 66
flowers 3ff, 18, 23, 24, 130, 263
   artificial 257
folk tales 167, 168ff, 174, 179, 216
Freud, Sigmund 22, 144, 171
funerals 27, 136, 138, 140, 142ff, 144ff, 147, 150, 164, 176, 209, 224, 259

games (*ludi*) 109ff, 114, 127
genitalia 235
   female 207, 216
genre 153ff, 163ff
God 11, 37, 38ff, 52ff, 154, 170, 172, 174, 176ff, 256ff, 258
   in Africa 56ff, 205
   imaging God 9
gods, communication with 52
graven and other images 12, 37, 68, 76
Greek drama 11, 27, 125

Heaven 83
heresy 267, 269
heretics 27, 44, 76, 91, 92, 115
Hindu sexual mysticism 211

history   171, 175, 178, 189, 190, 241, 199, 200
  drum   175 (Gonja)
  and the novel   186
homicide   17
homosexuality   222
  and theatre   217
host   27, 86
human body   205, 228, 237, 250
  female body   207
hysteria   38

icon   25, 35ff, 46, 51, 58, 60, 64, 113, 119, 259, 269ff
  defined   39
  marked icons   153
  materiality of   58
  return of   47
iconoclasm   13, 37, 43ff, 47, 55, 71, 73, 79, 91, 121, 151, 245, 258, 268, 269
  Andalusian   72
  Buddhist   48
  Confucian   62
  French school   69
  Harris in Ivory Coast   46
  of Kandinsky   68
  political   70ff
Iconodules   13, 44
iconography   39, 158
iconophobia   53
idolatry   37ff, 43ff, 45ff, 47, 55, 56, 60, 68, 72, 75, 91, 95, 125, 221
  and Jains   49
  and myth   156
  Vēda   50
illusion   22, 27, 61, 96, 111, 112, 118, 119, 131, 149, 150, 180, 198, 200, 217

  and allusion   122
  of narrative   177
image   39, 224, 233
image, religious   43ff, 47, 53, 58, 68, 75, 94, 115, 258, 268
  Buddhist   48–51
  Hindu   49–51
image and reality   25, 44, 51, 67
imagery   39
imitation   40, 113, 117, 120, 122, 135, 182, 201, 252
  China   200
imitator   103
Incarnation
  and images   47
intentionality   5, 24, 26, 63, 107, 145, 147, 214
Islam   35, 39ff, 43, 47, 53, 55, 58, 64, 95, 98, 106, 124, 142, 150, 151, 169, 175, 199, 214, 258, 263, 269
  and Jains   49
  Mogul   206

Jains   226, 258, 262
  and images   48, 206ff, 210
Johnson, Samuel   26, 154
Judaism   9, 19, 35, 39, 47, 91, 95, 106, 123ff, 126, 154, 199, 206, 228

*kabuki*   148–9
Keats, John   22
killing   260ff
knowledge   7, 172ff, 192, 229, 235ff, 237, 247, 252, 270
  book   202
  ontological   247

language, as representation  2, 9, 38
Laudians  45, 136
learning  251ff
legends (clan histories)  166, 175
Lévi-Strauss, C.  4, 157ff, 160ff, 163, 171, 175, 184, 190, 241, 242, 244ff
libraries  109
  lending  193ff
lie  44, 53, 71, 92, 104, 114, 120, 131, 156, 180, 193, 197, 203, 258
  fiction  182
  tales as  171
  theatre  108
lie and falsehood  26, 80, 122
luxury  4, 11, 13, 14, 19, 23, 44, 46, 71, 73, 87, 93, 109, 119, 120, 121, 129, 133, 136, 143ff, 195, 197, 203, 209, 212, 237, 263, 264ff
luxury cultures  24, 264ff

Malinowski, B  156, 167
male–female  222
Marx, Karl  266
masks  35, 36, 41ff, 55, 56, 64, 67, 99, 108, 110, 126, 130, 137, 139, 142, 145,
  Nō  150
Mass, the  80ff, 101, 108, 109
mass culture  13
mass media  21
mass production  18, 265
material–immaterial  10, 44, 48, 51, 53, 57, 64, 69, 87, 90, 91, 98, 148, 151, 244, 245, 256ff
material offerings  53–4, 65

materialism  125ff
medicine  251
'mentalités'  83ff, 85, 245ff, 260, 267ff, 269ff
mentality  159
metaphor  222
metaphorical and literal  25, 38, 170, 214
mimesis  2, 5ff, 103–4, 106, 116, 117, 118, 119, 122, 131, 134, 136ff, 141, 143ff, 145ff, 148, 150ff, 167, 200, 212
mimic  252, 259
mimicry  110, 114, 122, 127, 135ff, 139, 147, 149
miniature, the  40, 124, 212
miracles  77, 79ff, 88, 113
misrepresentation  26, 38
mode of communication  18, 246, 265ff, 270
modes of production  265
modes of thought  16
monotheism  37ff, 95, 154, 258
Muir, Edwin  19
music  19, 45, 53, 117, 124, 127, 128, 129, 133, 139, 142, 144, 164, 167
  and abstraction  70
  and mathematics  19
mystery plays  101, 123, 149
  Shi'ite  124
mysticism, sexual  231
myth  2, 14, 153ff, 244ff, 252, 270
  text-myths  160
  utterance-myth or *récit*  158, 160
mythology  2, 153ff, 175ff

narrative 153ff, 174ff, 177ff, 244
nationalism 246
natural–artificial 60, 61, 94
natural–divine 80
natural–supernatural 250ff
'neolithic thought' 246
neonates 247
Nō drama 127, 150
novel 153ff, 178ff, 182ff, 189, 228, 232
nudity 204ff, 214ff, 216, 218, 219ff, 220ff, 222ff
    Africa 215

opera 18
    Chinese 126ff
opposites, binary 23
ossuaries 86, 89

pantheism 60, 67, 78
pantheon 174, 177, 179, 267
paradox 83, 89–91, 98, 254ff
past, processing the 166, 194
past–present 80
'patriarchal culture' 222
perform, pressure to 116
performance 99ff, 122, 131, 136, 259
phallus 205, 211, 216, 222, 235
    Śiva as 210, 213, 220
philosophy, philosophers 8, 14, 23, 38, 49, 50, 53, 57, 120, 151, 174, 214, 237, 246, 262ff
picture recitation 129
pilgrimage 76ff, 92, 94, 96, 106, 126, 210, 213
    Jain 207
    objections to 78, 91

Plato 5ff, 10, 69, 103, 117, 119, 185, 218, 258
play–ritual 128, 134, 142
play–work 99ff, 102, 106, 109, 111, 112, 114, 142, 145, 147
poetry 124, 137, 161, 178, 195
pornography 196 224, 232
post-modern 28
prayer 57, 78, 91, 92, 143, 213, 268
praise-songs 164
printing 227, 230, 267
private–public 230, 233
prohibitions 17
projection 58, 161
'prose' 164, 189
proverbs 164, 171
puppets 137ff, 139, 140, 142
Purgatory 89, 268
Puritans, puritanism, puritanical 4, 18ff, 44ff, 67, 97, 110, 115, 116, 118, 119, 120, 136, 146, 151, 193, 197, 202, 206, 219, 228, 229, 233, 235, 236, 260, 267
    fundamentalism 125

quest 161, 172

rationality 14, 15, 27, 80, 92, 155, 197
    loss through reading 186
real presence 26, 27, 80
realism 7, 43, 110, 113,
    in novel 188ff
    revolutionary 122
reality, nature of 150, 199, 200
reality and appearance 103
reasoning, sequential 178

redistributive justice   264ff
refractions   56
    and spirituality   59, 60
Reformation   19, 62, 229, 267
    in Durham   44
    and relics   81
rejection   1, 23, 38, 42, 47, 52,
    58, 67, 71, 73, 82, 90, 93,
    98, 99, 116, 122, 123, 129,
    132, 143, 145, 151, 180,
    182ff, 185, 201, 203, 204,
    208, 233, 235, 255, 259,
    262, 264
relics   25, 45, 75ff
    bodily   84
    and memory   77
    and physical contact   78
    proliferation of   90
    subdivision of   82, 93
    theft of   90, 92
reliquary   26, 46, 75ff, 88
    Africa   98
    statue   87
Renaissance   267
represent, pressure to   58
Restoration   45
reverence–worship   60, 81, 84,
    89, 91, 92, 95
rich–poor   18, 265
ritual   99ff, 115, 125ff, 128,
    130, 131ff, 136ff, 138,
    142ff, 146, 150, 151, 157,
    161, 213, 218, 259, 263,
    268
ritual–secular   138, 147, 150
romance   186ff
romances   222
Rousseau, J.-J.   119, 147, 189ff

sacred–secular   127, 138, 151,
    157, 159, 174, 197

Jain   210
Sainte-Foy   75
saints, 80ff, 85, 88, 91, 134, 268
    Lives   197
scepticism   8ff, 170, 251, 256,
    260, 268
second burial   86
semen   231
sex manuals   223ff, 230, 232,
    236
sexuality   197, 201, 204ff,
    210ff, 215ff, 217, 218,
    222ff
    renunciation of   208
shadow puppets   125, 128, 130
shrine, as artefact   51–2, 64,
    213
skits   140, 216
social contradiction   265ff
soul   240, 250
spider, as intermediary   174
Soyinka, Wole   161
spel   113
stained glass   115
standard oral forms   153ff, 163,
    166, 172
symbol   39, 158, 161, 177, 210

'taboos'   17
tape-recorder   244ff, 252, 270
    and myth   173
temples   76ff, 92, 127, 130,
    149, 207ff, 235
    Indian   210ff
    and sex   212
text-utterance   28, 137, 156,
    158
thin versus thick action   4, 115,
    128, 151
three-dimensional forms   35,
    43, 73, 88, 123, 221, 235

tourism and figuration
    Africa   66
transformation   241
transubstantiation   26
tropes   101, 110, 114
truth   155, 156, 193, 200
    and appearance   69
    and falsehood   3, 9, 91
    and fiction   25, 156, 180ff, 182ff, 186, 193, 197, 199
truth-status   168, 170, 190, 203

urban drama   113, 149
usury   106

variants   162
Virgin Mary, cult   225
visible–invisible   56, 61
visual, the
    rejection of   45
    return of   46, 68

Weber, Max   14, 239, 249
witchcraft   142ff, 217, 240, 244, 250
women, as audience   184ff, 192, 203
    and sex   230ff
word, the   20, 40, 41, 46, 47, 53, 58, 67, 71, 92, 94, 124, 269
    Buddhist   48, 93, 224, 233
writing   7, 13, 15, 28, 41ff, 46, 51, 55, 61, 62, 64, 67, 73, 74, 95, 98, 100, 103, 108, 111, 128ff, 135, 136ff, 146, 150ff, 153, 154, 155, 156, 160, 172, 182ff, 202, 215, 227, 230, 233, 237, 239, 245, 249, 253ff, 258, 260, 262, 270
    book-burning   71
    and narrative   179
    and serious matters   185